Mental Health and Family Law

Mental Health and Family Law

Being

Papers given to the Family Justice Council's Interdisciplinary Conference for judges, directors of social services, mental health professionals, academia, guardians ad litem, panel managers and other professions, held at the Dartington Hall Conference Centre, Dartington Hall, Totnes, Devon, between 2 October and 4 October 2009, together with Resolutions adopted by the Conference.

Edited by

The Rt Hon Lord Justice Thorpe
and
Marina Faggionato
Barrister

Family Law

Published by Family Law
a publishing imprint of
Jordan Publishing Limited
21 St Thomas Street
Bristol BS1 6JS

Whilst the publishers and the author have taken every care in preparing the material included in this work, any statements made as to the legal or other implications of particular transactions are made in good faith purely for general guidance and cannot be regarded as a substitute for professional advice. Consequently, no liability can be accepted for loss or expense incurred as a result of relying in particular circumstances on statements made in this work.

Crown Copyright material is reproduced with kind permission of the Controller of Her Majesty's Stationery Office.

British Library Cataloguing-in-Publication Data

A catalogue record for this book is available from the British Library.

ISBN 978 1 84661 211 4

Typeset by Letterpart Ltd, Reigate, Surrey

Printed in Great Britain by CPI Antony Rowe, Chippenham, Wiltshire

Contributors

Dr Eia Asen
Clinical Director, Marlborough Family Service

Dr Diana Cassell
Consultant Child and Adolescent Psychiatrist, Tolworth Hospital

Sandie Chatterton
Service Manager, Lewisham CAMHS

Helen Clift
Office of the Official Solicitor

Karin Courtman
London Borough of Lewisham

Dr Sally Cubbin
Locum Consultant Psychiatrist, Maudsley Adult ADHD Clinic

Minna Daum
Head of Programme, Families at Risk, The Anna Freud Centre

Dr Nisha Dogra
Senior Lecturer in Child and Adolescent Psychiatry, University of Leicester

Peggy Ekeledo
Solicitor, Burke Niazi Solicitors, London

Dr Danya Glaser
Consultant Child and Adolescent Psychiatrist

Steve Goodman
London Borough of Hackney

Dr Nicola Graham-Kevan
Chartered Psychologist, School of Psychology, University of Central Lancashire

Professor Jane L Ireland
Chartered Forensic Psychologist

Dr James Jeffs
Honorary Specialty Registrar, Maudsley Adult ADHD Clinic

Janice Kaufman
Solicitor, Steel and Shamash, London

Dr David Lucey
Independent Clinical Child Psychologist, Yorkshire

Angela Nield
Circuit Judge, Manchester

Gillian Schofield
Professor of Child and Family Social Work, Centre for Research on the Child and Family,
University of East Anglia

Dr Mike Shaw
Consultant Child Psychiatrist, Tavistock Clinic

Dr Claire Sturge
Consultant Child and Adolescent Psychiatrist

Isabelle Trowler
London Borough of Hackney

Ann Tucker
Mother, Grandmother and Kinship Carer

Dr Judi Walsh
Lecturer in Developmental Psychology, Centre for Research on the Child and Family,
University of East Anglia

Dr Kiriakos Xenitidis
Consultant Psychiatrist, Maudsley Adult ADHD Clinic

Foreword

Although spoilt by attending all of the Dartington Conferences, I am each time impressed by the commitment of those who take part, and by the lively and thought-provoking exchanges the interdisciplinary environment promotes.

Mental health issues permeate the family law system. When the court is faced with parents or children with mental health difficulties it calls on the expertise of a wide range of specialists, working across various disciplines to try and help the family. At the Dartington Conference delegates from those disciplines join those who have carefully prepared the papers in this volume. Over 3 days we discuss important themes, and share our expertise and practical experiences of working with families. Together we formulate resolutions that reflect the consensus reached, and which we hope will inform the work of the Family Justice Council, Ministry of Justice, Department for Children Schools and Families and Local Authorities across the country.

I am grateful to all those that have contributed to this work, to Marina Faggionato for collating the conference materials and to Jordans for publishing them. I hope that this volume will be widely read and that the work of the Conference reaches all those involved in the family justice system.

The Rt Hon Lord Justice Thorpe
March 2010

Editorial Introduction

Family law proceedings are essentially interdisciplinary. They involve a wide range of professionals including judges, lawyers, social workers, guardians, Cafcass officers, psychiatrists, psychologists, and paediatricians. Each brings their own expertise to bear on these very difficult cases.

The theme of this interdisciplinary conference has to be chosen some 18 months in advance. We have occasionally found that our work comes too late, for example, by the time of the conference on 'The Future of the Family Law Act 1996' it was clear that the Act had no future. This year we have again returned to themes of mental health. I say again because the first Dartington Conference held in 1995 was entitled 'Rooted Sorrows'. At that conference we discussed the role, impact and importance of child psychology and psychoanalysis on the outcome of child protection issues. The success of that conference and the publication of the papers was due to the fact that it tackled a question of such importance to the family jurisdiction. Then, as now, mental health issues touch many of our cases. The Conference is, as an interdisciplinary conference, intended to bring together those who work in and around the family justice system, to nourish and sustain the collaboration between us.

Thanks to the hard work of our steering committee we were spoilt with papers of the highest quality, and speakers who are each at the forefront of their respective disciplines. This made for a lively and well-informed conference.

What we achieved at the conference is a fusion of the papers that were carefully prepared and disseminated beforehand, the oral presentations that amplified and developed the ideas in the papers, and the discussions in small groups in the Great Hall and in the gardens. Building on the work of the last conference we once again produced resolutions which serve as a monument to the discussions and debates. Thanks to Jordans, the papers and resolutions are collected here. The Family Justice Council will distribute copies to local branches, and I hope that what we publish will be widely disseminated and read by all those whose work brings them within the realm of Family Justice.

Once again I would like to express my thanks to the Family Justice Council Secretariat for their extremely efficient administration both before and during the conference, and to the staff of Dartington Hall. My particular thanks go to Joanna Wilkinson who has throughout taken the lead, guiding, supporting and deciding on all issues from great to small.

The Rt Hon Lord Justice Thorpe

CONTENTS

EIGHTH DARTINGTON CONFERENCE

OPENING ADDRESS

The Rt Hon Lord Justice Thorpe

A warm welcome to the 2009 Family Justice Council interdisciplinary conference. The first such conference was held in 1995; one of the things that make me realise how old I am becoming is the knowledge that our conference is now a teenager. Will I be here for the sixteenth birthday conference? That is a personal challenge that I will not now answer.

This conference is devoted to the overarching theme of mental health problems. The first conference was devoted to exploring the territory that is shared by psychoanalysis, mental health and legal practice. In 1995 the conference was interdisciplinary, but had not reached the stage of development that is now taken for granted, with its expression in the Family Justice Council giving its advice on all Family Justice issues. In 1995 we had a little society, a little committee, the President's Interdisciplinary Committee. Obtaining funding for the first conference was a complete nightmare. Now it is a given that we will have a funded conference every other year.

Many of you have attended past conferences (I note that there are a number of the old guard who instinctively signed up for the next conference as they left the last). For those who are new, the convention is that each paper is pre-read, with the sessions rapidly moving into discussion.

Our Rapporteur, Marina Faggionato is a rising young star of the family bar in QEB chambers. If any solicitors are taking note, that is her professional address. She will keep a record of our discussion, and help with the formulation of resolutions which have to be presented and agreed on the last day of the conference.

Yvonne Brown is chairing the Resolutions Committee (here she is in the front row). Each working group has one Resolutions Committee member, you only have to identify who it is and feed in your suggestions.

This conference is the product of 18 months of planning. The planning is done by a steering group, some of whom are members of the Council, many of whom are not.

To them we owe a huge debt of gratitude; they not only come up with the ideas as to the topics we should address but then go out into the professional world and recruit the speakers. It is thanks to their professional contacts and their charm that we acquire the professional support that we have today. Our thanks are due to Yvonne Brown, Helen Clift, Katherine Gieve, Danya Glaser, Ann Haigh, Angela Nield, Gillian Schofield and Claire Sturge for their outstanding contribution to the planning of this conference.

My last word is for Dartington. It is to me a place of unusual beauty and allure. The garden is historically important and presently immensely well maintained. So having listened carefully to the weather forecast on *Points West* I can tell you that a high wind is anticipated later in the day and torrential rain tomorrow. The prudent will look at the garden this evening. Jo has factored in a period of free time from 6pm to 6.30pm (she is indulgent in these small things) and so I would recommend the garden this evening.

No conference is perfect and we can always learn from experience. I see already that we made a blunder starting at 2pm when rooms are not available for occupation before then. I am sorry for the rush and delay, I think next time we will start at 2.30pm rather than 2pm. Jo is going to do some housekeeping, and then she tells me I am chairing the first plenary session so we will get the conference underway.

PLENARY 1

PARENTAL MENTAL HEALTH AND ITS
IMPACT ON CHILDREN

CLINICAL PSYCHOPATHY, PERSONALITY DISORDER AND RISK OF INTRA-FAMILIAL VIOLENCE

Professor Jane L Ireland

Chartered Forensic Psychologist

and

Dr Nicola Graham-Kevan

Chartered Psychologist, School of Psychology, University of Central Lancashire, UK

SUMMARY OF PAPER

Both personality disorder and clinical psychopathy have been related to violence. Although the association between these concepts is not necessarily straightforward, they need to be factored into any consideration of risk, particularly clinical psychopathy which is proving to represent a strong risk factor for violence at both the conceptual and empirical level. Robust assessments will account for personality disorder and clinical psychopathy and additional factors known to relate to recidivism.

Personality disorder is not a homogenous concept, but a disorder best described as an enduring, pervasive and stable pattern of experience and behaviour that deviates markedly from the expectation of an individual's culture. Clinical psychopathy is closely related to personality disorder and is conceptualised both in terms of personality and behaviour, closely related to histrionic, narcissistic and antisocial personality disorder. Both personality disorder and clinical psychopathy require careful diagnostic assessment involving lengthy clinical interview coupled with collateral and informant information.

There is an evidenced link between clinical psychopathy and violence which covers the full remit of aggression. There is a less well-researched link between personality disorder and violence, with a continuing agreement that this association may be an indirect one, with personality disorder more likely to feature as part of the route to violence in those who already have a history of violence, potentially acting through other important risk variables such as substance abuse. There needs to be more research into this area, particularly for more specific research exploring the association between these disorders and direct harm to children, including both physical harm and emotional harm.

THE PAPER

Personality disorder and clinical psychopathy have each been related to violence, featuring either in clinical risk guides for predicting and managing violence within the family home (eg the *Brief Spousal Assault Form for the Evaluation of Risk*: Kropp et al 2005), or in general aggression risk guides (eg *Historical, Clinical Risk Assessment Guide*: Webster et al 1997). The association between these concepts is also not necessarily straightforward, particularly with regards to personality disorder. For example, personality disorder is thought to have an *indirect* relationship to partner violence, and a more *direct* relationship with general violence; whereas the association between clinical psychopathy and general, sexual *and* partner violence is considered more direct. To aid an outline of the association between violence and personality disorder/clinical psychopathy, a definition of each concept is perhaps a valuable starting point.

Personality disorder is best described as an enduring, pervasive and stable pattern of experience and behaviour that deviates markedly from the expectation of an individual's culture. It manifests itself in areas such as cognition, affect, interpersonal functioning and/or impulse control, leading to significant distress or impairment (DSM-IV-TR 2000). It is not a homogenous concept; heterogeneity within those diagnosed with such disorders is high, with a number of specific disorders falling within this concept (eg anti-social, histrionic, borderline, paranoid personality disorder etc). Community prevalence rates for personality disorder are reported to be between 6% and 15% (Ekselius et al 2001), and between 64% and 78% for prisoner samples (McMurran 2003). The diagnosis of this disorder does, however, need to be completed carefully. It is not possible to determine the presence of this disorder based on limited information and from limited clinical contact, nor is it possible to diagnose among children and adolescents. The preferred assessments (eg International Personality Disorder Examination), require a lengthy clinical interview coupled with collateral and informant information.

A concept closely related to personality disorder is that of clinical psychopathy. This has been conceptualised both in terms of personality and behaviour, with Blackburn (2007) arguing for clinical psychopathy to relate closely to histrionic, narcissistic and anti-social personality disorder. Like personality disorder, the diagnosis of clinical psychopathy requires a detailed analysis. This includes an assessment of interpersonal and behavioural characteristics, with the current assessment of choice representing the Psychopathy Checklist Revised (PCL-R: Hare 1998), and focusing on adult populations only. Prevalence rates for clinical psychopathy vary across samples, although they tend to be higher among forensic populations – ranging between 12% and 30% (eg Huchzermeier et al 2006; Porter et al 2001; Tengström et al 2000). As with personality disorder, heterogeneity within the concept is high although it tends to be referred to globally (ie someone 'is' or 'is not' clinically psychopathic). There is, however, preference for reporting the psychopathic *profile* of an individual. The most common convention is to report the Factor I (interpersonal style) and Factor II (criminal history and lifestyle) scores since these both contribute to the overall PCL-R score. Finally, it is also important to make it clear that the concept being focused on here is that of *clinical* psychopathy and not 'psychopathic disorder'. The latter is a legal term that does not map onto a clinical diagnosis of psychopathy.

There is, however, consensus in the literature on the value of assessing for both personality disorder and clinical psychopathy when the issue under exploration is the future risk of aggression. Clinical psychopathy has been the most researched, leading some to argue that it is not possible to complete a violence risk assessment without attention to this concept (Hart 2001). The current paper aims to outline some of the findings across the literature with regards to their application to risk for violence, with particular reference to intra-familial violence. Psychopathy will be presented first, followed by personality disorder.

Studies of clinical psychopathy and re-offending report an overall tendency for such individuals to present with an increased risk for a range of offences, not just violence. Such individuals tend to commit more thefts, robberies, drug offences, escapes, kidnappings, obstructions of justice, and miscellaneous offences than non-psychopathic individuals. Of the most serious violent offences, clinical psychopaths have been found to demonstrate more gratuitous, sadistic, and instrumental offending than non-psychopaths (Porter et al 2000) and to recidivate more frequently and within a shorter time frame. Clinical psychopathy also outperforms mental illness and substance use as predictors for violent recidivism (eg Fullam & Dolan 2006; Tengström et al 2000). Scores on the PCL-R correlate well with violence risk guides (eg Webster et al 1997), and on occasion outperforming them as a risk predictor (Dahle 2006).

Although research on clinical psychopathy has focused primarily on men, there have been similarities reported for women with regards to the ability of the PCL-R to predict risk (eg Warren et al 2005). For women, however, personality disorder (notably borderline personality disorder) is presenting as a more robust risk factor for violence than clinical psychopathy. This is in part due to the assessment of clinical psychopathy – the PCL-R – which is arguably based on a male definition of psychopathy and anti-social behaviour. In short, the typology of a female clinical psychopath is less well known and researched, although some convergence is acknowledged.

The relationship between clinical psychopathy and sexual violence is more complex than that for nonsexual violence, with the prevalence of clinical psychopathy across types of sex offender differing markedly. For example, Porter et al (2000) found that 34% of non-sexual offenders were diagnosed with clinical psychopathy, whereas only 6% of extra-familial, 11% of intra-familial and 6% of mixed extra- and intra-familial were diagnosed as psychopathic. The prevalence of clinical psychopaths found in the group who targeted adult victims only was comparable to that found in non-sexually violent offenders (35%). The highest prevalence of psychopathy was found in the most criminally diverse sex offenders, the mixed adult and child offenders (64%). These results suggest that a diagnosis of clinical psychopathy increases the risk of recidivism in *some* types of sex offenders but not others. Therefore, a diagnosis of clinical psychopathy is important, but it is not as robust a predictor of future risk in all sex offenders as other factors (eg sexual deviance; substance use, relationship problems etc). There is, however, evidence suggesting that the heterogeneity of clinical psychopathy is particularly important to account for with sex offenders, and that whereas an overall clinical psychopathy score may not always distinguish sex from non-sex offenders, individual factor scores may. The Factor II (criminal history and lifestyle) component of clinical psychopathy appears particularly useful in distinguishing between these two groups, with adult sex offenders (ie those offending against adults) presenting with higher Factor II scores than non-sex offenders, with sex offenders who victimised children presenting with higher Factor I (interpersonal style) scores (Serin et al 2001).

There is also a researched association between clinical psychopathy and intra-familial violence, specifically partner violence. Although contrary to political conceptualisations of domestic violence as a crime motivated not by pathology but by patriarchy (eg Dobash & Dobash 1979; Pence & Paymar 1993), research suggests a diagnosis of clinical psychopathy is predictive of recidivism risk in domestic violence. Hilton et al (2001) investigated the rates of violent recidivism of men who had been convicted of a crime of violence against an intimate partner and compared them to a sample of non-domestic violence offenders. They found that among the domestic violence offenders, their PCL-R total score was positively associated with violent recidivism. This effect was found in spite of the fact that in comparison to non-domestically violent offenders these men had significantly lower PCL-R scores overall and evidenced less criminal lifestyles. In fact, clinical psychopathy features in all clinical risk guides for assessing partner violence, although in some they are merged within the description for the 'personality disorder' risk factor (eg Kropp et al 2005).

Thus there is an evidenced link between clinical psychopathy and violence which covers the full remit of aggression – general, sexual and intra-familial partner violence. The link between personality disorder and violence, however, has been less researched by comparison. The majority of research has been at a conceptual level, focused on cross-sectional research or the association between personality disorder and victimisation. There has also been a tendency for research to fail to separate out clinical psychopathy from personality disorder and instead to consider them both simultaneously. This is particularly the case for earlier research (ie in the 1990s).

At a conceptual level an association between personality disorder and violence is argued on the basis that there are direct indicators of an aggressive disposition in the clinical criteria for anti-social, borderline and paranoid personality disorders (Blackburn 1998). Hostile traits are also evidenced in a number of personality disorders (Widiger & Trull 1994). Hostility (eg rumination) is a factor known to raise the potential for aggression since it assists with the accessing of aggressive beliefs and associated aggressive scripts (Huesmann 1988). Thus there is sufficient reason to suppose a link, coupled further with the view that if a behaviour is repetitive then it is likely to be driven by personality. Thus, whereas a single incidence of aggression could, arguably, result from other factors (eg alcohol, an episode of psychosis), *repetitive* violence is thought to stem more from enduring personality characteristics.

Empirically, personality disorder has been found to correlate with a risk of violent recidivism in those presenting with a history of violence (Harris et al 1993), although most of the literature has focused on anti-social and borderline personality disorders, or failed to indicate the specific personality disorder under study (eg Harris et al 1993). A relationship between anti-social and borderline personality disorder is expected, nonetheless, owing to the fact that each of these disorders encourage a failure to inhibit aggression. Only one personality disorder, sadistic personality disorder, includes a clear *predisposition* to aggress. However, this disorder is no longer recognised, having been removed from the classification system, largely due to political reasons.

With regards to borderline personality disorder, the majority of research has focused on the association that it has with childhood victimisation, as opposed to adult engagement in perpetration. It is, however, considered to be associated with later adult perpetration through the risk factor of 'early maladjustment', which includes experiences of victimisation. Early maladjustment as a child is one of a number of identified risk factors known to elevate an individual's risk for future aggression perpetration (Kropp et al 2005). Borderline personality disorder is also considered related to aggression perpetration through an increased risk for poorly managed affect and impulsivity, with both of these elements known to increase the potential for an aggressive response (Ireland et al 2006).

Anti-social personality disorder has, however, been researched more. It is considered more closely associated with violence than borderline personality disorder (McMurran 2003), in part due to aggression representing a diagnostic feature. Even accounting for the fact that research has tended to look at anti-social traits as opposed to a full diagnosis, coupled with a tendency to discuss anti-social personality disorder in conjunction with clinical psychopathy, there remains evidence to indicate an association between this disorder and violence perpetration. Indeed, Scott and Resnick (2006) argued that the violence demonstrated by those with anti-social personality disorder presents with specific features, reporting that it is triggered by revenge, periods of heavy alcohol consumption, and a lack of emotion. Scott and Resnick (2006) further argue for the importance of anti-social *traits* as opposed to a full diagnosis, indicating that traits alone are a sufficient risk marker for future aggression.

There is, however, a continuing argument in the academic and clinical literature, that the association between personality disorder and violence (both general and intra-familial violence) may be an indirect one, with personality disorder working through other factors (Webster et al 1997; Kropp et al 2005). Taking intra-familial violence, specifically partner violence, as an example, it has been suggested that attachment styles may be one important correlating factor. The association between personality disorder and partner violence has drawn in particular on the creation of personality disorder through maladaptive attachment styles that an individual has developed during their childhood. For example, the 'preoccupied' attached individual whom presents with strong dependency needs is particularly prone to reactive aggression, with this associated with borderline personality disorder. The 'dismissive' attached individual whom is more withdrawn with low dependency needs is prone to more controlled aggression (if they are unable to withdraw), with this associated with anti-social personality disorder (Ireland et al 2006). The idea here is simply that personality disorder is developed in part by early childhood experiences which manifest themselves in poor interaction patterns with others (ie maladaptive personality). This personality can make an individual prone to responding negatively to events occurring within relationships, particularly if this threatens core schemas (beliefs) relating to attachment, such as a fear of being abandoned or a fear of being ignored. Equally it can encourage a re-expression in their current intimate relationship of the unhelpful behavioural patterns that they displayed as a child.

Research has generally reported that the most florid of personality disorders, specifically those most dramatic, are the ones most related to partner violence. This specifically includes those personality disorders which have a component of anger, impulsivity or behavioural instability, notably borderline, narcissistic, anti-social and histrionic personality disorders (Kropp et al 1995). As noted earlier, however, personality disorder does not *necessarily* have a direct link to a risk for partner violence; it is considered one of several pathways. Personality disorder can act indirectly through factors such as substance use (ie personality disorder plus difficulties in managing substances can raise the risk). Other factors thought to promote the risk for partner violence can act in a similar way, with mental illness and social disruption also acting through substance abuse (Hart 2001), with the mechanisms through which personality disorder is thought to promote the risk for partner violence including negative emotions, unstable attachment, impulsivity, suspiciousness and affect relating to entitlement (Hart 2001).

This paper has illustrated the importance of accounting for both personality disorder and clinical psychopathy in assessments of violence risk. Clinical psychopathy is the more robust *direct* risk factor, although personality disorder is more likely to feature as part of the route to violence in those who already have a history of violence, potentially acting through other important risk variables such as substance abuse. The importance of completing individual case formulations and avoiding making an automatic link to violence, particularly for personality disorder, is particularly important.

There is, however, a need for more research into this area. Little attention has been given to:

(1)   the association between personality disorder and clinical psychopathy across sex;

(2)   the dynamic nature of these concepts across time, with both currently considered to represent lifetime, stable, concepts;

(3)   which individuals with clinical psychopathy and/or personality disorder are *not* likely to recidivate violently; and

(4)   the relationship of these concepts to violence towards children.

With regards to the latter point, there remains a need for more specific research exploring the association between these disorders and direct harm to children, including both physical and emotional harm. A link is clearly expected and, indeed, it could be argued at a conceptual level that a child exposed to negative and disruptive parenting is likely to be in a higher risk category for developing attachment difficulties and later personality challenges.

Equally, there needs to be more attention given to what protects individuals who do present with personality disorder and/or clinical psychopathy from displaying overt or covert aggression within family settings, including exploring how some personality disorders may actually inhibit aggressive tendencies. Connected to this, the concept of heterogeneity is an important one; each case needs to be considered individually and there should be an avoidance of over-focusing on these concepts to the detriment of considering other important risk factors (eg substance abuse).

Nonetheless there does need to be more recognition of the importance of accounting for personality disorder and clinical psychopathy in any consideration of risk, particularly of clinical psychopathy which is proving to represent a very robust risk factor for violence at both the conceptual and empirical level. Furthermore, the most robust assessments will be those that account for personality disorder and clinical psychopathy, *and* additional factors known to relate to recidivism, such as substance abuse, employment problems and relationship difficulties etc. Indeed, some would consider it professional negligence not to include a concept such as clinical psychopathy in a violence risk assessment, although equally it would be negligent to base a risk assessment on a single risk factor alone (Hart 2000). The concern here is that merely demonstrating the absence of clinical psychopathy or personality disorder within a clinical presentation should not lead to a conclusion of low risk, rather the presence of these concepts can help with opinions on the severity, frequency and typology of risk.

CONFERENCE PRESENTATION

In her presentation Professor Ireland noted that in family settings both clinical psychopathy and personality disorder are seen. Professionals encounter parents that don't have a criminal background, but have some concerning interpersonal presentation; the traits are varied but can include callousness, impulsivity, lack of empathy and poor behavioural controls. Non-criminal psychopathy is now being researched. Personality disorder and clinical psychopathy are different, but they are often confused in instructions to experts; particularly antisocial personality disorder and clinical psychopathy which are often seen as the same thing. Professor Ireland expressed her concern at violence risk assessments that leave out the matter of clinical psychopathy; it has to be considered if only to screen it out. If clinical psychopathy is present this does suggest an elevated risk; the risk changes and becomes more versatile. If clinical psychopathy is not present, it does not mean that the risk is low, just that it is not a significant clinical fact for that individual.

REFERENCES

Blackburn, R 'Personality disorder and psychopathy: Conceptual and empirical integration' (2007) 13 *Psychology, Crime and Law* 7–18.

Dahle, K 'Strengths and limitations of actuarial prediction of criminal reoffence in a German prison sample: A comparative study of LSI-R, HCR-20 and PCL-R' (2006) 29 *International Journal of Law and Psychiatry* 431–442.

Dobash, RP and Dobash, RE *Violence against Wives: A Case against Patriarchy* (New York: Free Press, 1979).

DSM-IV-TR *Diagnostic and Statistical Manual of Mental Disorder, Text Revision* (American Psychiatric Association, 2000).

Ekselius, L, Tillfors, M, Furmark, T and Fredrikson, M 'Personality disorders in the general population: DSM-IV and ICD-10 defined prevalence as related to sociodemographic profile' (2001) 30 *Personality and Individual Differences* 311–320.

Fullam, R and Dolan, M 'The criminal and personality profile of patients with schizophrenia and comorbid psychopathic traits' (2006) 40 *Personality and Individual Differences* 1591–1602.

Hart, S 'Forensic Issues' in WJ Livesey (ed) *Handbook of Personality Disorders: Theory, Research and Treatment* (UK: Guilford Press, 2001).

Hare, RD 'Psychopathy, affect, and behaviour' in D Cooke, A Forth, and RD Hare (eds) *Psychopathy: Theory, Research, and Implications for Society* (The Netherlands: Kluwer, 1998) 105–137.

Harris, GT, Rice, ME and Quinsey, VL 'Violent recidivism in mentally disordered offenders: The development of a statistical prediction instrument' (1993) 20 *Criminal Justice and Behaviour* 315–335.

Hilton, NZ, Harris, GT and Rice, ME 'Predicting violence by serious wife assaulters' (2001) 16 *Journal of Interpersonal Violence* 408–423.

Huchzermeirer, C, Bruβ, E, Godt, N, and Aldenhoff, J 'Kiel psychotherapy project for violent offenders: Towards empirically based forensic psychotherapy – disturbance profiles and risk of recidivism among incarcerated offenders in a German prison' (2006) 13 *Journal of Clinical Forensic Medicine* 72–79.

Huesmann, LR 'An information processing model for the development of aggression' (1988) 14 *Aggressive Behaviour* 13–24.

Ireland et al *Life Minus Violence Treatment Manual* (Mersey Care NHS Trust and University of Central Lancashire, 2006).

Kropp, R, Hart, SD and Belfrage, H *Manual for the Brief Spousal Assault Form for the Evaluation of Risk: B-Safer* (Vancouver: Proactive Resolutions, 2004).

McMurran, M *Expert Paper on Personality Disorders* (Liverpool: NHS National Programme on Forensic Mental Health Research and Development, 2002).

Pence, E and Paymar, M *Education Groups for Men who Batter: The Duluth Model* (New York: Springer, 1993).

Porter, S, Birt, AR and Boer, DP 'Investigation of the criminal and conditional release profiles of Canadian federal offenders as a function of psychopathy and age' (2001) 25 *Law and Human Behaviour* 647–661.

Porter, S, Fairweather, D, Drugge, J, Hervé, H, Birt, AR and Boer, DP 'Profiles of psychopathy in incarcerated sexual offenders' (2000) 27 *Criminal Justice and Behaviour* 216–233.

Scott, CL and Resnick, PJ 'Violence risk assessment in persons with mental illness' (2006) 11 *Aggression and Violent Behaviour* 598–611.

Serin, RC, Mailloux, DL, and Malcolm, PB 'Psychopathy, deviant sexual arousal, and recidivism among sexual offenders' (2001) 16 *Journal of Interpersonal Violence* 234–246.

Tengström, A, Grann, M, Långström, N and Kullgren, G 'Psychopathy (PCL-R) as a predictor of violent recidivism among criminal offenders with schizophrenia' (2000) 24 *Law and Human Behaviour* 45–58.

Warren, JI, South, SC, Burnette, ML, Rogers, A, Friend, R, Bale, R and Van Pattern, I 'Understanding the risk factors for violence and criminality in women: The concurrent validity of the PCL-R and the HCR-20' (2005) 28 *Journal of Law and Psychiatry* 269–289.

Webster, CD, Douglas, KS, Eaves, D and Hart, SD *HCR-20: Assessing Risk for Violence (version 2)* (The Mental Health Law and Policy Institute, Simon Fraser University, 1997).

WORKING WITH FAMILIES WHERE A PARENT HAS MENTAL HEALTH PROBLEMS: RISKS, OPPORTUNITIES AND CHALLENGES

Dr Diana Cassell

Consultant Child and Adolescent Psychiatrist, Tolworth Hospital

SUMMARY OF PAPER

Whilst many parents with mental health difficulties do manage to parent to a level that is at least 'good enough' many of those families are 'in need'; with appropriately targeted support the likelihood of crises and negative outcomes is reduced. In order to determine whether a family needs help consideration of complex and dynamic models of risk (both acute and long-term) is required, balancing information from a variety of sources.

Families facing multiple adversities often feel overwhelmed by their difficulties, the complexities of their needs can similarly overwhelm professionals. Determining the family's current needs requires all those who know the family to pool their information.

Whilst knowing the diagnosis for an unwell parent helps (it provides guidance about what can be expected), this alone will not determine risk. In assessing the child's needs, it is important to find out how the child functions at school or nursery and to carefully consider whether the child has possibly as yet unrecognised needs of their own. Helping the child understand their parent's illness is an important building block, but one that can only be developed once the parent has a good understanding of their own illness.

Professionals often only have experience of their own systems: social workers with children's services often have limited experience of mental health systems, while professionals within adult mental health systems similarly often have little experience of children's services. Professionals tend to ally themselves with their core client group. Professionals in adult services should not be asked to give opinions about parenting or the children's needs: this puts them in a difficult position and interferes with the decision-making process; they should however share information about their assessment of the parent and treatment plans.

Families where a parent has a mental illness involve complex loops of adversity and require coordination from different services within complex systems with different priorities. In order for there to be progress, professionals need clarity about the family's predicament and useful interventions. They need to work across different agency cultures and collaborate with a common goal of thinking about the family as a whole.

THE PAPER

INTRODUCTION

Children whose parents have mental health problems face increased risks of poor outcomes. Progress over recent decades has improved awareness of the links between parents' mental health difficulties, child problems and safeguarding concerns; however, there are still considerable challenges for professionals working in these complex situations.

parenting & well-being

Parenting is a stressor for mental health as shown in increased rates of mood disorders in those with parenting responsibilities (Leigh & Milgrom 2008). Children who are stressed or unsettled become more difficult in their behaviour; cycles develop in which stressors affect the parent's health adversely, this leads to the child being unsettled, which in turn impacts adversely on the parent.

Mental health disorders are very common in the population; depression occurs in 20% at some point in the life span, psychoses in 2%, and personality disorders in around 10% (Royal College of Psychiatrists 2004–2008). Many of these parents may also have problems with substance misuse. However, the numbers of children identified as being at risk or requiring significant intervention for the family to stay intact are much lower than that, 54.6 per 10,000 population (Children Order Statistical Bulletin 2006); many parents with mental health disorders do manage to parent to a level that is at least 'good enough'. However, many of these families are among those identified as 'in need'; appropriately targeted support reduces the likelihood of crises and negative outcomes.

Diagnosis alone does not determine the extent to which parenting capacity or the children will be affected: one mother with a severe episode of depression felt worthless and so neglected herself, but kept her toddler safe and met his needs. The children of another mother with milder depression were at considerable risk due to her inattention to their needs.

practicality of assessing family – require of more intervention

Deciding which families need help requires consideration of complex and dynamic models of risk, balancing information from a variety of sources. The presence of a psychiatric problem makes assessing any problems in the parenting more difficult for professionals. Many of the children suffering adversity come from families without significant mental health problems in the parents; professionals do need to assess the whole situation and not allow the presence (or absence) of a psychiatric diagnosis to dominate the picture.

ACUTE RISK

Acutely the risk is of neglect or physical harm; assessing this requires careful consideration of the parent's current mental state and the specific symptoms the parent is experiencing, in acute illness these can change frequently requiring close monitoring. The recent behaviour of the parents will give a good idea of how they are likely to behave in the immediate future, historical information about behaviour in previous similar episodes is helpful too. Some specific symptoms imply very high risk situations: command hallucinations, the child included in the psychotic thinking and plans for suicide with altruistic killing (Rutter & Quinton 1984). In other situations the risk is less specifically linked to the mental state, but requires consideration of the level of insight and how the symptoms affect the parent's current range of behaviour.

LONGER-TERM RISKS

The risks are of neglect and emotional damage leading to suboptimal development, or poor outcomes in terms of the child's own mental well-being and social outcomes.

However, children are resilient, some will do surprisingly well despite adverse circumstances: this does not justify not offering help but reminds us of the need to be measured in response to the situation. Removing a child from their parent to the care system is fraught with risks and disruptive to the child's attachments, so whenever possible, other interventions need to be found. When the parent has long-term poor mental health impacting on their parenting, removing the child to an alternative family may be in the child's best interests; for some families providing support which can flex in response to changing needs is the better option.

The child's attachment status, in terms of the depth of attachments to their main caregivers and the extent to which that operates as a secure base for the child, has a significant impact on their future emotional and social development. A secure attachment acts as a protective factor for the child's emotional and social development, whereas the lack of one is a risk factor (Rutter et al 2009). The promotion of attachment formation with secure qualities requires the parent to provide consistent care, responsive to the child's needs and emotional state, thus helping the child to modulate their own levels of arousal and building positive templates for future relationships (Bretherton et al 2005). Occasions when the parent appears frightened, threatening or dissociated to the child tend to lead to a disorganised attachment pattern (Hesse & Main 2006). These problems can occur if the parent is disturbed, reacting to hallucinations or in response to stressors triggering dissociation as an abnormal response and so the risks to attachment are increased when the parent has a mental illness or personality disorder.

People with personality disorders often had damaging childhoods with poor parenting, they tend to have difficulties sustaining close emotional relationships and experience periods of emotional instability. These factors all contribute to a potential risk to the quality of their parenting and have been found to pose greater risk to the child's emotional development than psychiatric disorders (Norton & Dolan 1996).

Witnessing violence within the home constitutes emotional abuse which is especially troubling for children when their attachment figures are included within the violence, parents who have personality disorders, substance misuse or psychosis can be more prone to lives including violent incidents.

ASSESSING THE FAMILY SITUATION

Families facing multiple adversities often feel overwhelmed by their difficulties; the complexity of their needs can similarly overwhelm professionals. Knowing the parent's diagnosis will help; it provides guidance about what can be expected, but remember the diagnosis alone will not determine the level of risk. Plans need to include how any new information about changes in circumstances or behaviour will be reviewed.

A formulation of the family's current needs including these factors will provide structure to help this planning:

- A picture of the parent's illness: their mental state, how their symptoms affect parenting, the treatment plan and likely progress; with a holistic account of any learning difficulties, substance misuse concerns and physical health problems.

(handwritten in left margin: Consideration of mental health in families)

- Other pressures in the parent's life: domestic violence, financial or housing problems, family tensions etc.

- The child's mental and physical health and needs, behaviour profile, level of coping at school.

- The family's daily routines: things that cause common stresses.

- Consideration of the child as a young carer.

- Supportive factors: eg partner, extended family or other support.

Pooling the information from everyone who knows the family will give insight into the family members' resiliencies: how have they managed until now against all these odds? Developing plans that support and build on these factors will enhance family coping. Does the child appear to be thriving? Some will, especially if there is a well parent or other significant adult providing regular emotional support.

CONSIDERING PARENTING

Does the parent have any concerns about their parenting? Which professional should initiate these conversations? Most parents, including those with mental illnesses, want to talk about their children and to discuss the pressures of parenting. The opportunity to discuss these concerns helps parents with their own well-being. Parenting is highly stressful, yet this area is often neglected in fear that a parent with a mental illness will feel threatened that the children may be taken away, but parents will often have an awareness that things are not all right for their child. For some of these parents, the problem may be a lack of basic parenting skills, as opposed to those whose parenting capacity becomes affected during periods of illness which requires a different approach.

When the parent has a good understanding of their illness and how this affects their personal life, they can consider the issues which this presents for their child. Current initiatives for recovery-focused practice in mental health (Roberts et al 2008) empower service users to know more about their needs and to manage them. Prioritising attending to their own health care and getting greater stability in their mental state can then be an objective which also serves to help the children.

This discourse opens opportunities to identify specific problems and to find solutions; for example, if the parent struggles with basic daily routines this will add to their sense of inadequacy and the stress for all the family. Parenting programmes are readily available; the underlying message needs to be: these are common difficulties, addressing them will increase the chances of keeping their children and reduce their personal stress.

Practical support such as after-school clubs, help around bedtime etc, will often start the positive change for the family; working collaboratively with the parents to plan what is needed and using resources creatively can maximise effectiveness. A difficult cycle for a family where the mother became depressed when her teenage daughter with Aspergers would not go to school was broken when help to get the girl to school was provided.

THE CHILDREN'S NEEDS

In assessing the child's needs it is important to obtain information from nursery or school about how the child functions there, how they relate to the adults, how they get on with other children, any comments the child may make and how well cared for they appear to be. There should always be careful consideration of whether the child may have unrecognised needs of their own such as developmental disorders, health or education problems.

It is necessary to ask directly about any tasks the child may need to perform when the parent is distracted or lacks energy; uncovering what the child does to help on a practical level and how much the child ends up caring for, providing emotional support or reassurance to the parents; assists consideration of the child as a young carer.

Being in a caring role adds to the child's own stresses and can interfere with them seeing the parent as in charge; many of these children and young people do not want to lose this responsibility because of loyalty to their parents, also they may not want to lose their sense of power within the family. Depending on the age and developmental stage of the child, these matters will need delicate attention: for some it will be best to provide practical support or to join Young Carers groups, but not alter the dynamics; for others addressing this balance will be necessary.

Respite care to top-up the nurturing the child receives and time away from the worries can be very supportive. Research shows that having positive other adult caring relationships is the most important protective factor for the child's mental health outcomes (Kauffman et al 1979). This support can also be then used to infill with extra care at times when the family is in crisis.

Helping the child understand their parent's illness is an important building block; this can only be developed once the parent has a good understanding of their own illness. Parents often avoid talking about their illness with their children. Explaining that children who lack information tend to blame themselves can help parents see the need to find a way to do this (Cooklin 2008), leading to discussion about how best to explain their illness to the child.

PROFESSIONAL ROLES

Social workers within children's services often have limited experience of the mental health systems; the professionals within adult mental health services similarly often have little experience of children's services. The legislative frameworks differ: the Mental Health Act requires evidence that the parent appears to have an acute mental illness and that there is a risk to themselves or others; there can be high risk situations with parents behaving oddly and putting their child at risk, but who do not have an acute mental illness. The Children Act considers intervention is required because of significant harm and keeps the child's welfare central, so is often the framework required. The request for assessment of the parent's mental health often finds that they were not sectionable. Due to the high threshold needed for the Mental Health Act many whose functioning is impaired by distress, obsessive-compulsive disorder, agoraphobia or in less acute illness periods can not be forcibly treated or detained. Assessment drift occurs when professionals forget that the mental health assessment was requested because of concern for the child as a result of the parent's behaviour, and can lead to difficulties in effectively planning to safeguard the child.

Professionals tend to ally themselves with their core client group; adult mental health professionals act as advocates to champion the adult's rights for benefits or housing, it can be difficult for them to acknowledge concerns about the children. The rights of the parent need to be seen in terms of their right to maximise their personal functioning and the well-being of their family. When promoting the child's best interests requires alternative care for the child, an ill parent will find this very distressing; recognising that this is needed through no fault of their own, but because of how their illness affects their parenting, protects the family relationships. When there are Children Act proceedings the adult mental health professional's role must be to support the vulnerable ill parent through this stressful experience.

Professionals in adult services should not be asked to give opinions about parenting or the children's needs: this puts them in a difficult position and interferes with the decision-making process. Their main contribution to child safeguarding is to provide information about the parent's illness, treatment and prognosis and any risk presented by the parent's symptoms or behaviour. They may be in a strong position to encourage the parent to accept help around parenting and childcare and to contribute to the care plan for the family as a whole, they need to be empowered to focus on the areas related to their role with the parent; professionals within the system need to have discrete areas of responsibility.

CHALLENGES

The child's needs are paramount; it is not helpful to the parents for children to continue in adverse circumstances, but discussing the concerns can feel as if it will destabilise the family. Families where a parent has a mental illness, as described here, involve complex loops of adversity within the family and require coordination from different services within complex systems with different priorities.

Progress requires professionals to have clarity about the family's predicament and useful interventions; as well as how they can work together across different agency cultures and collaborate with a common goal of thinking about the family as a whole. Understanding the differences between the legal frameworks and respecting the area of focus for each professional's work supports effective collaboration. In a situation where the child's and adult's needs conflict, particular care is needed so professionals can focus on their core area of responsibility in line with their role whilst keeping communication open; at other times they may flexibly share tasks.

In a situation with conflicting needs, professionals working in adult mental health teams need to know that they can and should focus on the parent's needs, while providing information about their area of expertise to help those charged with prime responsibility for the children's well-being to safeguard the children (and at times make difficult decisions) – this will free them for the open collaboration and communication.

CONFERENCE PRESENTATION

In her presentation Dr Cassell highlighted the problems faced by such families. The parents feel frightened that they will lose their child; they feel they need the child's presence and support and assume that everyone is blaming them. Children are at risk of being confused and frightened but some are amazingly wise. If a child has a significant other who is offering emotional warmth they may be doing well notwithstanding their parent's difficulties. Highlighting the difficulties that may be caused by the division of the system, Dr Cassell suggested that matters would be improved if core roles were clarified and respected, and if each group of experts focused on their job: with good information sharing and coordination of plans difficult decisions can be taken about what is in the child's best interest. Dr Cassell invited delegates to consider how parents could be helped to think about their own mental health problems and how these impact on the children and to what extent services were currently acting in ways that were not conducive to that exercise.

REFERENCES

Bretherton, I 'In pursuit of the internal working model construct and its relevance to attachment relationships' in KE Grossman, K Grossman and E Waters (eds) *Attachment from infancy to adulthood: The major longitudinal studies* (New York: Guilford Press, 2005) 13–47.

Cooklin, A 'Children as carers of parents with mental illness' (2008) 8(1) *Psychiatry* 17–20.

Children Order Statistical Bulletin (Belfast: Department of Health, Social Services and Public Safety, Northern Ireland (DHSSPNI), 2006) 4.

Hesse, E and Main, M 'Frightened, threatening and dissociative parental behaviour in low-risk samples: Description, discussion and interpretations' (2006) 18 *Development and Psychopathology* 309–343.

Kauffman, C, Grunebaum, H, Cohler, B and Gamer, E 'Superkids: competent children of psychotic mothers' (1979) 136(11) *American Journal of Psychiatry* 1398–1402.

Leigh, B and Milgrom, J 'Risk factors for antenatal depression, postnatal depression and parenting stress' (2008) *BMC Psychiatry*, 8:24 doi:10.1186/1471-244X-8-24. Available from: www.biomedcentral.com/1471-244X/8/24.

Norton, K and Dolan, B 'Personality Disorder and Parenting' in M Gopfert, J Webster and MV Seeman (eds) *Parental Psychiatric Disorder: Distressed parents and their families* (Cambridge University Press, 1996) 219–232.

Roberts, G, Dorkins, E, Woolridge, J and Hewis, E 'Detained: what's my choice? Part 1: Discussion' (2008) 14 *Advances in Psychiatric Treatment* 172–180.

Royal College of Psychiatrists, Mental Health Information Leaflets: bipolar disorder (2007), depression (2008), personality disorder (2007) and Schizophrenia (2004). Available at www.rcpsych.ac.uk/mentalhealthinfoforall.aspx.

Rutter, M, Kreppner, J and Sonuga-Barke, E 'Attachment insecurity, disinhibited attachment and attachment disorders: where do the research findings leave the concepts?' (2009) 50(5) *Journal of Child Psychology and Psychiatry* 529–543.

Rutter, M and Quinton, D 'Parental psychiatric disorder: effects on children' (1984) 14 *Psychological Medicine* 853–880.

THE FAMILY DRUG AND ALCOHOL COURT: A NEW APPROACH TO SAFEGUARDING THE CHILDREN OF PARENTS WHO ABUSE DRUGS AND ALCOHOL

Dr Mike Shaw

Tavistock Clinic

SUMMARY OF PAPER

The Family Drug and Alcohol Court (FDAC) is a uniquely collaborative, interdisciplinary and interpersonal approach to improving the outcome for children with substance misusing parent. FDAC uses the authority of the court to support a highly coordinated and intensive therapeutic intervention, a package of treatment and support designed to improve children's chances to remain safe and thriving in their parent's care whilst making alternative plans as soon as possible for the families that fail.

The FDAC team comprises a small group of social workers, drug treatment workers, an Adult Psychiatrist, Dr Shaw (a Child & Adolescent Psychiatrist) and 'Parent Mentors' (recovered substances misusers who are often parents with experience of care proceedings). FDAC judges are particularly prepared for the task, with the same judge throughout proceedings. The judge tries to create a relationship with families by talking directly with parents on a fortnightly basis, and uses the authority of the court to keep the plan on track and maintain working alliances between the parties.

Experts are involved with the family from the outset; on the first day intervention team members meet families at court and answer questions, there follows daily contact for the first week (including a home visit and a whole day assessment) with an 'intervention plan' agreed the following week. The plan is designed to help parents overcome their drug and alcohol problems in the child's timeframe, broken down into a series of 2-3 month steps. Once parents have navigated the first stage of the intervention (achieving abstinence from street drugs and alcohol) the next is to see whether recovery can be sustained, whether parents can adopt a 'child centred lifestyle' and whether they can meet the child's needs.

THE PAPER

INTRODUCTION

This paper is based on my experience as the child psychiatrist and Clinical Lead for the intervention team of the UK's first Family Drug and Alcohol Court (FDAC). In essence FDAC attempts to improve outcomes for children with substance misusing parents, through a novel co-operation between the Family Court and other agencies. The court lends its authority to a highly coordinated intensive therapeutic intervention. Parents are given the best possible support to overcome their drug or alcohol problems and meet their children's needs in an appropriate time frame. The aim is to improve children's chances of remaining safe and thriving in their parents' care while making alternative plans as soon as possible for the families that fail. The FDAC model comes from the US where it has been running for about 15 years and large non-randomised trials have been encouraging (more parents recover, more children returned and less delay). At the time of writing, the UK programme is 18 months into a 3-year pilot.

THE SCALE OF THE PROBLEM

A surprisingly large number of children live with a parent who abuses drugs or alcohol. In England and Wales the Advisory Council on the Misuse of Drugs estimates that 2–3% of children (under 16) 'have a parent with serious drug problems' (Hidden Harm 2003). In the US the National Survey on Drug Use and Health also found 3% of young people (under 18 years) 'live with a parent who is dependent on, or abused, illicit drugs', while 10.3% 'live with a parent who is dependent on, or abused, alcohol' (2009).

Parental substance misuse is important to safeguarding authorities and the Family Courts because it accounts for so many children at risk. Forrester and Harwin (2006) studied 290 cases going for 'long-term allocation' in four London boroughs. Parental substance misuse was a concern in 34% of all cases, accounted for 40% of the children placed on the child protection register and represented 62% of those cases subject to care proceedings.

MODEL OF HARM

Effective intervention requires a model of how harm occurs, based on a sound understanding of child development and family function. Parents who misuse drugs and alcohol expose their children to multiple risks (see Figure 1 at the end of paper). First, the mixture of genetics, upbringing, culture, trauma and adversity that resulted in the parent's substance misuse conveys a risk to the child over and above the actual substance misuse.

Secondly, intrauterine exposure damages foetal growth and development (particularly in the presence of high maternal blood alcohol during pregnancy) and newborn babies can suffer withdrawal symptoms (especially with maternal misuse of narcotics and benzodiazepines).

Thirdly, parental intoxication and withdrawal (in combination with the parental vulnerability factors mentioned above) leads to problematic interpersonal relationships. Parents are less able to provide the 'sensitive responsiveness' required for children's healthy 'attachment' (Prior & Glaser 2006). Low levels of parental 'mentalising' (the ability to reflect on their own and other's thoughts and feelings (Allen, Fonagy & Bateman 2008) and closely related to 'sensitive responding') limit parent's ability to promote their child's capacity to tolerate, process and communicate painful thoughts and feelings. Harsh treatment and inconsistent discipline also lead to emotional and behavioural problems (Maccoby & Martin 1983). In more severely affected families there is a reduced capacity for mutually satisfying relationships and the dominant mode of interaction is coercion and exploitation (Patterson 1982). Finally children from substance misusing families are more likely to be exposed to the damaging effects of parental discord and violence (Friedman & Chase-Lansdale 2002).

Fourthly, parental intoxication and withdrawal particularly in the presence of high levels of parental dependence, leads to inadequate supervision and routines. Parents fail to keep children safe or feeling safe. There is a lack of developmentally appropriate routines and support for children's physical needs (eating, sleeping and washing). Parents fail to promote developmentally appropriate learning, play and interaction with peers. In severe cases parents don't promote adequate access to education and healthcare.

Finally, very high levels of dependence create a 'substance misuse centred lifestyle'. Parents spend the majority of the day acquiring, taking and recovering from drugs and alcohol. They lose the capacity to meet their own needs and keep themselves safe (therefore exposing their children to further risk). For example they damage their own health or are involved in accidents. Unable to hold down a job they resort to criminal activity (commonly theft and prostitution), thus putting themselves at risk to violence and exploitation and periods of imprisonment. Such families often have complex problems with accommodation. At the same time the social networks of such individuals become depleted and increasingly deviant. Severe substance misuse tends to alienate healthy family and friends. By necessity parents associate with other substance misusers and criminals, greatly increasing the risk to them and their own children.

WHO IS THE FDAC?

FDAC is a collaboration involving the Inner London and City Family Proceedings Court (Wells Street), Cafcass, three inner-London local authorities (Camden, Islington and Westminster), the Tavistock and Portman NHS Foundation Trust, and Coram. The three local authorities, the Home Office, Ministry of Justice and Department for Children, Schools and Families, fund it. There is an independent evaluation being conducted by Brunel University funded by the Nuffield Foundation.

The FDAC intervention team is a small group of social workers, drug treatment workers and 'Parent Mentors', myself (Child and Adolescent Psychiatrist) and an Adult Psychiatrist with an interest in substance misuse. The 'Parent Mentors' are recovered substance misusers who are often parents with experience of care proceedings and work on a voluntary basis. Some of the families we work with find them easier to relate to and they provide a role model of resilience.

ENGAGING AND SUSTAINING FAMILIES

Drug and alcohol misusing parents are difficult to engage. Traumatic backgrounds mean they tend not to trust others. They don't expect anyone to help them or believe they are helpable. What is more, dissembling becomes a very necessary skill for sustaining substance misuse.

Some parents are ready to confront their problems when the court removes their children (or they realise their children could be removed). To make the most of this opportunity the FDAC intervention team meets the families on their first day in court. Team members, including the 'Parent Mentors', introduce themselves and answer questions. There is then daily contact over the remainder of the week, including a home visit and a whole day assessment at the FDAC offices. The following week, parents join the FDAC intervention team, social workers, the Children's Guardian, drug workers, probation officers etc in agreeing an 'intervention plan'.

Nearly all parents want to overcome their drug and alcohol problems and be united as a family, and the initial intervention plan tries to make this possible. However these ambitions are only sustainable if they can be achieved in the child's time frame (for example we try to ensure that babies are permanently placed by their first birthday). The task and time available is broken down into a series of 2–3 month steps. We aim to mix optimism with a realistic appraisal of the challenge. Where the prognosis is poor the parents are told they will need to make better than expected progress. This allows us to present the court (at the second hearing) with a plan that has been agreed by the parents, local authority, Children's Guardian, FDAC intervention team and often other participating agencies (treatment services, probation etc).

Over the course of the intervention plan the families work with a number of agencies but continue to have contact with the FDAC intervention team once a week and the court once a fortnight. The intervention team use 'Motivational interviewing' (Miller & Rollick 2002) to build and sustain the momentum for change. While the court uses its authority to keep the plan on track and maintain working alliances between the parties. Lawyers are absent from these fortnightly hearings (although the Social Worker and Children's Guardian attend). Allowing the family and the judge 10–15 minutes to discuss what is going well, what is not going well and what needs to be done to overcome any obstacles or mishaps. Over time it becomes clear which families are making timely progress towards their goals. A contested hearing is usually required where families fail but many accept that they have been given a fair trial.

INTERVENTION ALGORITHM

The FDAC intervention follows an algorithm designed to test whether supported rehabilitation to the family or timely permanency elsewhere is the best for a particular child (see Figure 2 at the end of paper). The first step is to help the parents begin their recovery from substance misuse. In the first 3 months we expect them to achieve abstinence from street drugs and alcohol (some remain on prescribed narcotic substitutes such as methadone). To start to create a safer environment for themselves (getting away from a substance misusing lifestyle) and to begin to address some of the factors that have been driving their substance misuse (including practical skills for preventing relapse and insight into the vulnerabilities in their background). Usually the gravity of the risks means that the child has been temporarily placed elsewhere (with foster carers although not uncommonly with relatives). However this also frees up the parent to appropriately prioritise his or her own needs.

The FDAC team provides Motivational Interviewing, Social Behavioural Network Therapy (SBNT) (Williamson et al 2007, a new treatment that has performed well in at least one randomised controlled trial), testing and contact with the 'Parent Mentors'. As necessary they help the parent access (and coordinate) medically supervised withdrawal, methadone maintenance, relapse prevention or 3–6 month intensive rehabilitation programmes and help with housing. Failure to progress in the first 3 months normally means the parents are not going to be able to meet the child's time frame (for example, in the case of babies) or achieve enough progress in the maximum duration (10–12 months) of the court proceedings (in the case of older children where potentially the parents could take more time to sort themselves out and bring the matter back to court at a later stage). Occasionally one parent will be able to progress to the next stage while the other parent will not (and measures will be needed to avoid the second parent undermining the first).

Once parents successfully navigate the first stage of the intervention the next element is seeing whether recovery can be sustained (often in the more testing circumstances of living in the community), whether they can adopt a 'child centred lifestyle' (for example promoting developmentally appropriate learning, play, interaction with peers and access to education and healthcare), and whether they can meet the child's needs. Interventions include support sustaining drug and alcohol recovery (for example Alcoholics Anonymous), Family Group Conference, intra-family violence interventions (FDAC has its own programme run by colleagues from the Tavistock including multi-family systemic therapy), parenting classes (a version of 'Strengthening Families' adapted for substance misusing parents), child-parent interaction intervention, family therapy, adult psychotherapy, and advice on training and employment.

Whether a parent can meet their child's needs may depend on the extent of those needs, including whether there has been previous damage to the child's health and development. The FDAC intervention team assesses the child and makes recommendations about contact, counselling, psychotherapy or educational help.

PRELIMINARY FINDINGS

The first 50 cases suggest that most families want to engage but about a third fail in the first 3 months. Successful families would normally stay in proceedings for around 12 months and 'graduate' with a 'Supervision Order'. It is too soon to say but we anticipate that the majority of the families who get that far will be reunited with their child. The Brunel group is due to publish their initial findings in a few weeks and final report in a year's time. Longer-term research is needed as is an aftercare programme.

Figure 1

Model of Harm

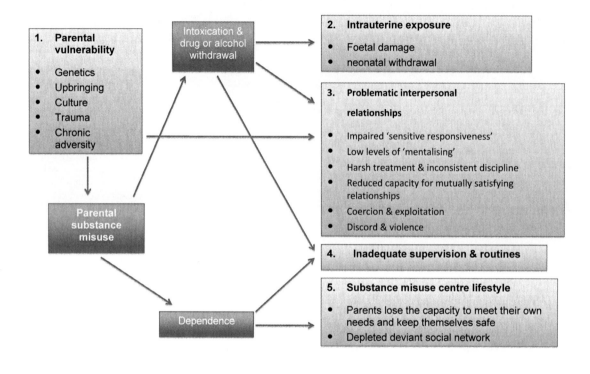

Figure 2

Intervention Algorithm

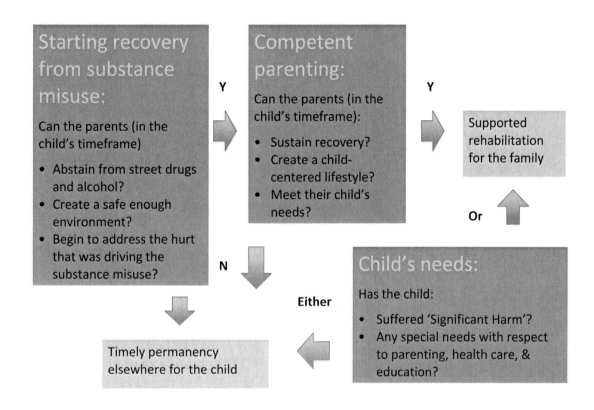

CONFERENCE PRESENTATION

At the conference Dr Shaw explained the working of FDAC and asked the delegates to consider: (a) whether it would be possible to intervene earlier; (b) whether the threshold for bringing matters to court was too high; and (c) whether the interdisciplinary cooperation of the model could be a bad thing – was it 'too cosy'?

REFERENCES

Advisory Council on the Misuse of Drugs *Hidden Harm: Responding to the needs of children of problem drug users* (2003) available at www.drugs.gov.uk.

Allen, JG, Fonagy, P and Bateman, A *Mentalising in Clinical Practice* (American Psychiatric Publishing, 2008).

Forrester, D and Harwin, J 'Parental substance misuse and child care social work: Findings from the first stage of a study of 100 families' (2006) 11(4) *Child and Family Social Work* 325–335.

Friedman, R and Chase-Lansdale, P 'Chronic Adversities' in M Rutter and E Taylor (eds) *Child and Adolescent Psychiatry* (London: Blackwell Science, 2002).

Green, B, Furrer, C, Worcel, S, et al 'How Effective Are Family Treatment Drug Courts? Outcomes From a Four-Site National Study' (2007) 12(1) *Child Maltreatment* 43-59.

Harwin, J *The Family Drug and Alcohol Court Evaluation Study Interim Report* available at www.brunel.ac.uk/research/centres/iccfyr/fdac (August 2009).

Kumpfer, K, DeMarsh, J and Child, W *Strengthening Families Program: Children's Skills Training Curriculum Manual, Parent Training Manual, Children's Skill Training Manual, and Family Skills Training Manual (Prevention Services to Children of Substance-abusing Parents)* (Social Research Institute, Graduate School of Social Work, University of Utah, 1989). (Now disseminated by Department of Health Promotion and Education, Call (801) 581-8498.)

Maccoby, E and Martin, J 'Socialization in the context of the family: Parent-child interaction' in PH Mussen and EM Hetherington (eds) *Handbook of child psychology: Vol 4 Socialization, personality, and social development* (New York: Wiley, 4th edn, 1983) 1–101.

Patterson, G *Coercive Family Process (Social Interactional Approach)* (Castalia Publishing Co, 1982).

Prior, V and Glaser, D *Understanding attachment and attachment disorders: theory, evidence and practice* (London: Jessica Kingsley, 2006).

Miller, WR and Rollnick, S *Motivational Interviewing: Preparing People to Change* (New York: Guilford Press, 2002).

National Survey on Drug Use and Health. The NSDUH Report. Children living with substance-dependent or substance misusing parents: 2002 to 2007, available at http://oas.samhsa.gov/2k9/SAparents/SAparents.cfm (19 April 2009).

Williamson, E, Smith, M, Orford, J, Copello, A and Day, E 'Social Behaviour and Network Therapy for Drug Problems: Evidence of Benefits and Challenges' (2007) 6 *Addictive Disorders and their Treatment* 167–179.

PLENARY 2

ASSESSING AND REPRESENTING PARENTS WITH MENTAL HEALTH ISSUES

ASSESSMENT AND DECISION MAKING – PARALYSIS IN THE FAMILY AND PROFESSIONAL SYSTEM IN PARENTS WITH PERSONALITY DISORDER

Minna Daum

Head of Programme, Families at Risk, The Anna Freud Centre

SUMMARY OF PAPER

Minna Daum runs a court assessment service specialising in personality disorder, working with a multidisciplinary team. In this paper she describes how families with parents with personality disorder often experience long involvement with social care services, marked by failed attempts at support and intervention, high anxiety and discord in the professional network and multiple assessments that do not lead to any change. Daum examines the interplay between parents' parental personality disorder and systemic failure, which she argues, can most usefully be understood in terms of bewildered, unthinking and disorganised responses to complex parental psychopathology. Professionals are subject to particular patterns of behaviour, characterised as responses to offers of care (often 'hostile/dependent') and an authoritative structure.

Professionals can be subjected to hostility and denigration, and the possibility that professionals can in turn become hostile and defensive. Such reactions arise from a lack of reflection by the professionals. This may be due to the overwhelming intensity of arousal in the personality disordered parent and the equally strong counter-response in the professional, anxiety about the risk to a child and an ambiguity in the role of child mental health or social care professional. Professionals have a dual role: caring/providing and assessing/judging. There are a number of problematic responses in the professional network (the professional becoming rigid or punitive in an attempt to get the parent to comply, the professional becoming delinquent themselves, or 'turning a blind eye'). A case management approach must be developed to mitigate these dangers. Professionals working with parents with a diagnosis of personality disorder must maintain a sense of the relational aspects of the parents functioning and maintain a position of thoughtfulness in relation to both parent(s) and other professionals.

THE PAPER

While the prevalence of personality disorder (PD) in the population is notoriously hard to assess, it is thought to be between 2% and 10%. Child and family social workers report that around 40% of their caseload involves a parent with PD. Meanwhile some estimates suggest that a much higher proportion of children in care proceedings have a parent with PD.

The families of parents with PD are characterised by long involvement with Social Care services, marked by failed attempts at support and intervention, high anxiety and discord in the professional network, and multiple assessments leading to no change. Typically, despite a staggering number of professional hours devoted to these families and the high level of anxiety within the network, no decision is made until children are removed in an unplanned way, on

Emergency Protection Orders, in response to a particular crisis. The impact on children of PD parents will have to be the subject of another paper (see Macfie 2009 for a recent literature review), but suffice it to say that a great deal of harm can be done by leaving children in the care of these parents without effective intervention.

This paper will examine the interplay between parental PD and systemic failure. It will be argued that such failure may most usefully be understood in terms of a bewildered, unthinking and disorganised response to complex parental psychopathology. Having detailed the nature of the challenge faced by professionals in their relationships with PD parents and with each other, I shall set out some principles for managing such cases in order to reduce the unacceptable delay often encountered in decision making around these families.

Personality disorder may most usefully be conceptualised as a disorder of social relationships. Its central characteristics relate to difficulties in interpersonal relationships, and it is defined primarily in terms of behaviour in relation to other people. Clearly, ways of relating have effects on every social context in which the PD parent operates, including any organisation s/he comes into contact with.

Some theorists and practitioners (eg Bateman & Fonagy 2004) characterise PD as a disorder whose environmental causes may be related to disorganised attachment relationships in childhood as a result of neglect and/or trauma. Space does not allow for a detailed consideration of this view. Two things are important to note here. First, the profound attachment difficulties experienced by adults with PD are activated in a particularly acute way when they become parents, and have a very significant impact on their relationships with their children. Second, the fact of having a child necessarily involves any parent in a set of relationships with professionals (from health visitors to school staff) who have a dual role: both caring and authoritative. I would contend that, given their attachment difficulties, it is particularly hard for parents with PD to relate in a straightforward way to professionals occupying this dual role, precisely because caring and authority constitute the central components of a parental, or attachment, relationship. These difficulties are particularly acute when PD parents come into contact with Social Workers, but are likely to be apparent in all their relationships with professional organisations.

An assumption being made here is that attachment patterns are played out not only in intimate relationships with children/partners/family members, but in all social relationships. This is in my view a useful paradigm within which to understand the destructive and confusing patterns of relating experienced by professionals attempting to negotiate with parents with PD.

In delineating the particular patterns of behaviour to which professionals are subject it may be useful to separate them into responses to offers of care on the one hand, and an authoritative structure on the other.

In response to offers of help, professionals are often met with what might be called a 'hostile/dependent' stance on the part of the parent with PD. Immense demands are made on the professional, but at the same time the help and attention offered is denigrated and characterised as 'not what I need'. This 'push-me-pull-you' attitude of overwhelming demand and simultaneous rejection of help is extremely frustrating for professionals.

In response to unboundaried demands on the part of the parent, professionals can find themselves responding in two potential ways. First, they may implicitly accept the responsibility for fulfilling the parent's unmet need by losing their own sense of boundaries and limitations. The net result of this is an exhausting attempt to 'rescue' the PD parent by making superhuman efforts to provide everything the parent insists they need. Professionals may find themselves fielding telephone calls at all hours of the day, chasing after allegations of unprofessional behaviour on the part of other agencies, and in essence buying into the implicit idea that it is the responsibility of the professional network to fill the yawning gaps felt by the PD parent. In psychological terms, what is apparent is the central fact of the PD parent's experience of unmet need associated with past relationships, but enacted in the present. This means that there is by definition no way that any professional can possibly satisfy the need expressed by the PD parent.

Despite these best efforts, professionals typically find themselves at the receiving end of hostility and denigration. In response, the professional can in turn become both hostile and defensive. In the face of aggressive onslaughts on the part of a parent one is trying to help, it is easy to feel aggrieved and rejected and to respond by taking words at face value and (for example) closing the case or, with some relief, referring it on to another professional.

What is missing in these responses is an attempt to reflect upon what is going on in the relationship between parent and professional. This is a situation in which the parent, by virtue of their personality difficulties, has a highly impoverished capacity to reflect in this way, particularly in the context of a relationship in which care is being offered, and which as a consequence arouses their attachment system. The onus is therefore on the professional to reflect upon the process on behalf of both the parent and themselves, and to try to help the parent manage this fraught relationship in a less destructive way.

It is worth thinking about why it is so difficult for a professional to maintain this capacity to reflect. I would suggest a number of internal and contextual reasons for this. First, and perhaps most simply, it is difficult to overestimate the overwhelming intensity of arousal in the PD parent, the equally strong counter-response this evokes in oneself, and the impact this has on one's capacity to think. Secondly, anxiety, in this case about risk to a child or children, in itself militates against clear thinking. Thirdly, there is an ambiguity inherent in the role of child mental health or social care professional, an ambiguity not removed by or articulated within the phrase 'working in partnership'. John Simmonds (2010) calls attention to the collision between imposing state authority and offering individual support inherent in the role of Social Worker, and it is uncontroversial to suggest that this is applicable to anyone working in a context in which children may be at risk. Put simply, no professional working with parents and children can do so outside the context of the Children Act. Professionals therefore have a dual role: caring/providing, and assessing/judging.

This gives rise to another aspect of relating that PD parents find especially difficult: negotiating with an authority structure. A mature relationship to authority is one that allows the authority to have a competence one may not possess oneself. This is difficult for all of us to negotiate, but for a parent whose early experience is of a corrupt, malignant or simply absent authority structure, this can be particularly problematic.

A common maladaptive response to authority on the part of parents with PD is paranoia. The parent with PD feels deeply mistrustful of those in authority, to the extent that they simply cannot conceive of the possibility that anyone in authority might be benign in intent. This fundamental mistrust impacts on parental responses towards any organisation that tries to set standards or boundaries of any kind. Parents may act variously in ways that are controlling, withdrawn, openly hostile, oppositional, passive-aggressive, falsely compliant, and/or dishonest. In response, one can feel bullied, rejected, and patronised.

Another response to authority is delinquency. Again, any attempt to impose boundaries will lead the parent overtly or covertly to attack or subvert whatever structure the professional attempts to put in place. Delinquency can be seen as an oppositional response to perceived neglect – the message is something like 'you don't care about me, so why should I do what you say?' Issues of importance are disregarded, and rules flouted. Again, at a personal level, it is hard to underestimate the level of frustration and anger engendered by such dismissive behaviour.

There are a number of problematic responses in the professional network to this delinquent and oppositional stance on the part of the PD parent. First, the professional may become rigid and punitive in an attempt to make the parent comply. Secondly, the professional may become delinquent themselves, joining with the parent against authority. Thirdly, professionals may 'turn a blind eye', pretending essentially that there has not been a breach of rules. Often in cases involving PD parents one will see different stances taken by different professionals within the network, or by the same agency (say a Social Services department) over time. Again, what is lacking on both sides is reflection about relational processes; the parent reacts in an unthinking way, and the professional response involves a kind of 'reciprocal mindlessness'. The net result is paralysis and delay in decision making.

It is perhaps self-evident that splits in the network occur very frequently in cases involving parents with PD. The term 'splitting' is often cheerily referred to but left at that, as if stating it as a fact will be sufficient to avoid its pitfalls. 'Splitting', referring to the idealisation of one person or part of an organisation and the denigration of another, may be most usefully thought about in terms of the parent's search for a safe relationship. Professionals working with PD parents will be familiar with the experience of being appealed to by the parent to be the 'good' person in contrast to another professional in the network who is denigrated. In psychological terms one may understand this as a reflection of the parent's profound difficulty in tolerating the idea that a relationship may contain positive and negative elements; a relationship that contains both feels unbearably risky and unsafe.

Again, what the professional experiences at point-blank range are unexamined, raw, infantile feelings of fear and helplessness on the part of the parent, and at an emotional level the temptation to react in a similarly unthinking way can be extremely strong. In terms of the family, one is there to help, the temptation is to collude with the parent's dismissal of issues of importance in relation to the child's needs in order to preserve the relationship with the parent. In terms of the network, the professional may get into a situation in which s/he feels s/he is the only one who truly understands this person, while others in the network are overly harsh and unforgiving. Again, what is most difficult for any professional involved in these relationships, whether they find themselves idealised or denigrated, is to hold a position of thoughtfulness, both in relation to the parent and to the network, which militates against the split and the conflict and paralysis that ensue.

CASE MANAGEMENT

The main principles here for any professional working with parents with a diagnosis of PD are:

- to maintain a sense of the relational aspects of the parent's functioning, rather than simply its phenomenology; and

- in doing so, to maintain a position of thoughtfulness in relation to both parent and other professionals, in the face of unthinking 'acting out'.

These principles apply both to individuals and to systems. What do they mean in practice? I would suggest the following.

Individual

(1) As suggested, it is useful to see any relationship between parent and professional as being in some sense an attachment relationship. It is therefore unhelpful to act in a way which denies this, ie by changing personnel working with a parent without acknowledging the potential difficulty of this for the parent. Such unthinking behaviour on the part of

professionals will arouse the parent's sense of abandonment and consequent aggression. More to the point, it makes no sense at all, when attempting to focus the parent's mind on attachment issues in relation to their own children, to act in a way that implies such issues are unimportant in one's own relationship with the parent.

(2)   Awareness of the impact of one's relationships with PD parents requires supervision which takes seriously relational aspects of behaviour, and supports one in managing one's own emotional counter-responses, eg frustration, despair, indifference, hostility.

System

(1)   The management of cases involving PD parents is likely to involve a hierarchy of interventions: these may overlap, and it is crucial to develop a structure to avoid chaos and conflict.

(2)   The importance of well-integrated, coherent, stable and well-supervised services cannot be overestimated.

(3)   Gathering information is vital. This requires the network to:
(a)   maintain awareness of gaps in information;
(b)   use all sources/informants;
(c)   build a picture of:
   (i)   adult functioning;
   (ii)   parental functioning;
   (iii) relationships; and
   (iv)   child functioning;
(d)   information must be well documented, detailed, and specific.

(4)   Establishing and maintaining a network is equally vital. This will require:
(a)   multi-professional/agency meetings;
(b)   inclusion of non-professionals in network;
(c)   agreed means of contact and communication; and
(d)   agreed roles and boundaries between agencies.

(5)   Engagement is an important issue and requires collective thought. Efforts should be made by all involved, and the network itself, to do the following:
(a)   maintain a positive and accepting attitude to help-seeking;
(b)   be accessible;
(c)   do outreach work where possible to minimise missed meetings and consequent delay/frustration;
(d)   form an authoritative structure that is clear and well-understood by all, including the parent; and
(e)   make sure limits are set in a clearly explained and non-punitive manner.

(6)   To have any hope of success, assessments/interventions need to be comprehensive. This means:
(a)   the case should have an agreed case manager;
(b)   the family's physical environment needs to be addressed: finances, housing, schooling, health;
(c)   the family's social/emotional environment likewise need to be addressed: safety, attachments, friends, activities;
(d)   short-term aims need to be established (crisis planning); and
(f)   long-term aims need addressing only after the situation has been stabilised.

The overall aim of these practical steps is to create a system around the family which has a clear structure and a capacity to think. I have argued that without such a structure, systems tend to become 'personality disordered' in response to PD parents and to flip backwards and forwards between over- and under-involvement, over-controlling and neglectful behaviour.

CONFERENCE PRESENTATION

In her presentation Daum painted a vivid picture of the challenges posed by parents with personality disorder, and the pattern too often seen in such cases, namely concerns about children leading to assessment and intervention, the failure of the parent to engage, disagreement between professionals, a change of social worker and concerns about child(ren) triggering the cycle once more.

REFERENCES

Bateman, A and Fonagy, P *Mentalisation-based therapy for Borderline Personality Disorder* (Oxford University Press, 2004).

Lyons-Ruth, K and Jacobovitz, D 'Attachment Disorganization: unresolved loss, relational violence, and lapses in behavioural and attentional strategies' in J Cassidy and P Shaver (eds) *Handbook of Attachment: Theory, research, and clinical applications* (New York: Guilford Press, 1999).

Macfie, J 'Development in Children and Adolescents whose mothers have borderline personality disorder' (2009) 3(1) *Child Development Perspectives* 66–71.

Simmonds, J 'Relating and relationships in supervision – supportive and companionable or dominant and submissive?' in G Ruch, D Turney and A Ward, *Relationship-Based Social Work: Discovering the Heart of Practice* (London: Jessica Kingsley, 2010).

REPRESENTATION OF PARENTS WITH MENTAL HEALTH ISSUES

Peggy Ekeledo
Burke Niazi

Janice Kaufman
Steel & Shamash

and

Helen Clift
Office of the Official Solicitor

SUMMARY OF PAPER

In this paper the authors consider the factors which impact on the legal representation of a parent with a mental health disorder, the framework(s) within which the solicitor may have to work and the role of the Official Solicitor when he acts as litigation friend.

Parents known to mental health adult services often come 'labelled': the solicitor needs to be alert to difficulties and the need for special arrangements. The solicitor will need to consider prognosis, the 'treatability' of the parent's mental health disorder and determine whether the timescale for the parent to recover and/or access the support or services with which they will be able to provide 'good enough' parenting is compatible with the timescale for the child. Where a parent is not known to mental health services or there is little or no information about their mental disorder, the solicitor is in a more difficult position.

Where a parent lacks capacity to conduct the proceedings (as defined by rules of court) they are a protected party, and must act by a litigation friend. The litigation friend must 'fairly and competently conduct the proceedings' in the best interests of the protected party in the proceedings: the litigation friend has a duty to inform himself of the issues and to instruct the solicitor of the course to be taken on behalf of the protected party.

The Official Solicitor is the litigation friend of last resort. It is not his role to pursue a case that is not reasonably arguable regardless of merit, cost and delay: his role is to ensure that the court process is fair to the protected party and (in children cases) that assessments are fair and properly take into account the parent's particular difficulties.

THE PAPER

This paper looks at factors which impact on the legal representation in children proceedings of a parent with a mental disorder ('a parent'); the emphasis is on public law proceedings but some are relevant to private law proceedings. It attempts to identify factors which the solicitor may need to consider and the framework(s) within which the solicitor may have to work.

A parent may, or may not, be known to services at the time the solicitor becomes involved; the challenges will differ depending on whether or not this is the case.

Parents known to mental health or adult services come 'labelled' and the solicitor should be alert to difficulties and the need for special arrangements. There may be a team in existence which knows the parent, and a wealth of available information, although the solicitor needs to be aware that diagnoses change, and that mistakes are made, and alert to challenge any preconceptions arising out of that 'label'.

The mental disorders which commonly feature are non-organic disorders which can be influenced by environmental factors such as stress, abuse or substance dependency. What is important is not so much diagnosis, but prognosis, and 'treatability' and/or support.

The timescale for a parent to recover, gain insight, comply with treatment, and therefore to have the proper opportunity to demonstrate they are able to parent their child, is outside the solicitor's control, and may not be compatible with the child's timescale. Some mental disorders are not treatable[1] but the parent may be able to provide good enough parenting with support. The search for support/services may also cause delay.

The solicitor will have to consider whether the delay is proportionate and the right balance being achieved.

Where a parent is not known to services, or there is no, or little information about their mental disorder, the solicitor may be unaware of the background and less able to consider and propose support both for assessments and in the proceedings. The parent may be resistant to any suggestion that they need special provision, fearful of the stigma, and may believe that it would be detrimental to their chance of parenting their child.

This situation is one of the more difficult that the solicitor may encounter: how to balance the client's wishes with the possibility of offering a better and fairer assessment.

How to tactfully explore the question of mental disorder?

If the parent has a mental illness the position is further complicated by the fact that different legal tests apply in relation to parent and child:

(1)   a parent may be too ill to look after their child, or to engage with social care professionals, and the threshold for court intervention met in respect of their child, but non-compliant with treatment and not ill enough to meet the criteria for detention for treatment;[2]

(2)   a parent may be well enough to leave hospital[3] but not well enough to meet the needs of their child and may, after a very short time need re-admission (the 'revolving door').

---

[1]   For example, learning disabilities.
[2]   Mental Health Act 1983, ss 2–3.
[3]   Ie not meet the criteria for detention under the Mental Health Act 1983.

Practically if a parent is detained for treatment, they may be simply too ill to engage in the court process, it may be impracticable for them to have contact with their child and the bond between them may be weakened.

FAIR ASSESSMENT – FAIR CHANCE?

A parent with a mental disorder is one for whom community care services[4] or health services can be provided on the basis of illness, disability, or both. Assessment of parenting ability[5] without first assessing the parent's own need for services may be unfair to that parent.

Effective services are those which the parent feels able to accept; and for that support to be flexible and available over time to meet the family's changing needs. Whilst a parent's mental health may deteriorate during proceedings, in many cases the difficulties are long standing and the parent has struggled without support until a crisis develops; their parenting ability is then assessed against a background of perceived failure. Far more effective if there can be early non-crisis driven identification of the need for support.[6]

Pre-proceedings

The Public Law Outline (PLO) emphasises the need for local authorities to undertake assessments and preparation pre-issue.[7] Parents with a mental disorder are disadvantaged in the pre-proceedings phase, they:

(1)   may be unrepresented because:
      (a)   less able to seek legal advice;
      (b)   detained in hospital;

(2)   may not appreciate that there is a real risk that their child(ren) will be removed;

(3)   may be reluctant to engage in, or lack understanding of the importance of participation in any Core Assessment or Family Group Conference;

(4)   may have different and lesser entitlement to legal aid (a modest fixed fee);

(5)   in proceedings may lack litigation capacity, but no provision for appointment of a litigation friend;

(6)   may have no Children's Guardian or solicitor for the child(ren).

When proceedings are issued, the outcome may appear at first glance inevitable, yet the parent may not have had legal advice and/or their difficulties not been properly recognised.

---

[4]   National Health Service and Community Care Act 1990, s 47.

[5]   Often unhelpfully referred to as parenting 'capacity'.

[6]   It has been interesting to note in cases under Part 4A of the Family Law Act 1996 (the forced marriage legislation) that the provisions of services, including special school education, has enabled vulnerable people to exercise their rights illustrating the benefit of a working relationship of trust established with professionals over a period of time in a positive environment.

[7]   The Pre-Proceedings Checklist includes any relevant assessment materials, initial and core assessments, section 7 and 37 reports, other relevant reports and records, single, joint or inter-agency materials (eg health and education/Home Office and Immigration documents), records of discussions with the family and key local authority minutes and records for the child.

In proceedings

There is no 'specialist' approach to these parents other than that provided by the Family Drug and Alcohol Court (FDAC)[8] which works with parents dependent on drugs and/or alcohol. The FDAC multidisciplinary team provides support to the family and coordinate the process and Intervention Plan; progress is closely monitored by the court.[9] However, so great is the need in London, the demand was not anticipated and (at the time of writing) FDAC had to stop taking new referrals until at least mid-September.

The following should be considered (relevant factors to that consideration are listed):

(1) Support from the *parent's* social worker or AMHP:[10]
 – known to parent;
 – may have continuing involvement with them;
 – may know them when they are mentally well or not under stress;
 – may have influence over resources available for parent's treatment and care plan;
 – may be perceived by parent as coercive;
 – may be involved in compulsory detention of parent;
 – may be uninformed about child protection and the Children Act;
 – parent may be opposed to disclosure of confidential information into court proceedings.

(2) Request for a community care assessment:[11]
 – parent is likely to require support temporarily or over a long period if they are to meet their child(ren)'s needs and their parental duties and responsibilities;
 – support may come from a partner, family or friends but often parent is isolated and reliant on professional support;
 – assessment of parent is necessary, if the support and services are to be right for that parent, and if assessment of their parenting ability is to be properly informed about that parent *and* about the availability of services;
 – parent with a mental disorder may have least familial or community support but be most suspicious of professionals;
 – the value of an offer of support/services made for the first time in proceedings and in the context of court assessment may be undermined by the context in which it is made;
 – the statutory duty is to assess – provision of services depends on local authority's eligibility criteria;
 – many parents with learning difficulties are 'too able' to meet the eligibility criteria; similarly the Community Mental Health Team supports people with severe mental illness or complex mental health conditions: parents who may, with support, have the best chance of being good enough parents may not meet criteria for services.

(3) Disability Discrimination Act issues?

(4) Advocacy Support:
 – can provide uncritical support;
 – may be able to spend time with parent explaining issues/orders – time which the Legal Services Commission (LSC) may challenge as unreasonable if spent by solicitor;
 – should have experience of working with adults with mental disorder;
 – may be able to provide relevant information to solicitor;
 – solicitor is parent's legal representative, not their support worker;

---

8 Still in the pilot phase and based in the Inner London Family Proceedings Court.
9 For more information see the Leaflet for Service Professionals at Appendix 1.
10 Approved Mental Health Professional.
11 National Health Service and Community Care Act 1990, s 47.

- may provide valuable support to parent during *and* after the proceedings;
- no national advocacy service; often difficult to obtain local advocacy services;
- who will fund?
- likelihood advocate will need to commit considerable time;
- need for a single individual to save repetition of personal/confidential information.

(5) Involvement of family member/friend:
- parent may have confidence in them;
- may have long-term involvement in parent's life;
- may have important role in child(ren)'s life;
- no cost implications;
- could be conflict of interest;
- confidentiality;
- are they playing a 'constructive' role?

(6) Accessible information in easy to understand words and pictures:
- may make a difference to parent's understanding of both issues[12] and court process;[13]
- can be valuable support to parent and helpful working tool for both parent and professionals[14] working with that parent;
- may not be free;[15]
- often not available until after a crisis point has been reached, and then in the context of child protection and court proceedings.[16]

Information/recommendations which arise in the context of expert assessments can also be relied on to try and secure health/social care support and services for the parent.[17]

Legal aid

Although it is non-means and non-merits based for parents in care proceedings, there are a number of issues surrounding legal aid:

- non means and non merits for parents in care proceedings;

- LSC is seeking increased control over the work done by solicitors;

- solicitor needs prior approval from LSC for experts' fees and assessments which takes time;

- solicitors are paid under 'standard fee' regime for many care cases and cannot know at outset whether a case will escape 'standard fee'; solicitors stand to make substantial losses in work that will not be remunerated by LSC;

---

[12] For example: the Personal Child Health Record ('the red book') given to all new parents offers advice on health and development matters but that advice may be inaccessible to a parent with learning difficulties.

[13] Are the FJC's own easy-read information leaflets: *The Court and your child: When social workers get involved* and *The Court and your child: When mum and dad split up*, as well known to the legal profession (and to social workers and children's guardians) as they should be?

[14] For example: the community midwife, health visitor, general practitioner, social worker, children's guardian, family support workers, Sure Start workers, etc.

[15] Easy-read publications such as those published by Change – *My Pregnancy, My Choice, You and Your Baby 0–1* and *You and Your Little Child 1–5*, the development of which was funded by central government, cost £38 each – a sum likely to be unaffordable for any low income parent.

[16] The Official Solicitor has his own easy-read leaflet commissioned from Change.

[17] FPR 1991, r 11.4 allows a party to communicate any information relating to proceedings to a healthcare professional or a person or body providing counselling services for children or families to enable that party to obtain healthcare or counselling.

- • LSC questions the need to spend time explaining evidence to, and advising such parents; the demand on time/skill in representing a parent with a mental disorder and possibly other difficulties, in a sophisticated process, is substantial;

- • solicitors firms are more and more using inexperienced or less qualified staff to undertake legally aided work;[18]

- • a parent with a mental disorder may be least able to articulate their own case but the most challenging for the solicitor to work with; they need the most experienced representation.

Litigation friend

The law presumes that an adult has capacity to conduct proceedings ('litigation capacity'). A parent with a mental disorder does not necessarily need to act through a litigation friend.[19] Court rules[20] provide that a party or intended party who lacks capacity within the meaning of the Mental Capacity Act 2005 (the MCA) to conduct the proceedings is a protected party.[21] A protected party must act by a litigation friend.

The MCA Code of Practice refers to a two-stage test for capacity: a 'diagnostic test' (is there an impairment of, or a disturbance in, the functioning of the mind or brain?) and a 'functional test' (does that impairment of, or disturbance in, functioning mean the person is unable to make a decision when they need to?) – the Code emphasises that all practical and appropriate support must be given to enable that person to make a decision for himself.[22]

Case-law established that the test for capacity is issue specific and the requirement is to consider capacity in relation to the particular transaction (its nature and *complexity*)[23] in respect of which the decision as to capacity falls to be made[24] – in this context the transaction is the litigation in question and not 'by reference to each step in the process of litigation'.[25] If it were otherwise there would be significant practical and resource implications for the conduct of proceedings. The protected party's capacity would have to be positively reviewed before each significant step in the proceedings – either the solicitor would be the 'decision maker' for that purpose, or repeated reference back for further expert assessment. The conduct of proceedings by the litigation friend would be frustrated and decisions made in relation to different steps during the proceedings may be incompatible with each other.

---

[18] They may have little or no knowledge of, or experience of, working with people with a mental disorder.

[19] In family proceedings known as a guardian ad litem or next friend.

[20] In family proceedings, FPR 1991 and FP(A)R 2005. There is no provision under the Magistrates Courts Rules 1981 or the Family Proceedings Courts (Children Act 1989) Rules 1991 for the appointment of a litigation friend. Cases where there is a reason to believe a party is a protected party are transferred to the county court.

[21] The FPR 1991 and FP(A)R 2005 do not import any other provisions of the MCA or its Code of Practice. In particular they do not import section 4 'best interests' – section 4(1) starts: *In determining for the purposes of this Act* – the conduct of proceedings in other courts is not one of the purposes of the MCA.

[22] The Official Solicitor has had referred to him a couple of cases where the initial evidence has been that the party would have litigation capacity if that party had at all times the assistance of a lay advocate. Those cases were rejected pending further investigation as to whether the appointment and attendance of a lay advocate was a practicable step which could be taken and (if need be) funded as a disbursement on the legal aid certificate.

[23] The test adopted by Kennedy J in *Masterman-Lister v Brutton & Co* [2003] 3 All ER 162 (see para 26) focused on the complexity *not* the gravity of the decisions in question in the litigation.

[24] Kennedy LJ, *Masterman-Lister v Brutton & Co* [2003] 3 All ER 162; *Sheffield City Council v E and another* [2004] EWHC (2808) Fam, paras 38–39; *Bailey v Warren* [2006] EWCA Civ 51; *Lindsay v Wood* [2006] EWHC 2895 (QB).

[25] Kennedy LJ, *Masterman-Lister v Brutton & Co* [2003] 3 All ER 162.

Case-law has held that the pre-existing common law test for lack of capacity and the statutory definition are essentially the same test.[26] For the full statutory definition and the case-law guidance on litigation capacity see Appendix 2.

It is unlikely that the party concerned will assert their own lack of capacity;[27] the absence of litigation capacity is likely to first be apparent to their legal advisers:[28]

> '... the test of mental capacity should be such that, in the ordinary case, the need for a next friend or guardian ad litem should be readily recognizable by an experienced solicitor ...'[29]

The rules do not provide for judicial determination of litigation capacity, or specify what evidence is required. Neither the court nor the solicitor should however conclude that a party is a protected party without proper enquiry as the appointment of a litigation friend removes the right of that party to make their own decisions about the conduct of the proceedings.

There are cases where litigation capacity is in issue but the parent refuses assessment; the court has then to arrive at a determination having regard to the evidence as a whole.

The overriding duty in all proceedings in which litigation friends may be appointed is to 'fairly and competently conduct the proceedings' in the best interests of the protected party in those proceedings; therefore the litigation friend has a duty, under proper legal advice, to inform himself of the issues and to instruct the solicitor of the course to be taken on behalf of the protected party.[30]

The role of the litigation friend is conceptually different from that of the children's guardian appointed in specified proceedings[31] or that of the lay advocate;[32] if the litigation friend's decisions are determined by the views and wishes of the protected party he simply acts as an advocate.

The role and choice of litigation friend is not prescribed by the nature of the proceedings.[33] Any adult may act as litigation friend if he can fairly and competently conduct proceedings on behalf of the protected party and has no interest adverse to that of the protected party, *if* the solicitor is willing to sign the certificate of suitability,[34] *and* the court to accept it.

---

[26] *Local Authority X v MM* [2007] EWHC 2003 (Fam); *Saulle v Nouvet* [2007] EWHC 2902 (QB).

[27] Although not unknown – see, for example, *Phillips, Harland & Others v Symes & Others* [2004] EWHC 1887 (Ch).

[28] The solicitor needs to be alert however to the risk of concluding that the 'difficult' or 'chaotic' client lacks litigation capacity.

[29] *Masterman-Lister v Brutton & Co* [2003] 1 WLR 1511, Chadwick LJ.

[30] Sir Robert Megarry V-C said in *Re E (mental health patient)* [1984] 1 All ER 209 at 312–313: 'The main function of a next friend appears to be to carry on the litigation on behalf of the plaintiff and in his best interests. For this purpose the next friend must make all the decisions that the plaintiff would have made, had he been able. The next friend may, on behalf of the plaintiff, do anything which the Rules of the Supreme Court require or authorise the plaintiff to do, though the next friend must act by a solicitor: see Ord 80, r 2. It is the next friend who is responsible to the court for the propriety and the progress of the proceedings. The next friend does not, however become a litigant himself.'

[31] Whose role and duties are defined by statute and court rules.

[32] Whose role is to support the person in their contact with professionals, who may attend meetings with the person and who will help the person to articulate their concerns or wishes.

[33] The choice of litigation friend is immaterial to the question of whether or not a party is a protected party.

[34] FPR 1991, r 9.2 and FP(A)R 2005, r 54.

The Official Solicitor

No special rules apply to the Official Solicitor when he acts as litigation friend[35] – he is simply the litigation friend of last resort.[36]

Unsurprisingly in many children cases, a parent, irrespective of the weight of the evidence will want to care for their child(ren), and will be opposed to any other plan for placement whether with the other parent, or outside the family. Children proceedings engage the Article 8 rights of parent and child but precedence is given by domestic law to the child's welfare and whilst the litigation friend's duty is to represent the interests of the protected party/parent in the proceedings, that parent's own interests are not at issue in the proceedings. This can give rise to a tension in the relationships between parent and litigation friend *and* between parent and solicitor, as the solicitor has to act on the instructions of the litigation friend.

The Official Solicitor has taken the view (in all proceedings) that it is not his role as litigation friend, to pursue a case that is not reasonably arguable regardless of merit, cost and delay. His concern is to ensure that the court process is fair to the protected party, and (in children cases) that assessments are fair and properly take account of the parent's particular difficulties. It remains for the parent to work with the social care professionals and counter evidence that the parent is not able to be a 'good enough' parent.

The Official Solicitor's standard instruction to solicitors whom he instructs for the parent[37] is that he will, on their legal advice, present any realistic arguments and relevant evidence – the criterion being whether a point is reasonably arguable, *not* whether it is likely to succeed at trial.

It is not always easy for the Official Solicitor to persuade courts that he should have permission to instruct independent experts on behalf of the parent particularly if a parent has already had a child removed into care and/or if he becomes involved at a late stage of the proceedings. He therefore welcomed the Court of Appeal's recent decision in *M (A Child)* [2009] EWCA Civ 315.[38]

The parent's wishes and feelings must be put before the court; this need not mean the protected party giving formal evidence. A protected party is not exempt from the general principle that all competent witnesses are compellable witnesses, subject to the court's residual discretion to refuse to compel a compellable witness.[39] There may be good reasons however why the parent should not give evidence including:

- if, on the evidence, the criteria for a care/placement order are made out, raising unrealistic expectations that the case is realistically arguable;

---

[35] Save that he is exempt from filing some documents.

[36] Although unhelpfully 'litigation friend' and 'Official Solicitor' (OS) are often used interchangeably – a litigation friend will not necessarily be the OS and the OS carries out many functions other than acting as litigation friend of last resort.

[37] When he acts as litigation friend the OS sends out 'Standard Instructions' to solicitors in proceedings under the Children Act 1989, the Adoption and Children Act 2005, the Matrimonial Causes Act 1973, and Part IV of the Family Law Act 1996. They are intended to provide a robust framework for the working relationship between the OS's lay case manager and the solicitor. The solicitor is responsible for legally advising the OS through his case manager. The relationship between the OS and the solicitor is *not* an agency relationship as when he acts as litigation friend the OS is not (save in exceptional circumstances) the solicitor on record. The interest which the solicitor serves remains that of the protected party as his client and not that of the litigation friend.

[38] Thorpe LJ: '. . . if the Official Solicitor, with the responsibility that he holds in the litigation, requires that assessment, it seems to me that a judge should be slow to refuse it ...' and Wall LJ: '... the Official Solicitor has a plain duty to investigate the case on the mother's behalf and to obtain whatever evidence he thought appropriate to do so'.

[39] If to do so would be a fishing exercise, speculation or oppression.

- if there are concurrent criminal proceedings or a police investigation the protected party may struggle to understand the distinction between the criminal proceedings/investigation, and care proceedings, and to understand a relevant warning;[40]

- the expert advice may be that it will be harmful to the parent's own mental health to give evidence.

Whether or not a protected party is a competent witness is a question for the judge; consideration should however be given not only to competence but also as to whether special measures should be introduced.

There is no statutory guidance in family proceedings as to the issue of 'competence'. The Youth Justice and Criminal Evidence Act 1999 gives statutory guidance in relation to a witness in criminal proceedings (other than the accused)[41] and as to 'special measures'. One such 'special measure' is the Witness Intermediary Service (see Appendix 3) which has also been successfully used in at least two care cases, in one of which the Official Solicitor was involved. His experience of the service was very positive and he would hope that it will be used in more cases.

The Official Solicitor's appointment and approach as litigation friend was considered last year by the Court of Appeal in the case of *Re P (a child)(care and placement order proceedings: mental capacity of parent)* [2008] All ER (D) 102 (May). In that case permission to appeal to the House of Lords was refused. It is now before the European Court of Human Rights under the name of *RP v UK*.

The Official Solicitor welcomes the initiative taken by the Safeguarding Committee of the Family Justice Council, following on from the decision in *Re P*, which has recently (July 2009) circulated a paper: *Parents Who Lack Capacity to Conduct Public Law Proceedings* to the local Family Justice Councils (FJCs) for consideration. A copy of that paper is annexed as Appendix 4.

CONFERENCE PRESENTATION

In her presentation Peggy Ekeledo highlighted the problems parents with mental health difficulties experience. In accordance with the Public Law Outline local authorities do a lot of work 'behind the scenes' with parents with mental health difficulties. The parents do not engage, the children are not represented and there is no legal advice before the matter goes to court. Parents don't appreciate the importance of engaging with the local authority and by the time the matter comes to court parents feel as though the decision has already been made and they are being presented with a fait accompli. Peggy Ekeledo advised delegates not to be distracted by the diagnosis of mental health disorder: the important questions were those of prognosis, of 'treatability' and what support there was for the parent/family.

---

[40] See Children Act 1989, s 98(2): 'A statement or admission made … shall not be admissible in evidence against the person making it or his spouse or civil partner in proceedings for an offence other than perjury.' It will however be the criminal court which decides on the degree of protection afforded by s 98(2) in any one case. See also *Re EC (Disclosure of Material)* [1996] 2 FLR 725; *Re X (Disclosure for Purposes of Criminal Proceedings)* [2008] 2 FLR 944 and others.

[41] (1) persons of any age are competent to give evidence (s 53(1)) unless, (2) the person is not able to 'understand questions put to him as a witness, and give answers which can be understood' (s 53(2)), (3) a person may not be sworn to give evidence 'unless he has attained the age of 14, and he has sufficient understanding of the solemnity of the occasion and of the particular responsibility to tell the truth which is involved in taking an oath' (s 55(2)), (4) a person 'shall, if he is able to give intelligible testimony, be presumed to have a sufficient appreciation of those matters if no evidence tending to show the contrary is adduced (by any other party)' (s 55(3)), (5) a person is 'able to give intelligible testimony' if 'he is able to: (a) understand questions put to him as a witness, and (b) give answers to them which can be understood' (s 55(8)), (6) if a person is competent to give evidence but, by virtue of section 55(2) is not permitted to be sworn, then his evidence may be given unsworn (s 56(1) and (2)).

Janice Kaufman highlighted the difficulties that parents experience:

> 'legal representatives have to be very aware that inferences may be drawn about a parent who needs or wants a lot of support in proceedings. The professionals may take the view that a parent who says they cannot or will not attend a child protection conference or a meeting with a social worker without support is unlikely to be able to care for their child(ren). It is difficult to expect a parent to treat the social worker who may have been involved in the assessment of the parent for detention under the Mental Health Act 1983 as a professional that the parent can trust and rely on. However, that social worker may have known the parent over a period of time and have good access to the parent's support network of family and friends. The social worker should have knowledge of, and access to statutory and voluntary agencies, and can be the best person to facilitate contact and negotiation with the children's team. '

Helen Clift explored the role of the Official Solicitor. She commended to delegates the Family Justice Council's consultation paper 'Parents Who Lack Capacity to Conduct Public Law Proceedings' which considers the approach to the assessment of capacity to conduct the proceedings and the role of the litigation friend. She went on to consider the Witness Intermediary Scheme established for use in criminal proceedings. Given the success of the pilot scheme it is to be rolled out across the country. Unfortunately the funding of a Witness Intermediary is not considered by the Legal Services Commission to be a proper disbursement on a legal aid certificate and there is therefore a practical problem in funding for a Witness Intermediary in children proceedings.

APPENDIX 1 – FAMILY AND DRUG ALCOHOL COURT (FDAC)

The Family Drug and Alcohol Court (FDAC) - Leaflet for Service Professionals

Who this leaflet is for?

This leaflet is aimed at any service professional that wants information about the FDAC or has been asked to become involved in any aspect of the process.

It is particularly relevant for social workers whose cases get put forward for the FDAC and for key workers in drug, alcohol, housing, domestic violence or any other wrap around service involved in the treatment of someone going through the FDAC process.

Introduction to the Family Drug and Alcohol Court (FDAC)

The Family Drug and Alcohol Court (FDAC) is a pilot project that has been based on an American model. Specialist drug and alcohol courts are used widely across the USA, where early findings have suggested they have been successful in enabling more children in care to return home because their parents have engaged with substance misuse services.

The aim of the FDAC is to help parents stabilise/stop using drugs/alcohol and, where possible, to keep families together. Instead of a normal care proceedings court process, a family chosen for the FDAC process will go through a slightly different process, with more regular court hearings with the same judge for the whole process.

The process has been set up specifically to help tackle any drug or alcohol problems. The process involves co-ordinating a range of services so that the family's needs, concerns and strengths are all taken into account, with everyone working towards the best possible outcome for the children - a stable and safe family which is able to stay together.

Selection - the cases that go through the Court

The FDAC is a pilot project, so cases are being selected for the court each week by the Listings Office on a first come first served basis. The usual threshold for proceedings applies to these cases and if they do not get chosen for the FDAC they will enter the usual family proceedings court instead, or be offered a place the following week.

There are no acceptance criteria to become a potential FDAC case, but there must be a history of drug or alcohol misuse in the family and this should be the main factor impacting on parenting ability. There are some exclusion criteria however;

- a history of severe physical or sexual abuse of the children
- ongoing domestic violence, where the safety of the Parents/Children cannot be established or supported
- parents experiencing florid psychosis which would prevent them from being able to engage purposefully or meaningfully in the project

Where these criteria apply, they will usually be a more pressing concern than the substance misuse within the family. At the moment, during the pilot, the criteria is being kept as wide as possible so that an assessment can be made of the types of family which are able to make best use of the process.

There are only a limited number of places available in the pilot scheme. Of all the potential cases, only 1 or 2 are selected each week. When a case gets to the stage of legal planning, if substance misuse is a key presenting issue, this will be indicated on a front sheet. When the case gets to court, the listings office will place all potential FDAC cases together and will choose 1 or 2 to enter the FDAC. At this stage the family will be notified that they have been selected for the FDAC and given written information about it before the first hearing, and at the first hearing by the FDAC team. The FDAC is

coram better chances for children since 1739   **The Tavistock and Portman** **NHS**
NHS Foundation Trust

voluntary and if parents do not wish to proceed, their case will be heard in the usual family proceedings court.

Choice for the Families

A family may choose not to go through the FDAC process, instead opting to go through the normal care proceedings route. They might do this for any number of reasons, but wherever possible, they should be encouraged to see the FDAC process as a real opportunity to get things back on track.

Like any care proceedings, there is still a potential for the family to lose their children, but the FDAC process has been set up to encourage success and to be as supportive as possible. Whilst they must take the process seriously, as they would do for normal care proceedings, families need not be fearful that the FDAC is there to trap or trick them in any way.

Once a family is chosen they do not have to make a decision immediately. They will be asked at the 1st Hearing on a Monday if they want to commit to the process; it begins immediately if they do. If they feel they need more time to think about it, they can ask the Court for another week. The family will be encouraged to talk to their Social Worker, and the FDAC team, if they have any doubts or questions over the process.

If the family sign up to enter this Court, they will have Court hearings fortnightly every Monday, starting 2 or 3 weeks after the first hearing. Between the first and second hearing they will be asked to take part in an assessment day by the FDAC team, who will formulate an intervention plan by the second Court hearing. After the second hearing, interventions will begin and the subsequent fortnightly hearings will be used to provide encouragement, review progress, review the intervention plan, problem solve any difficulties that arise and make decisions in order to reach permanency as quickly as possible.

Support given to the Families

- Support from the FDAC team who will coordinate the process and Intervention Plan. It is a multi-disciplinary team which includes: a Service Manager, a Nurse, a Drugs Worker, Senior Practitioner and Social Worker. There are sessions from Child and Adolescent Psychiatrist, Adult Psychiatrist and family therapist. There are also named links in the Housing and Domestic Violence Teams within the Local Authority

- A comprehensive assessment will include the family's strengths as well as concerns. The assessment will take into account any existing assessments/information and look at current needs.

- The FDAC team can help tackle issues around drug and/or alcohol use, physical and mental health, relationships with children and other family members, parenting, and issues with housing and domestic violence. The team will put in place a range of services in the family's Borough of residence to meet their needs.

- Depending on what the assessment results recommend, the Court will be able to monitor what the FDAC team identifies and refer the parent/s quickly to an appropriate treatment provider for counseling, community prescribing or inpatient detoxification and rehabilitation

- There may be access to Family therapy including play therapy for children and appropriate assessment and work to be undertaken by the psychologist / psychiatrist

- A Parent Mentor will be present during the Court and assessment period to provide support, encouragement and reassurance. Following the assessment phase a parent mentor may be assigned to the family. This person will have had similar experiences to the family and will be able to offer encouragement and advice

- Support will be offered for any current or previous issues of domestic violence

- Help with accessing employment and training will be offered

The Court Process

The FDAC is based in the Inner London Family Proceedings Court at Wells Street.

Once the process has started, there will be frequent Court hearings, every 2 weeks until the final review. The whole process will take around 9-12 months, but may be shorter, depending on progress.

The same District Judge, or one of a small team of District Judges, will oversee the whole process and will be able to review progress at the hearings and offer support and encouragement.

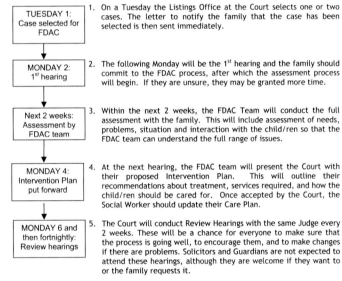

TUESDAY 1: Case selected for FDAC	1. On a Tuesday the Listings Office at the Court selects one or two cases. The letter to notify the family that the case has been selected is then sent immediately.
MONDAY 2: 1st hearing	2. The following Monday will be the 1st hearing and the family should commit to the FDAC process, after which the assessment process will begin. If they are unsure, they may be granted more time.
Next 2 weeks: Assessment by FDAC team	3. Within the next 2 weeks, the FDAC Team will conduct the full assessment with the family. This will include assessment of needs, problems, situation and interaction with the child/ren so that the FDAC team can understand the full range of issues.
MONDAY 4: Intervention Plan put forward	4. At the next hearing, the FDAC team will present the Court with their proposed Intervention Plan. This will outline their recommendations about treatment, services required, and how the child/ren should be cared for. Once accepted by the Court, the Social Worker should update their Care Plan.
MONDAY 6 and then fortnightly: Review hearings	5. The Court will conduct Review Hearings with the same Judge every 2 weeks. These will be a chance for everyone to make sure that the process is going well, to encourage them, and to make changes if there are problems. Solicitors and Guardians are not expected to attend these hearings, although they are welcome if they want to or the family requests it.

Expectations of the Families

The most important thing is that they engage with this process. There will be an expectation that the family is honest with the Court and the Professionals involved, and that they engage with the relevant treatment services to address their substance misuse

 better chances for children since 1739 The Tavistock and Portman
NHS Foundation Trust

issues, as well as any other relevant services identified for them. They will also be expected to attend the fortnightly Court hearings to review progress of the case. These hearings provide the opportunity to address problems as they arise and review the Intervention Plan. It is anticipated that legal representatives, guardians and other professionals will not need to attend every hearing; however, they will be welcome if they wish to be present.

If the parent drops out of the process at any time, the case returns to a regular family proceedings court in a seamless manner, without the need to instigate a whole new set of proceedings. However, families should be reminded that the FDAC offers a good opportunity for them to take the support being offered and work with professionals to address their issues.

Role of Lawyers in FDAC

As the Court proceedings continue and whilst the FDAC assessments are ongoing, each parent involved in the project will have their own Solicitor. Their job is to put across the position of the parent to the Court and other parties in the context of providing legal representation. It is envisaged that the Solicitor will attend the first two Court hearings whilst the assessment is being conducted and the Intervention Plan agreed. Once the intervention plan has been agreed the Solicitors will not have to attend the fortnightly Review Hearings unless there is a problem which the parents wish their Solicitor to raise with the Court and the other parties. If the "problem" cannot be dealt with either through correspondence or at the review hearing the Court will adjourn the matter for a hearing in front of the Judge with all the parties present at the earliest possible opportunity. The Solicitors are allowed to attend the Review Hearings as an observer if they wish to, or if their client wants them to attend.

The Court proceedings will continue in line with the new Public Law Outline in respect of Case Management Conferences, Advocates Meetings and Issue Resolution Hearings - although these will be dictated to by the progression of the FDAC assessments.

Guidance from the Legal Services Commission regarding identification of FDAC cases and remuneration of legal representatives

Identification of cases:

Legal representatives who are instructed in FDAC cases should identify them to the Legal Services Commission at the earliest opportunity. This should be done by marking the relevant application "FDAC Pilot" at the top of the standard form. This will enable LSC staff to consider funding issues in the context of the FDAC pilot and avoid queries and delays. The notification may be in the course of the case or even on its conclusion.

Remuneration:

The Legal Services Commission considers it justified to remunerate the attendance of legal representatives at those hearings where it is reasonable to anticipate in advance of the particular hearing that the representative will be required to provide advocacy services for the funded client(s) at the hearing. This may include the first review hearing but not subsequent review hearings which are listed as such and conducted by the Court with the client(s).

If any issues arise at a review hearing which the Court considers require its consideration or the provision of legal advice to the client(s), the hearing will be adjourned to another date. If issues requiring the consideration of the Court are identified by any of the legal representatives involved in the case in advance of a review hearing, then the Court should be requested to list the case for a directions or other hearing.

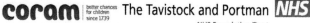

If a publicly funded representative chooses to attend a review hearing where it is not reasonable to anticipate the provision of advocacy services (including a review immediately preceding a directions hearing or other substantive hearing), then any time spent must not be included in any costs claim or calculation of the threshold for exceptional cases.

Any queries regarding this guidance should be addressed to family@legalservices.gov.uk.

Involvement of Parent Mentors

Parent Mentors are there to give the families support, help, encouragement and advice. They are not trained professionals, but they can offer invaluable informal and practical support.

All the Mentors are people who have had similar life experiences to those experienced by the families in the FDAC. They may not have been through exactly the same set of circumstances, but they will understand the issues the families are facing, and have a good knowledge of the treatment services, the Court and Social Services.

Contact details for further information

Sophie Kershaw
Service Manager, Family Drug and Alcohol Court Team
Coram Campus, Gregory House
49 Mecklenburgh Square
London WC1N 2QA
Tel: 0207 278 5708
Fax: 0207 278 4763
Email: info.FDACteam@coram.org.uk

APPENDIX 2 – CAPACITY TO CONDUCT PROCEEDINGS – THE RULES AND CASE-LAW

The relevant rules are rule 9.2 of the Family Proceedings Rules 1991 (FPR) and rule 50.2 of the Family Procedure (Adoption) Rules 2005 (FP(A)R).

Before 1 October 2007 the rules defined incapacity by reference to section 1(2) of the Mental Health Act 1983 and contained no statutory guidance. The guidance was supplied by case-law. the leading case being: *Masterman-Lister v Brutton & Co* [2003] 1 WLR 1511.

The FPR and the FP(A)R provided that:

> '"patient"' means a person who, by reason of mental disorder within the meaning of the Mental Health Act 1983, is incapable of managing and administering his property and affairs.'

Section 1(2) of the Mental Health Act 1983 (MHA) defines 'mental disorder':

> '"mental disorder" means mental illness, arrested or incomplete development of mind, psychopathic disorder and any other disorder or disability of mind and "mentally disordered" shall be construed accordingly;'

With effect from 1 October 2007 and the implementation of the Mental Capacity Act 2005 (MCA) the rules were amended. A party who lacks capacity to conduct proceedings is now a 'protected party' and the rules define a protected party as:

> 'a party or intended party, who lacks capacity (within the meaning of the 2005 Act [the Mental Capacity Act 2005]) to conduct the proceedings.'

Section 2(1) of the MCA sets out the statutory definition for lack of capacity:

> 'a person lacks capacity in relation to a matter if at the material time he is unable to make a decision for himself in relation to the matter because of an impairment of, or a disturbance in the functioning of, the mind or brain.'

Section 3(1) is the key section of the MCA; it provides that a person is unable to make a decision for himself if he is unable:

> '(a) to understand the information relevant to the decision,
> (b) to retain that information,
> (c) to use or weigh that information as part of the process of making the decision, or
> (d) to communicate his decision (whether by talking, using sign language or any other means).'

The common law test for litigation capacity is set out by Kennedy LJ at paragraph 26 of *Masterman-Lister*:

> '... the mental abilities required include the ability to recognise a problem, obtain and receive, understand and retain relevant information, including advice; the ability to weigh the information (including that derived from advice) in the balance in reaching a decision, and the ability to communicate that decision ...'

APPENDIX 3 – WITNESS INTERMEDIARY SCHEME

The Witness Intermediary Scheme – a background note

The Witness Intermediary Scheme was set up initially because, under the Youth Justice and Criminal Evidence Act 1999, vulnerable witnesses are able to give evidence with the assistance of an intermediary. However, it is not widely known that the scheme will also assist in other courts not just the criminal jurisdiction. There can be some confusion as to what a witness intermediary is. They are not from the local advocacy service but are specially trained and accredited professionals whose role is specifically aimed at assisting people in the court process. They do not replace foreign language/BSL interpreters. They have been described as an independent 'go-between' for the witness, helping children and people with mental or physical disabilities and disorders to understand the questions they're being asked and assisting them in communicating their answers, without influencing the content of the evidence. Their role is to facilitate communications without changing the substance of the evidence. Intermediaries can work with witnesses at each stage of the process, from police investigations and interviews, through pre-trial preparations to court. Intermediaries assess the individual abilities and needs of the witness to determine how they communicate and their level of understanding and advise the agencies on how to best question them and get their best evidence. The intermediary will meet the client in advance of the hearing to assess the best way to help them to give their evidence. They will then write a brief report for the court and advocates to consider with recommendations as to how the court should try to conduct things to ensure they got the best possible evidence from the witness. The intermediary will offer their view to the court when they think that the witness had not understood the question or even suggesting ways that the question could be rephrased so the witness does understand it. They will want to sit next to the witness and will be able to assist them with finding documents in the bundle etc. There is a code of practice and ethics for intermediates. They are accredited through the witness intermediary scheme and swear their own oath at the start of the evidence. The intermediaries are all self employed but are booked through the central matching service. They come from a variety of backgrounds – there are a lot of speech and language therapists involved but there are other disciplines too and the matching service will attempt to match up the client's needs with the skills of the intermediary.

The Witness Intermediary Service – a practical experience

This was a finding of fact hearing in the county court concerning serious injuries to a young baby. The protected party was a grandmother who was a possible perpetrator of the injury with the only other possible perpetrator being her daughter, the child's mother. A psychologist had assessed the protected party's competence to give evidence and recommended the appointment of a witness intermediary. On the basis of this recommendation the court agreed to an intermediary being instructed and this week the grandmother gave oral evidence with the intermediary's assistance.

Prior authority from the LSC to fund the intermediary had been obtained.

The intermediary had never acted in a civil case before but was experienced in the criminal courts and in assisting witnesses when they were interviewed by the police and had no difficulty in acting in discharging her role in a family case.

The intermediary met the grandmother in advance of the hearing to assess the best way to help her when she gave evidence. The intermediary then provided a brief report for the court and advocates with her recommendations as to how the court should try to conduct the hearing to ensure the best possible evidence was obtained from the witness. They were fairly basic recommendations but it was noticeable that the advocates found it difficult to follow that advice – for example to just ask a straight question about one thing at a time.

The intermediary had no problem intervening when she thought that the witness had not understood the question or even suggesting ways that the question could be rephrased so the witness did understand it. She sat next to the witness so could tell if the witness needed a break or detect that the witness had not understood what she was being asked. She also assisted the witness with finding the correct pages in the bundle so it was one less thing for the witness to worry about and get in a panic over.

It obviously slowed the process down considerably and it took a whole day for the grandmother's evidence alone but in my view, and that of the court and other advocates, it was really useful to have the intermediary there. It helped enormously that the judge was positive about the role of the intermediary and the room was organised so the witness did not feel overwhelmed by all the advocates present.

Although the witness was very anxious about giving evidence at least with this special measure she had the chance to tell the judge herself that she did not injure the baby and I thought she came across very well in the witness box – an impression the judge may not have got just from the papers and without hearing directly from her.

Attached are a brief note about the scheme, the intermediary Code of Practice and Code of Ethics, the form to request their service and some frequently asked questions (which deal mainly with the criminal jurisdiction mainly but include some general points). The information refers to it being a pilot scheme but it is now to be rolled out across the country due to its success.

The way to refer to the scheme will be changing very shortly (as it is now to be a permanent scheme).

The Code of Practice and Code of Ethics for Intermediaries (reproduced below) are included with the application to become an intermediary, available at: http:// insidejustice.cjsonline.gov.uk/getinvolved/careers/Intermediary_Info_Pack_08.doc

The Code of Practice for Intermediaries

1. The primary responsibility of the intermediary is to enable complete, coherent and accurate communication to take place between a witness who requires special measures and the court.

2. Intermediaries must have a clear and comprehensive understanding of the responsibilities and duties of their role within the criminal justice system, including their primary responsibility to the court.

3. They must conduct themselves in a professional and courteous manner at all times.

4. They must be familiar with and observe the terms and conditions and procedures that govern their assignment.

5. They should identify the sources of advice, information and materials required in order to ensure a clear understanding of the special needs of the witness.

6. They must carry out a functional assessment of the communication needs of the witness and make an informed professional judgement of the time required to enable them to carry out the assessment satisfactorily.

7.	They will use the background information provided and will meet with the witness, his or her relatives, supporter, carer or relevant professionals to acquaint themselves fully with the knowledge and understanding required to carry out the assignment successfully.

8.	They must not enter discussions, give advice or express opinions concerning the evidence the witness is to present or any aspect of the case that could contaminate the evidence or lead to an allegation of rehearsing or coaching the witness.

9.	They must keep the co-ordinator and other appropriate parties informed of any difficulties that may arise in the course of the assignment that may affect the prospects of best evidence being given.

10.	They must hold meetings with witnesses within a time-scale agreed with the co-ordinator and in appropriate venues.

11.	They must make clear the purpose of the meetings and structure meetings in a way that allows sufficient time to assess the needs of the witness and to gain the confidence and trust of the witness.

12.	They must record and communicate to the co-ordinator any dissatisfaction expressed by the witness with either the intermediary or the procedure being followed.

13.	They must ensure the witness is satisfied with the outcome of the assessment and understands the role of the intermediary, particularly in the context of the court appearance.

14.	They must conduct themselves in court in a manner that facilitates accurate and coherent communication between the witness and the court.

15.	They must not change the content of what is being said or attempt to improve or elaborate what has been said. Any actions that may improve understanding without changing meaning or the sense of what is being said, such as conveying the meaning of gestures the witness may make, must be taken only with the explicit understanding and consent of the court.

16.	They must disclose to the court any difficulties encountered, such as limitations in their professional experience and training, and seek the court's guidance about action that may be taken that is consistent with best evidence.

17.	They must intervene only to seek clarification from the court or to draw the court's attention to any difficulty the witness may be experiencing in understanding what is being said or that may be distressing the witness.

18.	They must respect at all times the authority and judgment of the court.

19.	They must complete, at the conclusion of each assignment a monitoring and evaluation form that will contribute to efforts to improve the quality of the service.

20.	They must recognise that an intermediary's duty to the court remains paramount.

21.	They must understand the different obligations regarding disclosure of information between the prosecution and the defence legal teams and must maintain their professional integrity in relation to these different obligations.

22. They must notify the Intermediary Registration Board immediately of any criminal investigation or proceedings against them or any other complaint or investigation into their conduct or competence.

23. They must notify the Intermediary Registration Board of the result of any adverse Criminal Records Bureau disclosure check carried out on them (ie any result where a conviction is recorded other than already disclosed to the Intermediary Registration Board).

The Code of Ethics for Intermediaries

1. Definition: in this code, intermediary means any person who is registered on the national register as an intermediary in the criminal justice system as specified in Section 29 of the Youth Justice and Criminal Evidence Act 1999.

2. Intermediaries will consider at all times the potential for conflict of interest and the need to act in the public interest and will conduct themselves responsibly and professionally using reasonable skill and care in the performance of their duties.

3. This includes:
    *   Seeking to increase their professional communication skills and knowledge and their skills as an intermediary eg court skills, through training and research.
    *   Ensuring they have adequate and sustained professional support for their own role.
    *   Safeguarding professional standards in every practicable way.
    *   Offering other intermediaries reasonable and appropriate assistance.
    *   Respecting the ethics and professional practice of other professions.
    *   Endeavouring to the best of their ability to enable communication to be complete, coherent and accurate.
    *   Only accepting work for which they are appropriately qualified and they judge to be within their professional competence.
    *   Accepting only in exceptional circumstances, an assignment for which no entirely suitable intermediary is available, with such acceptance being subject to the informed consent of all parties.
    *   Acknowledging and seeking to overcome in a professional manner, such as through professional advice and guidance or support networks, any unforeseen difficulties or limitations in knowledge or practice that may become apparent in the course of an assignment.
    *   Promptly notifying the co-ordinator of any matter, including conflict of interest or lack of suitable qualifications and experience, that may disqualify or make it undesirable for them to have continued involvement in the assignment.
    *   Treating as confidential any information that may come to them in the course of their work including the fact of their having undertaken a particular assignment, although assignments may be used as evidence for continued registration but not in other (to be defined) circumstances. However, this does not preclude disclosure when legally required to do so or when failure to disclose information could render the intermediary liable to prosecution.
    *   Disclosing before commencing an assignment or as soon as practicable any vested or material interest that the intermediary may have in the assignment.
    *   Not using any information or knowledge gained during the course of their work to benefit themselves or anyone else improperly.
    *   Not giving advice or offering personal opinions in relation to the evidence presented by the witness nor concerning people present during an assignment.
    *   Making appropriate efforts to facilitate communication between people who have differing communication and cultural characteristics

- Making all reasonable effort to be available for all meetings, hearings, trials and other appointments for which adequate notice has been given.
- Not cancelling or postponing meetings that are part of the assignment without good reason and where possible, the consent of the people concerned.
- Respecting the decisions taken by other professionals, particularly criminal justice decisions.

APPENDIX 4 – PARENTS WHO LACK CAPACITY TO CONDUCT PUBLIC LAW PROCEEDINGS

The following is a reproduction of The Safeguarding Committee of the Family Justice Council's paper prepared in July 2009 which was circulated to Family Justice Council branches.

The difficult issues arising in public law care cases where a parent lacks capacity to conduct the proceedings have been referred to the Family Justice Council for consideration by the Family Procedure Rules Committee. There have been a number of developments which render such consideration timely: the decision of the Court of Appeal in *Nottingham CC –v- RP* (2008) (EWCA Civ 462); the emphasis on pre-proceedings work with parents contained in the Public Law Outline issued in April 2008; the implementation of the Mental Capacity Act 2005.

What follows is an attempt to summarise current good practice in procedural terms followed by a number of specific questions and a more general opportunity to express the views of your local Family Justice Council.

Part 1 – Current practice

1. The Mental Capacity Act provides at s2(1) that a person lacks capacity in relation to matter if at the material time he is unable to make a decision for himself in relation to the matter because of an impairment of or disturbance in the functioning of the mind or brain, whether the impairment or disturbance is permanent or temporary. There are parents whose lack of litigation capacity is lifelong, for example those with profound learning disabilities or dementia. There may be other individuals whose lack of capacity is associated with, for example, specific acute periods of mental illness or following brain injury, and who may regain capacity as their health improves. In the latter type of case it important that the issue is kept under close review.

The Local Authority – pre-proceedings

2. There are many groups of parents who are vulnerable in the context of social work involvement. This paper purports only to deal with a limited and specific group, those whose disabilities are sufficiently severe that they lack the capacity to conduct legal proceedings. Thus for example the detailed guidance issued by the DCSF in 2007 entitled 'Good Practice in Working with Parents with a Learning Disability' is useful by way of background and in terms of setting broad standards for Local Authorities to achieve but does not directly address the issue of parents who lack litigation capacity.

3. Where a parent lacks litigation capacity it must be appreciated that it is very improbable that s/he has the capacity to consent to their child being accommodated under s20 of the Children Act. If the child is plainly at risk, the Local Authority should issue care proceedings.

4. Obviously it is important that a parent's particular difficulties are recognised and properly taken into account from the outset of the Local Authority's involvement. As the Official Solicitor advises *'This recognition should not focus on the issue of litigation capacity, as (a) the intention is to try and work with the parents to avert litigation, and (b) to concentrate on the issue of litigation capacity can give rise to the risk that a parent feels that the local authority is seeking to disempower the parent in the decision making process with regard to the child.'* Whilst an early cognitive functioning assessment could not provide a definitive diagnosis, it may be particularly helpful in enabling the Local Authority to undertake parenting and other social work assessments on an informed basis.

5. If a parent's difficulties are not recognised, any assessment conducted by the Local Authority may be vitiated and will certainly be susceptible to subsequent challenge. There will also be unnecessary delay in ensuring that an appropriate assessment of the parent's own need for support is obtained eg under s47 of the National Health Service and Community Care Act 1990.

6. Once it is clear that proceedings are likely to be necessary, the Local Authority must bear in mind that the PLO will require the Local Authority to file a case summary which includes 'a summary of any concerns which the Local Authority may have about the mental capacity of an adult to care for the child or prepare for the proceedings'. In the Nottingham case, Wall LJ concluded that judgments on litigation capacity should not be made by social workers from the child protection team. He suggested that where a Local Authority had such concerns prior to the issue of proceedings 'it should refer the parent to the Adult Learning Disability Team *(or presumably an appropriate mental health resource?)* for help and advice. If that team thinks that further investigations are required it can undertake them; it should moreover, have the necessary contacts and resources to commission a report'. The referrals proposed will not necessarily provide information which clarifies the issue of litigation capacity because the person referred may not meet the criteria for the service or may not take up the referral. But if a referral does prove successful and proceedings are subsequently issued, the more detailed information will enhance the parent's solicitors' ability to advise and to address the question of a litigation friend promptly.

7. Good Local Authority practice would include:
    7.1 Jointly agreed referral and assessment procedures between Children's Social Care Services and Adult Learning Disability teams/Mental Health Services and any other partner agencies eg maternity services. This is likely to involve commissioning decisions at a senior level
    7.2 Appropriate support for parents, such as the provision of a lay advocate during meetings such as child protection conferences and FGCs
    7.3 The provision of documentation in an accessible form. [The FJC has supported the publication of suitable booklets about care proceedings for parents with learning difficulties which are currently being translated into a wide range of languages]

Once proceedings are issued – The Local Authority

8. The Local Authority issuing care proceedings should complete Section 5 of the Case Summary (concerns re: mental health) attaching any available evidence as to any potential lack of litigation capacity and within Section 6 of their Case Summary, should identify the directions sought to resolve this issue.

9. The Local Authority 'Allocation Record and Timetable for the Child' should indicate a request for immediate transfer with a First Hearing in the Care Centre if there is evidence as to lack of capacity to conduct the proceedings and the need for an appointment of a litigation friend.

Family Proceedings Courts

10. If there is evidence as to lack of parental capacity to conduct the proceedings, the FPC should transfer the case immediately for first appointment in the Care Centre.

11. If there is insufficient information for the FPC allocator to make a properly informed decision, the FPC should retain the case and give Directions in order to fulfil its duty to

investigate the issue of capacity at the earliest opportunity (unless there are other grounds which require the case to be transferred to the Care Centre).

12.   If the issue of capacity to conduct the proceedings arises unexpectedly, or the mental health of a party deteriorates during proceedings being conduced within the FPC, then again directions should be given as above and if evidence of lack of capacity to conduct the proceedings is available, then the case should be transferred urgently to the Care Centre.

Care Centre/High Court

13.   Unless the Family Proceedings Court has already given appropriate directions, on receipt of an application with evidence of lack of capacity to conduct the proceedings, the Care Centre should give directions urgently in order to resolve the identity of the litigation friend/guardian ad litem.

14.   If an issue of capacity to conduct the proceedings arises unexpectedly then urgent directions should be given in order to obtain an appropriate assessment and resolve the issue.

15.   Standard Directions, if a professional litigation friend or the Official Solicitor is to be invited to act, should be as follows:

'That X (named party) forward to Y/Official Solicitor forthwith

(a)   a copy of the order appointing the litigation friend/inviting the Official Solicitor to act
(b)   a detailed letter of background information, including the stage of proceedings reached and the date of any pending hearing
(c)   a paginated bundle with summary, statement of issues, and chronology'

The Parent's legal representatives

16.   The assessment of capacity to conduct the proceedings involves consideration of whether the party is capable of understanding issues 'with the assistance of such proper explanation from legal advisors and experts in other disciplines as the case may require'. Sometimes, particularly patient, careful and repeated explanation and discussion with a solicitor/ barrister may enable a parent, with even significant degree of learning disability, to participate in proceedings without a litigation friend. By s1(2) of the Mental Capacity Act a person is not to be treated as unable to make a decision unless all practicable steps to enable him to do so have been taken without success.

17.   It may be helpful if a solicitor can provide a parent with accessible written information and also give consideration as to whether a lay advocate might assist the parent during their more formal dealings with the Local Authority or in discussions with their legal representatives or during any attendance at court.

18.   Once instructed, if there is doubt as to capacity to conduct proceedings, the legal representative of a party is under a duty to draw it to the attention of the Court. See para 47 Wall LJ's judgment in *RP-v-Nottingham CC* 2008 EWCA Civ. 462

'Both the relevant rules of Court and the leading case of *Masterman-v-Lister (2003) 3 All ER 192* make it clear that once either counsel or (the solicitor) had formed the view that … (the protected party) … might not be able to give them proper instructions, and might be a person under a disability, it was their professional duty to have the question resolved as quickly as possible'

19. The party concerned should always be informed of any worries the legal representative has about capacity to conduct the proceedings, the purpose of any assessment directed at the issue, and the implications if they are found to lack such capacity. Particular difficulties do arise if a parent refuses to be assessed by an appropriately qualified expert.

20. It is the responsibility of the parent's solicitor to obtain an opinion on litigation capacity. There may be occasions when it is appropriate to seek an opinion from a treating clinician otherwise an appropriately qualified independent expert must be identified. The solicitor must ensure that the assessor receives appropriate and adequate information about the legal framework for the assessment. The Official Solicitor's standard letter of instruction, pro formas and questions should be used. Unless a treating clinician is instructed, the PLO Practice Direction in relation to Experts should be drawn to the attention of any assessor.

21. Once received, the expert's report should, if possible, be explained to the parent. This can be a difficult task and the relevant expert may be able to assist. The solicitor must advise the parent that s/he is entitled to dispute any opinion to the effect that they lack capacity. If the parent wishes to assert his/her own capacity the case must be listed urgently for the issue to be determined by the court. It may be necessary for the court to hear evidence from the expert and the parent concerned and any relevant witnesses. If the parent has declined professional assessment it will be for the court to determine the issue on the best evidence it has available.

22. Initially the identity of the 'litigation friend' is a question for the protected parent and his/her solicitor. It is not an inter-partes issue. The solicitor should explore whether there is any person the protected party would suggest in their circle of family and friends. If so, and the solicitor feels able to provide the certificate under Rule 9.2(7)(c) FPR 1991, then it is for the Court to decide whether or not to accept that certificate.

23. It is only if there is no one identified to act, or the solicitor feels unable to provide the R9.2 certificate or the court refuses to accept the R9.2 certificate that the case becomes a 'last resort' case and an invitation may need to be extended to the Official Solicitor.

24. On average, the Official Solicitor receives 20 invitations each week from courts to act as litigation friend for a parent involved in proceedings under the Children Act 1989 and the Adoption and Children Act 2002. There appear to be no records available referring to litigation friends other than the Official Solicitor but in our experience such appointments are rare.

25. Unless there is clear evidence that particular information would be *harmful* (not simply distressing) the solicitor should inform the protected party:
    25.1 About the appointment of a litigation friend
    25.2 About the role of a litigation friend
    25.3 That the solicitor remains the protected party's solicitor although acting upon the instructions of the litigation friend.
    25.4 That whilst the litigation friend makes decisions about the conduct of the proceedings, it is for the parent to demonstrate that he/she is able to meet the welfare needs of their child
    25.5 About steps in the proceedings
    25.6 Of court dates
    25.7 About orders of the court.

26. If there is credible reason to suggest that a party may have regained capacity then it may be necessary for a further assessment to be conducted. In some cases it may be appropriate to ask an expert instructed during the course of the case to conduct that review depending on the nature of their primary instructions. If the party's capacity to conduct the proceedings is

regained then the litigation friend/guardian ad litem should immediately apply for his or her discharge so that the party can resume personal conduct of the proceedings. The court should give priority to such an application.

The Parent who acts as a Litigant in Person

27. A lack of litigation capacity must *not* be assumed simply because a litigant in person [LIP] is difficult/hostile etc. The presumption of competence can only be rebutted on the balance of probabilities having regard to the evidence.

28. Where the capacity of a LIP is to be assessed, the standard letter of instruction/pro forma certificate should be sent to the expert by whoever the court directs although this is likely to be the children's guardian. The letter of instruction should include the LIP's own comments on the issue.

29. In relation to the letter of instruction, additional information to the expert should include that the LIP will generally be at a disadvantage facing professional legal representatives but that this does not of itself give rise to a lack of litigation capacity.

30. If the LIP is found to lack capacity to conduct proceedings he should be informed, as directed by the court, of the issues set out at 25 above.

The role of the Official Solicitor.

31. 'The Official Solicitor: Appointment in Family Proceedings' is the current Practice Note issued April 2001.

32. If the Official Solicitor agrees to act, it would be usual for him to ensure continuity of representation by instructing the solicitor chosen by the protected parent. The solicitor remains the primary point of contact for the parent.

33. It is the duty of any litigation friend, including the Official Solicitor, to fairly and competently conduct the proceedings on behalf of the protected party. Given the implications of Art 6 and the disempowering effect of the involvement of a litigation friend, the role of the Official Solicitor is a complex and sensitive one.

34. Sections 2 and 3 of the Mental Capacity Act refer to a lack of capacity to make specific decisions. That reflects the *Masterman-Lister* approach which refers to capacity as 'fact specific'. The Official Solicitor's pro formas for expert assessors do not separate out the capacity to make specific decisions potentially arising within the proceedings but consider the proceedings as a whole.

35. The Official Solicitor will consider the protected party's views and wishes as communicated via the solicitor as the case progresses. Those views, wishes and feelings will be set out in the Official Solicitor's final report. However they will not be determinative of the Official Solicitor's approach. Tensions will inevitably arise where the Official Solicitor's assessment of the parent's best interests in the litigation differ from the parents own view. The Official Solicitor is committed to presenting any realistic arguments and relevant evidence in relation to the issues before the court, the criterion being whether the point is 'reasonably arguable' not whether it is likely to succeed.

36. There is a distinction between the capacity to conduct proceedings and the capacity to give evidence. It should not be assumed that a parent who lacks litigation capacity cannot give

evidence. There may be occasions, for example during a fact finding hearing where a child has suffered injury or has been sexually abused, where a parent's factual evidence of events may be very important for the protection of the child. The court should strive to facilitate the giving of the best possible evidence by any parent with a disability.

Intervenors

37. This paper is concerned principally with *parents* who lack capacity. There may also be circumstances in which an intervener to the proceedings, for example someone who is a potential perpetrator of injuries to a child, does not have the capacity to conduct the proceedings. Very similar considerations, for example as to the role of the party's solicitor would apply.

Part 2 – Specific questions

1. Could any further steps appropriately be taken by a Local Authority pre-proceedings where is suspected that a parent lacks capacity?

2. Within many Local Authorities there appears to be limited communication and differing thresholds for intervention and/or eligibility criteria between the Children Social Care Services and Adult Learning Disability Teams/mental health services. How can that be improved? How can links with existing services be enhanced? Are there areas where relevant services simply don't exist?

3. Are pre-proceedings letters always desirable, for example when a parent suffers from severe mental health problems and the receipt of such a letter is likely to prove positively damaging to their health?

4. We are aware of occasions upon which a parent who lacks capacity has 'agreed' to s20 accommodation and found their child removed from their care without legal or other professional support. What additional safeguards might be put in place to protect both parent and child in his situation? Should the Local Authority always be required to issue public law proceedings if there are significant child protection concerns in the context of a parent who lacks capacity? Is there a particular role for the Independent Reviewing Officer?

5. Would it be helpful if there were standard directions which could be issued by either the FPC or the Care Centre in cases where parental litigation capacity is an issue

6. How might delay in determining issues around the appointment of a litigation friend best be avoided? In practical terms are there stages within this process which give rise to particular difficulty?

7. Are lay advocacy services readily available within your area?

8. Are any additional safeguards necessary to protect the position of an unrepresented party or of an intervener who lacks litigation capacity?

The role of the Official Solicitor

We recognise that some of these issues will properly remain matters for the Official Solicitor's professional judgment. We are also aware that the ECHR is to hear a relevant case towards the end of this year and that the FJC may need to revisit some of these issues following the judgment in that case.

9.   Sometimes the solicitor originally instructed by a parent may not have any specialist expertise or even basic competence in conducting family proceedings. Do the advantages of continuity of representation outweigh the potential benefits of an arrangement whereby for example the Official Solicitor might restrict instructions to solicitors from the Law Society Family Panel?

10.   It would be impracticable to seek to assess capacity by looking at every single step in the proceedings. Some stages could not in any event readily be anticipated in advance. Is the present relatively 'broad brush' the best approach?

11.   In the normal course of civil and family proceedings it seems unlikely to be in a protected person's interests for a litigation friend to seek to present a case which is not reasonably arguable. There are disadvantages to a parent being caught up in protracted proceedings and subjected to repeated assessment which result in no better outcome. On the other hand, there is an argument that in care and placement order proceedings the consequences for a parent are so far reaching and drastic that unless they positively express a wish to agree to the making of such orders, it may generally be in their best interests for the case to be actively contested. That would probably require a different set of rules specifically distinguishing public law cases from all other form of litigation. In practical terms the courts are not likely to welcome the Official Solicitor fully contesting hopeless cases and it would not be a proportionate use of scarce resources. Is there actually any evidence that the Official Solicitor's current approach gives rise to injustice? Is there any realistic alternative?

12.   Should courts be more willing to permit a parent who lacks litigation capacity and is represented by a litigation friend to give evidence? Indeed, should there be a presumption that a parent who wants to give evidence should be allowed to do so? Is there information which could better be circulated as to the range of special measures now readily available in the criminal courts, including trained witness intermediaries?

Part 3 – Wider responses

Are there any other issues which arise in care proceedings where a parent lacks litigation capacity which you wish to draw to our attention? We would welcome your experiences, both positive and negative, of the current system and any concrete suggestions for improvement. It would be helpful to receive any feedback by **Friday 30 October.**

CARING IN THE FAMILY

Ann Tucker

SUMMARY OF PAPER

Ann Tucker, mother, grandmother and kinship carer gave a very personal insight into the complex relationship between mental health issues, the law and the family. Sharing her experience with the conference, she considered the institutionalised attitudes she encountered, the benefits of kinship care and made some suggestions for changes to improve the kinship care environment.

THE PAPER

I welcome the opportunity to participate in the bi-annual Mental Health and Family Law conference, and to share my experience even though I feel somewhat like a 'living case study'. On the other hand perhaps it also brings a sense of reality to the conference which in some way will help to improve the current situation for the many thousands of 'family and friends carers' like myself and the children they care for.

THE STORY

It is only a potted version but my story begins over 16 years ago when my eldest daughter was in her first year at Art College and had a psychotic episode. She never recovered from that first episode and after 16 years of being in hospitals and various hostels she still suffers from mental ill health.

This was a devastating experience for all the family, especially my younger daughter who adored her older sister but was too young to understand what was happening and why her sister had become someone she hardly recognised anymore.

Eleven years ago my older daughter had a child, my grandchild.

It is quite common for new mothers to revert to mental ill health, as the hormones that are released during childbirth can be detrimental to mental well-being. My daughter became extremely ill after the birth and 6 days later she was taken back into hospital, removed from our home, handcuffed and escorted by eight police officers, an action I still question.

My husband and I had agreed I would take a year off work to look after our grandchild and help support our daughter to be a mother.

Due to my daughter's mental health condition, my granddaughter was immediately put on the 'at risk register'. This meant she was assigned a social worker; in fact she was assigned two, one before the birth and another after. We also had a Child Protection Conference when our granddaughter was about 6 months old, when she was taken off the register; a huge relief to us all.

We were advised by the second social worker to seek a residence order (which gave us shared parental responsibility with our daughter) to safeguard the welfare of our grandchild. We were not told it meant there would be no support whatsoever after this as the child would then be our responsibility. The procedure cost us about £1,000 and a lot of emotional heartache knowing we were taking on a role that should have been our daughter's.

Meanwhile my husband and I were juggling caring for our granddaughter, working, caring for our teenage daughter, visiting our daughter in hospital daily and supporting her relationship with her daughter.

My daughter's consultant reluctantly agreed that I could bring my granddaughter to visit her mother twice a week. We would be allocated a room for an hour with a member of the nursing staff always present. We were not supported by my daughter's consultant who was of the opinion that women with mental health problems were not really fit to care for their children and when I asked about my daughter's lack of progress in the hospital the consultant replied 'what can you expect when you keep putting that baby in her face'. She later opposed a placement for my daughter in a supported mental health mother and baby unit.

My daughter valued these early visits with her child and no matter what situation my daughter has been in during the last 11 years I have maintained the contact between my daughter and her own daughter. It has not always been easy but they continue to spend quality time together and it means my granddaughter knows her own story and can talk about it, which I believe is very important.

When my grandchild was 2, my husband of 33 years left us. He said he wanted a new life, which is hardly surprising given the life we had. He has not seen his grandchild since but has regular contact with his two daughters.

Interestingly enough during our divorce in 2004, when maintenance was mentioned, the judge deemed the case to be very complicated. Because our granddaughter was not legally ours (a residence order is not the same as adoption) I was told that I was not entitled to child maintenance. This presented another problem as I consequently needed to work full time in order to support my family. Thankfully I reached retirement age in April of this year and now work part time supporting other kinship carers.

My story is not unique but it demonstrates the effects and sometimes the consequences of caring within the family. I would love to be a regular grandmother enjoying my grandchild, having her to stay at weekends, taking her on holiday, having that special relationship grandparents have with their grandchildren. Instead I'm a tired, older, working, single 'mum' who feels harassed and sometimes overwhelmed by the enormity of my responsibilities and feel constantly concerned as to how she will cope with her own life once she fully comprehends it.

As a kinship carer you do it because it is your family and you love them, you want the best for them and you will do whatever you can to achieve it. Yes, we should have received better information from the services. Yes, we should have received some financial help to undergo the legal procedures to ensure our granddaughter was safe and secure. Yes, we should have received better support from the social services department but having experienced this service through caring for my daughter I didn't relish or trust that intervention. My concerns were later confirmed by a social worker himself.

INSTITUTIONALISED ATTITUDES

My granddaughter's father also has mental health problems but has found himself in the 'care' of prisons as well as hospitals. I have also maintained contact with him so my granddaughter knows both her parents. Whether one agrees or not I believe that to be as honest as possible, within a sensitive framework for the child, is the best policy. By being open there is always a platform for discussion later.

I had occasion to speak to his social worker about seeing his daughter. The social worker asked if it was best to go through the child's social worker and I said she doesn't have one. He replied – 'that's good there will be no stigma attached to her later in life' and sadly that summed it up.

Another incident occurred about 9 months ago reminding me how far apart the social worker's agenda is and the needs of the client are and how easy to it to see only a caseload and not a whole person.

As a result of my own experiences of mental health services I have been involved in many things including training sessions at Goldsmith's College to student social workers. Through this work I was asked to give a presentation to social workers in Lewisham and Southwark. I talked about my experiences and afterwards a man came up to me and asked if I remembered him as he had been my granddaughter's social worker. I had to confess I didn't remember him visually though of course I remembered vividly my encounter with him. My presentation had not been terribly complimentary about the services I had received and his next question to me was 'how had he been as my social worker?' I had to confess my experience had not been good. He had come into our lives for 6 months, visited twice and was very obviously inspecting my grandchild for signs of physical damage. He had recommended we apply for a residence order saying it would prevent my own daughter being able to take her child away and once the case conference had taken place to remove my grandchild from the 'at risk register' I never saw him again.

Eleven years later I was actually able to tell him I hadn't felt supported by him and he replied 'but you were such an easy case'. This epitomised so many of the issues and problems I had encountered during my 16 years of involvement with both the mental health and social service systems.

I was momentarily silenced by his few words but then I understood his perspective was so different from mine. My family had been willing to take on the baby so he could close the case and think no more about it. To him I was an easy, straightforward case. The child was placed and he had the added benefit of dealing with 'a family of professionals' who could comprehend the jargon and understand reports and processes whereas for me I was in the middle of a crisis with no help and no one I could trust to even ask for help. For me it was yet another painful decision and a lifetime commitment alongside the devastation I was already experiencing at the prolonged mental ill health of my daughter. Trying to come to terms with the abuse she had suffered whilst in the mental health system, dealing with her pregnancy, coping with the daily visits, taking on the responsibility of a baby and the financial implications of this. And of course I still had a 15-year-old adolescent at home who herself was still trying to understand what had happened to her sister, dealing with a new baby in the family whilst coping with her own adolescent transition.

THE BENEFITS

Despite what might seem a difficult and tragic story there are of course many benefits – the greatest of all being my granddaughter herself and the fact that we have remained a loving, supportive family, albeit in a new format.

My granddaughter has a strong sense of her own identity within that family and feels secure enough to talk about her own parents and though she might not fully understand their situation knows the family is a safe place where these issues can be shared and discussed.

Being brought up within the extended family is not new – I was brought up by my grandparents and parents and spent all my early years being loved and cared for by them all. My middle years were with my grandparents then when I became an adolescent I moved back with my parents.

This experience was neither detrimental nor disturbing and I only have a sense of my childhood as being one where I was surrounded by love, had endless adventures, was thoroughly spoilt and now have nothing but happy memories.

IMPROVING WHAT WE HAVE

Caring within families and friends contributes greatly to the total number of children who are actually cared for by someone other than their parents, yet this contribution is often unrecognised and in many cases is even unknown.

The government has begun to take more notice of the crucial role family and friends carers have in the care of children but many of their proposals remain discretionary. This means that not all carers experience the same support.

Data has been collected highlighting the care provided by family and friends and the benefits that are gained. This information should be used to create the necessary services to support this work. Care amongst family and friends should be seen as a legitimate and respected alternative to institutional care and as such should be recognised, supported and financed. Especially remembering that up till now caring in the family has probably saved the government and the country millions of pounds and has always been regarded as a cheaper and preferable option.

- Family and friends carers should receive financial support for legal procedures in applications for residence and special guardianship orders or provision for fees to be at least greatly reduced as well as receiving financial support with caring for the child or children that is consistent and at a statutory requirement throughout the country.

- Family and friends carers should not be seen as part of the regular 'client mentality' within the social services structure; they should be recognised for the valuable and often difficult job they do and should be regarded as partners in the care process.

- Family and friends carers should receive a carer's assessment, if they want one, and this should not become a paperwork exercise that feeds the 'system' but is backed by real resources and support networks.

- Consideration should be given to the creation of a 'One Stop Service' that supports family and friends carers, this would incorporate health/social services/education and become a government-funded body but without the stigma attached to being involved in the service.

I believe these recommendations need to be included within the very structure, framework and concept of any document or policy that purports to use the term 'Care Matters' along with a serious examination of the attitudes that underline any implementation of such policies.

I don't want to appear too idealistic because family and friends care doesn't work for everyone and there will be children and young people for whom being looked after within the family is not the best scenario. However, most findings suggest that the majority of children cared for within families don't just survive better but they positively thrive and at the end of the day I would have thought that is what we are all striving for.

PLENARY 3

SPECIFIC ISSUES RELEVANT TO MENTAL HEALTH

YOUNG CARERS – OR CHILDREN IN NEED OF CARE? DECISION MAKING FOR CHILDREN OF PARENTS WITH MENTAL HEALTH PROBLEMS

Gillian Schofield

Professor of Child and Family Social Work

and

Dr Judi Walsh

Lecturer in Developmental Psychology, Centre for Research on the Child and Family, University of East Anglia

SUMMARY OF PAPER

Children of parents with mental health problems who offer various forms of support and care to their parents have acquired the label 'young carers'. The extent to which this caring role may be acceptable or may, on the other hand, interfere with children's development is not always easy to determine. In complex families with multiple risks to child well-being, it may be difficult to distinguish the impact of individual risk factors, including that of being a 'young carer', or whether a child may be experiencing or at risk of significant harm. This paper reviews the range of research on the impact of parental mental problems on children and considers the risks that may need to be taken into account when children become young carers, but do not receive adequate care themselves.

Children of mentally ill parents are particularly at risk of insecure attachment. The paper explains that it is important to understand that a 'strong' attachment may not be a secure attachment when children are pre-occupied with their mentally ill parents' well-being and even survival. This issue can be important not only when decisions are made about the significant harm threshold, but also when considering the care plan and the importance of constructive birth family contact and achieving permanence.

Research discussed here suggests that there is a very wide spectrum of experience for young carers: some children thrive in families providing excellent care notwithstanding the presence of a parent with significant mental health problems; some children are entirely vulnerable to absent, neglectful or abusive parenting in the context of parental mental health problems compounded by multiple additional risks and adversities. There is therefore a wide range of 'young carers' from the secure, competent child who offers a parent support at times, to the insecure, anxious, traumatised and pre-occupied child who is not fulfilling his or her potential. The impact of multiple and cumulative risk and protective factors need to be carefully assessed if the right decisions are to be made.

THE PAPER

It has been estimated that two million children live in households where at least one parent has a mental health problem (Social Care Institute for Excellence 2008b). The majority of these children will be parented adequately and will not come to the attention of professional agencies. Those children who do come to the attention of children's social work services, education departments, health services and, in a small minority of cases, the courts, will do so for very different reasons. These range from perhaps occasional absences from school through to such significant concerns for the child's physical and emotional health and well-being that separation through a care order or adoption order will be needed in order to meet the child's needs. The parent's mental health is unlikely to be the only problem facing the family or affecting parenting (Social Care Institute for Excellence 2008a, Walsh et al 2009), but it can be a significant factor.

Among this group of children will be a number who may provide care for their mentally ill parent and acquire the designation 'young carers'. Their caregiving roles can range from occasional support to many hours a week of physical and emotional caring commitments. Children who care range in age from 5 to 18 and the 2001 census reported 175,000 young carers, with nearly a third providing care for someone with a mental health problem (Social Care Institute for Excellence 2008b). However, it is suggested that this is likely to be an underestimate, as family members, including children, will often conceal mental health problems and their consequences.

The terminology 'young carer' is now commonly used in this context to recognise and legitimise the child's role as caring for their mentally ill parent. A corollary is that, like other carers, young carers are seen as having *rights*, for example to practical and emotional support, perhaps including respite from this role and opportunities to mix with other young carers. However, as the Social Care Institute for Excellence (2008b: 2) reports, there are 'important practical and ethical questions about the competency of the child as carer and the age-appropriate nature of the caring tasks being undertaken'.

From the perspective of professional agencies and courts, defining young carers and their needs in a rights context must be set alongside *developmental* expectations that children are generally seen as being *cared for by* rather than *being a carer for* their parents. Many factors will affect the child's well-being and development and in the most difficult cases, where the child's future is to be decided in court, they may have experienced a range of other risk factors (eg drug use or family violence) or protective factors (eg stable other parent or involved grandparent) that interact in complex ways with the impact of parental mental illness to increase or decrease the potential negative consequences.

This paper will review the evidence on children with mentally ill parents who may be described as 'young carers' and consider at what point, in the more extreme and complex cases, being a young carer may slip over the threshold into experiencing or being at risk of experiencing significant harm. It will then consider the next stage, how care planning for children of parents with mental health problems may be affected by beliefs about the nature of their relationships with their parents, including decisions about foster care, adoption and contact. Finally, it will look at those children growing up in foster care who continue to have contact and a relationship with parents with mental health problems. It will draw on the research literature and a series of projects at the University of East Anglia, including studies of foster care, care planning and birth parents of children growing up in foster care.

One of the helpful theoretical frameworks used here will be attachment theory, since attachment theory helps to explain the quality of different child-parent relationships, and since questions of security and insecurity of attachment are an important part of both assessment of emotional harm and care planning for permanence.

RESEARCH CONTEXT

Families where a parent has a mental health problem have long struggled to have the needs of both parents and children understood and recognised (Sheppard 1994, Smith 2004, Tunnard 2004). Social workers and other professionals who work with adults and with children need a good understanding of all aspects of the psychosocial impact of parental mental health problems on children and other family members in order to target their assessment and intervention – and to make decisions about the risk of significant harm.

Research, which tends to focus on mothers, has pointed to a number of ways in which mothers with mental health problems experience very particular parenting difficulties, which may require a range of support targeted at improving outcomes for their children (Smith 2004). Maternal depression, for example, has long been known to be associated with children's cognitive, emotional and other developmental problems (Murray et al 1993, Cunningham et al 2004, Leschied et al 2005) and also with an increased risk of abuse and neglect (Sheppard 1997). But although the need for intervention and help is recognised, it is also known that mothers suffering from depression will find it especially difficult to work in partnership with social workers in order to protect their children's development (Sheppard 2002).

When depression combines with other problems, the impact on children can be particularly severe. As Woodcock and Sheppard (2002: 242) describe in their study of mothers who were depressed and also alcohol dependent, 'a central concern for social workers, with this group, was with the woman's capacity to empathise with and respond to their children's needs, overwhelmed as they were by their own needs'. Such parental problems in engaging with the mind of the child are likely to impact on all aspects of parenting and attachment relationships. They may, in some cases, contribute to children experiencing physical and emotional neglect or abuse (Howe 2005). Although there is generally a low risk of physical abuse where parents have mental health problems, this risk increases where parents have a personality disorder or psychosis, particularly in combination with drug or alcohol misuse (Hall 2004).

In some families, particularly where parents lack other sources of support, children may find themselves drawn into a caring role during periods when maternal – or indeed paternal – mental health problems make it difficult for the child to get their own physical and emotional needs met, but also make it likely that the child's anxiety about the parent will lead to the child attempting to meet some of the physical and emotional needs of the parent. The child's caring role may be continuous or may be periodic. So it is important to consider whether there are times when the parent resumes the role of providing a secure base for the child in such a way as to promote exploration and learning and for the child to fulfil their potential (Bowlby 1973), whether there are other adult caregivers who can provide a secure base for the child and the parent *or* whether, even when the parent is relatively well, the child's caring role, concern for, and preoccupation with the parent have a limiting effect on their peer relationships, school achievements, participation in activities and so on.

Research suggests that when mothers with a range of mental health problems do become subject to child protection investigations, they find it particularly difficult to trust and engage with services. Interventions that then focus solely on maternal mental health needs will not necessarily produce the required improvement in parenting, in part because parents sometimes find it difficult to acknowledge that their mental health problems may be having an effect on their children (Stanley et al 2003, Stanley and Penhale 1999). It is not unusual for adult services who work with parents in this context to share this tendency to deny the impact of adult mental health problems on parenting (Stanley and Penhale 1999). On the other hand, there is also evidence that child focused social workers will often take insufficient account of the mental health needs of the parent, even though changes in the parent's mental health and functioning need to occur before change in the parenting will be possible (Sheppard 2002). For both child and adult workers, the concept of 'child as carer' (which may have positive or negative connotations for different workers) can be a difficult factor to take into account when judging the appropriateness of the parenting or of the child's development within the family.

Although this tension between parent focus and child focus has been recognised for some time and is an international phenomenon (Sheehan 2004), there has been little specific focus on the impact of parental mental health problems on children's coping skills – which will often be at the heart of what we define as the tension between caring and suffering harm.

ATTACHMENT SECURITY AND CHILDREN OF PARENTS WITH MENTAL HEALTH PROBLEMS – CARE SEEKERS AND CAREGIVERS

Research suggests that children whose mothers have mental health problems are more likely to be classified as insecurely attached than children whose mothers do not have mental health problems. For example, Cicchetti et al (1998) found that toddlers whose mothers had depression showed more insecure attachments than toddlers whose mothers did not have depression, and that this difference was not accounted for by contextual risk factors like marital discord, stress, or lack of social support. Research on parental mental health and attachment has primarily looked at maternal depression, but the impact of other psychiatric disorders, such as anxiety, has also been investigated. Manassis et al (1994) found insecure attachments in 80% of children whose mothers had anxiety disorders. Thus, whatever the parent may be trying to offer, however much they may love the child, their ability to offer a secure base, which reduces the child's anxiety and promotes development, is likely to be limited by the mother's difficulty in managing their own low moods or anxieties. Parents who need a high level of reassurance from their children that there is nothing to worry about (ie need the child to provide a secure base for them) may create a situation of *role reversal*, which may be more obvious in older children, but can start as early as 4 or 5 years old. This is not by any means characteristic of all or even most relationships where children offer some care or support to parents with mental health problems (Aldridge 2006). But where parents are also highly stressed *and* have unresolved traumatic early histories that make them vulnerable, role reversal may occur.

The overall finding that parental psychiatric disorder may increase the likelihood of insecure attachments has implications for other areas of children's development. For example, studies looking at the consequences and correlates of insecure attachment have suggested that children classified as insecurely attached are at a greater risk of emotional and behavioural problems (see Greenberg 1999, for a review), and deficits in emotional understanding (Fonagy et al 1997) than are children classified as securely attached. However, it appears that of particular concern is a classification of disorganised attachment, hypothesised to develop where caregivers are frightened or frightening, and where the child, who would ordinarily seek proximity to the attachment figure as a safe haven, cannot use them to resolve the threat, as they cannot find a solution to the paradox that their haven of safety is also the source of the fear (Main and Hesse 1990). Frightened or frightening caregivers are not necessarily abusive or neglectful, but may have unresolved traumas and difficulties from the past that in the context of a close attachment relationship can affect children's mental representations of themselves and of other people: their internal working models (Bowlby 1973, Howe et al 1999).

As children develop, the disorganised behaviours that characterise infancy become more organised, resulting in controlling strategies in middle childhood and adolescence which are either punitive and coercive, compulsively self-reliant or directing and caregiving (Main and Cassidy 1988, Lyons-Ruth et al 2004). Studies suggest that maternal depression may be strongly linked to disorganised attachment (Radke-Yarrow et al 1995, Teti et al 1995), but also with parents' own unresolved loss and trauma, and anomalous and disrupted behaviours characteristic of psychotic disorder (Wan and Green 2009). Thus it is not parental depression per se that links to more extreme problems in children, but certain unresolved experiences that may contribute to and interact with the depression, leaving the parent less able to keep the child's needs in mind. As depression is a very common diagnosis and covers a wide range and degree of difficulty, it is therefore essential to establish the whole picture of the parent's history, functioning and current parenting behaviour when considering the impact on children.

Jonathan Hill (2004) proposes four mechanisms by which parental mental illness might affect attachment processes. First, Hill suggests that the risks for parental mental health (eg marital discord, other psychosocial stressors such as lack of social support or loss of employment) might also affect the parent-child relationship and therefore attachment processes. Secondly, the parent-child relationship might be affected by a combination of the disorder and other pre-existing or concurrent psychosocial risks. Thirdly, the parent-child relationship may be affected solely by the disorder, independently of other contextual factors, and lastly, that a parents' capacity to retain factors associated with security of attachment, such as sensitivity and responsiveness, regardless of the disorder, might serve as protective in the context of a mental health problem. Hill suggests that helping a child integrate unresponsive or frightening episodes in the caregiver into their overall framework of a secure attachment may help to preserve the relationship. The importance of others (fathers, grandparents, older siblings), within the child's attachment hierarchy (Kerns and Richardson 2005, Kobak et al 2005) is therefore crucial here, as are other supportive factors, such as the child's age and developmental capacity and the availability of supports within other areas of the child's life, such as school (Tunnard 2004). In this context, the social worker may have a role both through their direct work with the child and/or through supporting others in the child's network who can offer a secure base (Bowlby 1973). Since role reversal is a feature of disorganised attachment behaviours, in some cases children will cope with their anxiety about their parents by becoming compulsive caregivers, a more disturbed form of caregiving for a parent that is a strategy by which the child attempts to reduce risk of harm or danger.

The research on children of mentally ill parents suggests that it is important to see where other factors may be protective and promote resilience. Many studies on the effects of mental health on children's attachments and relationships assume that the primary attachment figure for these children is the mother, especially longitudinal studies which predict later outcome from infant attachment classification. However, most children in a study of families where mothers were hospitalised, were found to have close relationships with other family members – fathers, grandparents and family friends, who not only offered direct care to the child but provided a secure base for the mother so that the child did not have to (Walsh et al 2009). In this context, the emotionally available caregiver provides a bridge for the child while a parent is unwell, which protects the child's well-being *and* preserves the relationship with the parent during the episode. As a result, most children whose mothers have mental health problems do not develop lasting attachment difficulties (Wan & Green 2009).

However, it is equally important when making decisions in complex children's cases in the family justice context to consider factors that may add further risk for the child, often by interacting with the risks presented by the mental health problems. In a recent study of birth parents of children who had come into foster care, mental health problems, particularly depression and anxiety, were often in the context of childhood trauma, domestic violence and substance misuse (Schofield & Ward in preparation). This finding is reflected in other studies of children coming into care, where cases of multiple parental difficulties that include mental health problems are the majority (Schofield et al 2000, Sinclair et al 2008). The impact on the quality of the parenting of cumulative factors of this kind will always be a far greater risk to children's well-being than any one factor on its own. It is important that neither the parent's mental health nor the child's caring role should be seen in isolation from other risks to the quality of the child's physical and emotional health, and educational progress.

What emerges from this evidence is a very wide spectrum of experience. At one end of this spectrum we have children who thrive in families which provide excellent care, even when a parent has a significant mental health problem, and where the child's awareness of the need to be more sensitive and even supportive to the parent at certain times may actually be an important learning experience (Aldridge & Becker 2003). At the other end of the spectrum we have children who are entirely vulnerable to absent, neglectful or abusive parenting in the context of parental mental health problems that are generally compounded by multiple additional risks and adversities, such as violence and substance misuse, and which in combination leave the child developmentally harmed and struggling to care for the parent in order to survive.

IMPLICATIONS FOR THE COURT AND THE CARE PLAN

Having considered the research on issues that affect assessment of harm, it is important to look more specifically at some of the planning decisions that face the court. In cases where a parent has a mental health problem, where the significant harm threshold criteria are judged to be met and where a court has deemed that the child needs to be placed for permanence outside of the family, a decision will need to be made about whether adoption or fostering will be in the child's best interests. It is not unusual for this decision to be linked to other related decisions, eg should the sibling group be kept together? How, for example, should relationships between individual children and their parents be weighed where parental mental health problems are a factor? What are the implications for contact?

One key issue for decision makers to determine in relation to 'young carers' will be the difference between, on the one hand children who are getting their own emotional needs met, but show appropriate concern or undertake certain tasks for their mother or father, and on the other hand, children who are so practically and emotionally preoccupied with their parent's needs and well-being that they are unable to function and develop appropriately themselves. One difficulty for assessment and decision making may be that a child who is highly preoccupied with the parent's whereabouts and welfare may be described as having a 'strong' attachment. At a common sense level this terminology appears to suggest that (a) this is a positive relationship and (b) that it would be too damaging to disrupt. However, this may be a child who is insecurely attached and has become preoccupied with the availability of care and affection because the caregiving has been inconsistent and anxiety provoking. Insecure attachment is not in itself pathological, but where the caregiving has not only been inconsistent but has included elements of *fear*, this is likely to have had more troubling consequences for the child, as discussed above in relation to disorganised attachment. Fear can arise in many different circumstances; in particular, children may experience fear not only in the face of direct threat, but when they are profoundly neglected (especially in early childhood) or if they are exposed to parenting that is unpredictable. So, for example, neglected babies and young children who have spent long, isolated periods shut in bedrooms experience profound existential fear – and often show behaviours such as self-harming that indicate the extent of their distress (Howe 2005).

In sibling groups where there are serious concerns about neglect in the context of mental health problems, it will often be the eldest child who has become a physical and emotional carer – not only for the parent but also for the younger children. The notion of a 'strong' attachment in such cases can lead to the older child or children being inadequately protected from the harmful impact of the relationship with the mentally ill parent. This is a case example from a longitudinal study funded by the Nuffield Foundation (Schofield et al 2000, Beek & Schofield 2004, Schofield & Beek 2009).

Katie was 6 years old when she and two younger siblings became subject of care proceedings following an extended period of emotional abuse and physical neglect by her mother, who had a personality disorder. The care plan, proposed by the local authority and the Guardian, was that because of her 'strong attachment' to her mother the care plan for her would be long-term foster care, while her younger siblings would be adopted. Initially she settled well in a foster family, but during the contact with her birth mother – both in person and on the telephone – Katie continued to bear the burden of her mother's disturbance, distress and troubled life. At subsequent stages of the research (when she was 11 years old and 16 years old), Katie was increasingly unable to take any pleasure in her own life in the foster home, to make friends or to benefit from school. She was described by her carers as being like 'an empty box'. Her adopted siblings who had no contact had thrived.

This is not in itself an argument for adoption or against contact, but there must always be an important question asked about the role of contact and the quality of the relationship that is being preserved (Schofield & Stevenson 2009). Children will form very 'strong' attachments to abusive or neglectful parents – and the strength of this bond will be increased where the child also feels anxious about and responsible for not only the parent's well-being, but the parent's survival in the context of mental illness. Thus the current 'strength' of relationship, including caring roles and preoccupations, is less helpful in decision making than a broader based assessment of the contribution that the relationship will make to the child's well-being into the future.

PERMANENCY IN FOSTER CARE WHERE PARENTS HAVE MENTAL HEALTH PROBLEMS – THE ROLE OF THE PARENT AND THE QUESTION OF CONTACT

If the permanency plan for the child is to grow up in foster care, the question will arise as to how the relationship with the parents, where one or both has mental health problems, needs to be managed. This in turn will have an impact on the kind of support that is available for parents and the kind of contact that it will be reasonable for social workers to recommend and courts to approve in the care plan.

Research funded by the Economic and Social Research Council (ESRC) and by the Nuffield Foundation at the University of East Anglia (both led by Gillian Schofield) has suggested that it is, perhaps inevitably, hard to predict the course of the mental health difficulties experienced by parents and the role that they may be able to play during the long-term foster placement of their children. Mental health is not static in any population (Butcher et al 2009). This diversity may include, for example, a short depressive episode or chronic and recurrent depression, recovery after a single psychotic episode or chronic schizophrenia. When parents with mental health difficulties of different kinds are separated from their children, this can lead to a downward spiral into drug and alcohol misuse, depression and hospitalisation (Schofield & Ward in preparation). But for some parents it can lead (rapidly or over time) to a decision to put their previous lifestyle behind them, part from a violent partner, give up drugs and seek help for the mental health problems that had contributed to the break-up of their family.

Our research has shown that even some parents of children in foster care who suffered many interconnecting difficulties, including mental health and drug misuse, and who feel a continuing sense of loss and even some degree of anger, are able to appreciate the benefits that foster care has given to their child. For these parents, it is possible to develop a collaborative relationship between the parents and the foster carers that will include negotiated and constructive contact, to the benefit of the children. In some cases, contact can be informal, but even in collaborative situations there may be a need for supervision and contact may include visiting parents in secure psychiatric care (Beek & Schofield 2004).

However, other parents of foster children do remain fixed, angry, and unable to be empathic towards the children or to compromise and co-operate. Of these parents, several in our recent study (Schofield & Ward in preparation) were said to have a diagnosis of personality disorder, but for others, 'disturbed' behaviour was not necessarily associated with a particular diagnosis – and this makes planning even more complex. Reliance on a formal diagnosis can oversimplify a complex situation (Hill 2004).

As children in foster care move into adolescence, there is a risk that a number whose parents have mental health problems will get drawn back into the role of carer that they had left behind when they were taken into care as young children.

Jane came into care at the age of 6 because her mother had significant alcohol and mental health problems and she was at times starting to look after her mother. Contact was controlled over the years. Jane remained concerned about her mother's welfare, but as a 13-year-old she was thriving in a positive foster placement. However, by the age of 16 she was having more flexible contact, staying with her mother most weekends – and was effectively taking back the role of carer for her mother. There was a risk that her significant developmental and social gains in foster care would be lost if she were to be drawn back via this caregiving role to her former chaotic family environment.

This scenario, once foster children reach adolescence, is far from unique in our experience – and is a key example of the way in which care plans that are made in early childhood need active work with young people, foster families and birth families right through adolescence if the child is to truly have benefited from their care experience as they move into adulthood.

CONCLUSION

There is little doubt that most parents with mental health problems parent their children effectively and that these children experience few adverse effects (Smith 2004). It is also likely that the majority of children who offer some degree of care to a parent with mental health problems are nevertheless able to develop and function well, with support (Aldridge & Becker 2003, Social Care Institute for Excellence 2008b). However, in the complex cases that come before the courts – in private as well as public law proceedings – it is important that the concept of 'child as carer' is looked at critically in each case and that the full range of attachment, developmental and social functioning issues are explored. The impact of multiple and cumulative risk and protective factors – of which the parent's mental ill health and the child's caring role are unlikely to be the only ones – need to be carefully assessed if the right decisions are to be made.

CONFERENCE PRESENTATION

Professor Schofield invited the delegates to consider the following questions:

(a) *In what circumstances is the role of 'young carer' acceptable or harmful?*

(b) *What kind of harm might be significant?*

(c) *How can we distinguish between secure attachments and 'strong' but insecure attachment?*

(d) *What are the implications of the young carer role for permanence/ residence plans and contact?*

REFERENCES

Aldridge, J 'The experiences of children living with and caring for parents with mental health problems' (2006) 15 *Child Abuse Review* 79–88.

Aldridge, J and Becker, S *Children caring for parents with mental illness* (Bristol: The Policy Press, 2003).

Beek, M and Schofield, G *Providing a secure base in long-term foster care* (London: BAAF, 2004).

Bowlby, J *Attachment and Loss: Vol 2 Separation* (New York: Basic Books, 1973).

Butcher, JN, Mineka, S and Hooley JM *Abnormal Psychology* (Boston: Pearson, 2009).

Cicchetti, D, Rogosch, FA and Toth, SL 'Maternal depressive disorder and contextual risk: Contributions to the development of attachment insecurity and behaviour problems in toddlerhood' (1998) 10 *Development and Psychopathology* 283–300.

Cunningham, J, Harris, G, Vostanis, P, Oyebode, F and Blissett, J 'Children of mothers with mental illness: attachment and emotional and behavioural problems' (2004) 174(7–8) *Early Child Development and Care* 639–650.

Fonagy, P, Redfern, S and Charman, T 'The relationship between belief-desire reasoning and a projective measure of attachment security (SAT)' (1997) 15 *British Journal of Developmental Psychology* 51–61.

Greenberg, MT 'Attachment and psychopathology in childhood' in J Cassidy and PR Shaver (eds) *Handbook of attachment: theory, research and clinical applications* (London: Guilford Press, 1999).

Hall, A 'Parental psychiatric disorder and the developing child' in M Göpfert, J Webster and MV Seeman (eds) *Parental Psychiatric Disorder: distressed parents and their families* (Cambridge University Press, 2nd edn, 2004).

Hill, J 'Parental psychiatric disorder and attachment' in M Göpfert, J Webster and MV Seeman (eds) *Parental Psychiatric Disorder: distressed parents and their families* (Cambridge University Press, 2nd edn, 2004).

Howe, D *Child Abuse and Neglect: attachment, development and intervention* (Basingstoke: Macmillan, 2005).

Howe, D, Brandon, M, Hinings, D and Schofield, G *Attachment, Child Maltreatment and Family Support; a practice and assessment model* (Basingstoke: Macmillan, 1999).

Kerns, KA and Richardson, RA *Attachment in Middle Childhood* (New York: Guilford Press, 2005).

Kobak, R, Rosenthal, N and Serwick, A 'The attachment hierarchy in middle childhood: conceptual and methodological issues' in KA Kerns and RA Richardson (eds) *Attachment in middle childhood* (London; Guilford Press, 2005).

Leschied, AW, Chiodo, D, Whitehead, PC and Hurley, D 'The relationship between maternal depression and child outcomes in a child welfare sample: implications for treatment and policy' (2005) 10(4) *Child and Family Social Work* 281–291.

Lyons-Ruth, K, Melnick, S, Bronfman, E, Sheey, S and Llanas, L 'Hostile-helpless relational models and disorganized attachment patterns between parents and their young children: review of research and implications for clinical work' in L Atkinson and S Goldberg (eds) *Attachment issues in psychopathology and intervention* (New Jersey: Lawrence Erlbaum Associates, 2004).

Main, M and Hesse, E 'Parents' unresolved traumatic experiences are related to infant disorganized attachment status: is frightened and/or frightening behaviour the linking mechanism?' in MT Greenberg, D Cicchetti, and EM Cummings (eds) *Attachment in the Preschool Years: Theory, Research and Intervention* (Chicago: University of Chicago Press, 1990).

Main, M, Kaplan, N and Cassidy, J 'Security in infancy, childhood, and adulthood: a move to the level of representation' in I Bretherton and E Waters (eds) *Monographs of the Society for Research in Child Development* (1985) 50, (1–2, Serial No 209), 66–104.

Manassis, K, Bradley, S, Goldberg, S, Hood, J and Swinson, RP 'Attachment in mothers with anxiety disorders and their children' (1994) 33(8) *Journal of the American Academy of Child and Adolescent Psychiatry* 1106–1113.

Murray, L, Kempton, C, Woolgar, M and Hooper, R 'Depressed mothers' speech to their infants and its relationship to infant gender and cognitive development' (1993) 34 *Journal of Child Psychology and Psychiatry* 1083–1101.

Radke-Yarrow, M, McCann, K, DeMulder, E, Belmont, B, Martinez, P and Richardson, DT 'Attachment in the context of high-risk conditions' (1995) 7 *Development and Psychopathology* 247–265.

Schofield, G, Beek, M, Sargent, K and Thoburn, J *Growing up in Foster Care* (London: BAAF, 2000).

Schofield, G and Beek, M 'Growing up in foster care: providing a secure base through adolescence' (2009) *Child and Family Social Work* (online access or from author g.schofield@uea.ac.uk).

Schofield, G and Stevenson, O 'Contact and relationships between fostered children and their birth families' in *The Child Placement Handbook* (London: BAAF, 2009).

Schofield, G and Ward, E *Working with Birth Parents of Children Growing up in Foster Care* (Jessica Kingsley Publishers, in preparation).

Sheehan, R 'Partnership in Mental Health and Child Welfare' (2004) 39(3–4) *Social Work in Health Care* 309–324.

Sheppard, M 'Maternal depression, child care and the social work role' (1994) 24 *British Journal of Social Work* 33–51.

Sheppard, M 'Double jeopardy: the link between child abuse and maternal depression' (1997) 2 *British Journal of Social Work* 91–109.

Sheppard, M 'Depressed mothers' experience of partnership in child and family care' (2002) 32(1) *British Journal of Social Work* 93–112.

Sinclair, I, Baker, C, Lee, J and Gibbs, I (2008) *The Pursuit of Permanence: A Study of the English Child Care System* (London: Jessica Kingsley Publishers, 2008).

Smith, M 'Parental mental health: disruptions to parenting and outcomes for children' (2004) 9 *Child and Family Social Work* 3–12.

Social Care Institute for Excellence *Stress and resilience factors in parents with mental health problems and their children* (London: SCIE, 2008a).

Social Care Institute for Excellence *Experiences of young people caring for a parent with a mental health problem* (London: SCIE, 2008b).

Stanley, N and Penhale, B 'The Mental Health Problems of Mothers Experiencing the Child Protection System: identifying needs and appropriate responses' (1999) 8 *Child Abuse Review* 34–45.

Stanley, N, Penhale, B, Riordan, D, Barbour RS and Holden, S (2003) *Child Protection and Mental Health Services: Interprofessional Responses to the Needs of Mothers* (Bristol: The Policy Press, 2003).

Teti, DM, Gelfand, DM, Messinger, DS and Isabella, R 'Maternal depression and the quality of early attachment: an examination of infants, preschoolers, and their mothers'(1995) 31 *Developmental Psychology* 364–376.

Tunnard, J *Parental mental health problems: key messages from research, policy and practice* (Dartington: Research in Practice, 2005).

Wan, MW and Green, J 'The impact of maternal psychopathology on child-mother attachment' (2009) 12 *Archives of Women's Mental Health* 123–134.

Walsh, J, Schofield, G, Harris, G, Vostanis, P, Oyebode, F and Coulthard, H 'Attachment and coping strategies in middle childhood children whose mothers have a mental health problem: implications for social work practice' (2009) 39(1) *British Journal of Social Work* 81–98.

Woodcock, J and Sheppard, M 'Double Trouble: Maternal Depression and Alcohol Dependence as Combined Factors in Child and Family Social Work' (2002) 16 *Children and Society* 232–245.

CULTURE IN CHILD AND ADOLESCENT PSYCHIATRY

Dr Nisha Dogra

Senior Lecturer in Child and Adolescent Psychiatry, University of Leicester

SUMMARY OF PAPER

There are many definitions of culture: a patient-centred definition of culture allows patients to define which aspects of their whole are important to them and when these factors are relevant to them; children often find that choices are made for them. Although culture itself does not cause mental health problems, the concept of mental health is culturally influenced. Whilst there are few culturally specific mental health problems, some disorders are more likely to occur in some contexts than others, and clinicians need to be aware of how culture may influence the diagnostic process. The higher level of unmet health needs among ethnic minority clients may reflect differential access, referral pathways and service utilisation.

Adopting a 'cultural sensibility' places the practitioner in a position of learning about the unique cultural situation of the child and his or her family, using the assessment process to gain the information needed to ensure that any management plan incorporates the cultural perspective of the family and is thereby acceptable to them. Clinicians need to be aware of their own perspectives and hope these interplay with those of the family.

THE PAPER

INTRODUCTION

This paper is in part based on Nisha Dogra's chapter 'Culture and child psychiatry' in R Bhattacharya, S Cross and D Bhugra (eds) *Clinical Topics in Cultural Psychiatry* (London: Royal College of Psychiatrists Press, in press).

DEFINING CULTURE AND CHILDHOOD

As readers will no doubt be aware, there are many definitions of culture. For the purposes of this chapter, the following definition is employed:

> 'Culture may be best defined by each person in relationship to the group or groups with whom he or she identifies. An individual's cultural identity may be based on heritage (by factors such as race, ethnicity, language, country of origin) as well as individual circumstances (age, gender, sexual orientation, socioeconomic status, physical ability) and personal choice (religious/spiritual beliefs). These factors may impact behaviours such as communication styles, diet preferences, health beliefs, family roles, lifestyle, rituals and decision-making processes. Culture, while not always tied to race or ethnicity, defines how we interpret and interact with others through these and many other factors.' (As derived from the Association of American Medical Colleges (AAMC 1999: 25).)

As this definition is patient-centred it allows patients to define which aspects of their whole are important to them and when these factors have relevance (Dogra & Karim 2005; Dogra et al 2007). Clearly children also make some choices about the aspects outlined above but they may often find that choices are made for them without their involvement. There can be great pressure on children to 'act out' the most obvious aspect of themselves such as their 'ethnic' or 'cultural background' even if that is not how they feel about themselves. This pressure unintended or intended may come from the family, peers and even professionals. Children of mixed racial heritage can often be forced to identify with one part of their heritage than others (eg Lincoln 2009).

The concept of childhood is itself also culturally influenced. In 'Western' cultures as a more autonomous sense of self has developed, the rights of children have been increasingly recognised; a process which started in Victorian times (Heywood 2001). This in turn means that the expectations of children's behaviour and protection are also culturally influenced. Family structure and expectations are also culturally influenced.

CULTURE AND MENTAL HEALTH PROBLEMS

Some of the issues discussed here are not specific to child psychiatry. Culture itself does not cause mental health problems, and as such these may not be responsive to change. However, an understanding of the cultural context may help clinicians present the issues in ways that are acceptable to the family and thereby amenable to intervention.

It is worth noting that the concept of mental health itself is culturally influenced. Confusion about what mental illness is and stigma about it is widespread across different cultures (Ronzoni et al 2009). Young people also often confuse mental illness with learning disability (eg Dogra et al 2007).

There are very few culturally specific problems. However, some disorders are more likely to occur in some contexts than others (Dogra et al 2007a). For example, the eating disorder anorexia nervosa is more common in Western contexts than others. Rousseau et al (2008) surveyed the literature on culture and DSM-IV in child psychiatry. They concluded that although the DSM-IV diagnostic categories may be found cross culturally, clinicians need to be aware of how culture may influence the diagnostic process.

The Office for National Statistics (ONS) Survey (2004) highlights that children living within the same environment of the UK had different prevalence rates of psychiatric disorders, with those of Indian girls being considerably lower than other groups. However, the small numbers of ethnic children represented makes it difficult to be conclusive. Goodman et al (2008) in a systematic review (included the ONS data) noted that there was evidence to suggest that there are inter-ethnic differences for prevalence of mental health problems in children in the UK but that the differences were largely unexplained. Klineberg et al (2006) found that differences in social support did not explain ethnic differences in psychological distress in an ethnically diverse adolescent group. Low social support in common with other studies was associated with poor mental health; however this relationship did not vary with ethnicity.

Culture may influence the development of mental health problems by the influence it has on how gender roles, parenting styles and so on are enacted. Culture and religion may also influence how mental health problems and the interventions used to address them are viewed (Yeh et al 2004). Meltzer et al (2008) found that for children's fears, the most marked associations were fears of the dark, loud noises, imagined supernatural beings in younger children and fear of animals among girls and all non-white groups. They concluded that children's fears differ in nature across different ethnic groups. Culturally mediated beliefs, values and traditions may play a role in their expression. Not only is culture a relevant factor in the development of factors, it can be relevant in whether children are presented to services or not. Hackett and Hackett (1993) found differences between how Gujarati and English parents viewed normal and deviant behaviours with respect to conduct and bedwetting, but not in self care, but as immigrants adapt their views change. Pumariega et al (2005) also reported that Latinos and African-Americans were perhaps more accepting of hyperactivity than Caucasian and Asian-Americans. This in turn could affect prevalence rates.

Professional perspectives may also influence whether children are referred or not. When referral patterns were analysed for different agencies and professional groups, Daryanani et al (2001) found that general practitioners were more likely to over-refer white children, while paediatricians referred Black and South Asian children, education services referred Black children, and social workers referred mixed race children. This may say more about the professional's bias than the child's problems or presentation. Thus clinicians must be aware of their own perspectives and how these influence their interactions with culturally diverse groups.

There is often a higher level of unmet health need among ethnic minority clients, which may reflect differential access, referral pathways and service utilisation (Dogra 2004; Pumariega et al 2005). It may also reflect different patterns of care even when services are accessed. Culture not only influences the presentation of problems but also influences the interpretations of symptoms, who is accessed first (for example for some ethnic groups religious leaders may be the first point of access when there are concerns about children's behaviour) and which treatment options the family may accept (some of the principles of family therapy may be unacceptable to authoritarian parents).

IMPLICATIONS FOR PRACTICE

A 'cultural sensibility' approach with the AAMC definitions places the practitioner in a position of learning about the unique cultural situation of the child and his or her family, and use the assessment process to gain information that will ensure any management plan incorporates the cultural perspective of the family and is thereby acceptable to them (Dogra & Karim 2005; Dogra et al 2007). The choices children make about how they play, the structure their lives take, their investment in education and so on are all influenced by parental and cultural and economic choices.

It is important that clinicians identify their own biases and prejudices about children and families. This is crucial as this is the baggage taken into the clinical or consultation context. Personal perspectives are important not only because they may lead to less good care to those towards whom there is prejudice. However, there may also be overcompensation through guilt, for example if clinicians are uncomfortable dealing with a particular group but do not acknowledge this, they may be sympathetic and supportive in a context when the more appropriate response may have been to expect the young person to take some responsibility. In training this is often glossed over as 'awareness'. It needs to be more critical and clinicians' assumptions need to be challenged as routine practice.

Garland et al's (2004) findings that adolescents, caregivers and therapists have different expectations for outcomes of the consultation can also highlight how culture might influence who is allowed to express themselves at meetings. Family expectations may mean that the therapist is not supposed to give as much weight to the young person's perspective as that of adults, or the father's view may override the maternal perspective. All these require careful negotiation and sensitivity but cannot be ignored. Dogra (2007) addresses in detail how to ensure that those working in child psychiatry make sure that the care they provide is 'culturally appropriate' using vulnerable children as an example.

system overview

It is important to avoid making assumptions or trying to explain things in a way that supports one's own world view. The 'cultural sensibility' framework outlined earlier is adaptable for this audience. It has not yet been formally tested but, at face value, it is an approach that focuses on the needs of the child and acknowledges that the provider is not a neutral being but a real person who is flawed.

CLINICAL CASE EXAMPLE

At a workshop, a clinician asked how to manage a situation where a Pakistani Muslim father spoke for his female child. The clinician was unsure as to whether it would be appropriate for him as a male to offer to see the child alone.

There are of course, different ways to this potential dilemma. A way forward is to consider for whom the clinician has primary responsibility. Whilst child psychiatrists have a responsibility to ensure that parental perspectives are heard, the overriding responsibility is to the young person. The young person should be offered an opportunity to meet alone with the clinicians and if neither the child nor parent felt this was appropriate, this would be acceptable, unless there were other concerns such as abuse. However, that does not mean there is no need to explore what worries the parent has about the child being seen alone. If the parent does not wish for the child to be seen alone but the child indicates that they would like to take this option, weight has to be given to the child's view, especially the older they are. Some clinicians fear that this will set up tensions in the family; it is likely that this only illustrates what is already happening or what underlies the presentation. The Convention on the Rights of the Child (CRC) (1989) covers all children in the UK irrespective of race, ethnicity or religion. Whether authoritarian parents want their children to have a viewpoint or not is not the point, children have a right to be heard. There are legislative frameworks that we are obliged to work within in the UK.

Younger children will often accept what they are told about their families and the values the family has although this may vary if the larger societal or cultural expectations vary from those of the family. As they move into adolescence, cultural expectations are likely to influence their developing sense of identity and they may challenge and question the values that they have grown up with. Assumptions are often made that there are more likely to be 'cultural differences' between parents and young people from ethnic minority families, especially when children experience one culture at home and another outside the home. The explanation given is that the parents may hold views consistent with their ethnic origin, whereas adolescents face the task of integrating the wider culture in which they have grown up with their family's culture. This is often presented as 'Eastern cultures' having a more collective sense of identity, whilst 'Western cultures' are more focused on the individuals. In practice, most families have a unique culture of their own. Cultural practices often vary between the private (usually the home) and public domains (school or work). Different families and young people manage in diverse ways. Some may integrate the culture of origin and the culture of the new country, others may switch between cultures depending on the context, and others may fuse elements of both cultures to produce a unique culture of their own (Dogra in press).

Issues that may give rise to problems are:

- pressures to conform to practice their family's religion or other practices that the young person cannot reconcile with their own beliefs;

- pressures to conform to expected gender roles (boys wanting to pursue careers generally considered to be in the female domain such as nursing, childcare and vice versa);

- pressures to conform to the family social norms (eg the expectation that a young person will go on to further education despite this not being what the young person wants);

- pressures to conform to family expectations that differ from what the young person wants (eg an expectation that the young person will work in the family business);

- sexual orientation;

- impending forced marriages;

- difficulty in reconciling the culture in the private and public domains.

The young person may respond by challenging their parents, rebelling and becoming non-compliant, self harming and/or becoming moody and withdrawn. They may become depressed especially if they feel there is no possibility of resolution. Bhui et al (2005) investigated cultural identity as a factor for mental health problems among adolescents. Integrated friendships (that is friendships across groups) conferred advantages across all cultural groups. Bangladeshi and South Asian adolescents with integrated friendship choices had lower mental health problems than white pupils. Girls with integrated clothing choices and boys with integrated preferences had fewer mental health problems. This highlights how young people have to negotiate their way round a public world and their private lives. Referring back to the AAMC definition, it enables us to see that young people have a myriad of options and depending on the context will express different parts of themselves.

CONCLUSIONS

Culture influences child psychiatry perhaps even more so than in other areas given that the view of children and their behaviour is to a lesser or greater extent culturally influenced. Children are dependent on their families and the meaning of family and how families respond to children is a complex relationship between the wider culture and the micro familial culture. This has several implications for practising child psychiatry. There is a need to strike a balance between understanding parental concerns and perspectives but also those of the child which are no less important. Negotiating this with families requires sensitivity but cannot be ignored. In trying to balance the wider culture and the culture of their family, young people may face challenges which lead them to mental health services. To initiate appropriate interventions, clinicians need to ensure that they are mindful of their own perspectives and how these interplay with those of the family. Only if these issues are acknowledged and addressed will it be possible to devise management plans that are clinically sound but also acceptable to the family.

CONFERENCE PRESENTATION

In the course of her presentation Dr Dogra reminded delegates that culture can sometimes be used as a way of not accepting painful issues: children's welfare is put secondary to political correctness about the parent's cultural needs. The professional's fear or lack of knowledge should not prevent them from tackling serious matters; professionals should ask those they are working with about the meaning of culture to them, to find out where they are on the 'cultural spectrum'.

REFERENCES

Bhui, K, Stansfield, S, Hood, J, Haines, M, Hillier, S, Taylor, S, Viner, R and Booy, R 'Cultural identity, acculturation, and mental health among adolescents in east London's multiethnic community' (2005) 59 *Journal of Epidemiology and Community Health* 296–302.

Daryanani, R, Hindley, P, Evans, C, Fahy, P and Turk, J 'Ethnicity and the use of a child and adolescent mental health service' (2001) 6 *Child Psychology and Psychiatry Review* 127–132.

Dogra, N 'Problems related to culture' in S Bailey and M Shooter (eds) *The Young Mind* (London: Bantam Press).

Dogra, N 'Cultural diversity issues' in P Vostanis (ed) *Mental health interventions and services for vulnerable children and young people* (London: Jessica Kingsley Publishers, 2007) 233–243.

Dogra, N, Vostanis, P, Abuateya, H and Jewson, N 'Children's mental health services and ethnic diversity: Gujarati families' perspectives of service provision for mental health problems' (2007) 44(2) *Transcultural Psychiatry* 275–291.

Dogra, N, Vostanis, P and Karnik, N 'Child and adolescent psychiatric disorders' in D Bhugra and K Bhui (eds) *Text book of cultural psychiatry* (Cambridge University Press, 2007a) 301–313.

Dogra, N and Karim, K 'Training in diversity for psychiatrists' (2005) 11 *Advances in psychiatric treatment* 159–167.

Dogra, N 'Commissioning and delivering culturally diverse child and adolescent mental services' (2004) 17 *Current Opinion in Psychiatry* 243–247.

Garland, AF, Lewczyk-Boxmeyer, C, Gabayan, EN and Hawley, KM 'Multiple stakeholder agreement on desired outcomes for adolescents' mental health services' (2004) 55(6) *Psychiatric Services* 671–676.

Goodman, A, Patel, V and Leon, DA 'Child mental health differences amongst ethnic groups in Britain: a systematic review' (2008) 8 *BMC Public Health* 258.

Hackett, L and Hackett, R 'Parental ideas of normal and deviant child behaviour: A comparison of two ethnic groups' (1993) 162 *British Journal of Psychiatry* 353–357.

Heywood, C *A history of childhood: children and childhood in the West from medieval to modern times (Themes in history)* (Cambridge: Polity press, 2001).

Klineberg, E, Clark, C, Bhui, KS, Haines, MM, Viner, RM, Head, J, Woodley-Jones, D and Stansfield, S 'Social support, ethnicity and mental health in adolescents' (2006) 41 *Social Psychiatry and Epidemiology* 755–760.

Lincoln, B 'A mixed race experience' (2009) accessed on 9 February 2009 at www.intermix.org.uk/Events/Bradley%20Lincoln.asp.

Meltzer, H, Vostanis, P, Dogra, N, Doos, L, Ford, T and Goodman, R 'Children's specific fears' (2009) 35(6) *Child: Care, health and development* 781–789.

Pumariega, AJ, Rogers, K and Rothe, E 'Culturally competent systems of care for children's mental health: advances and challenges' (2005) 41(5) *Community Mental Health Journal* 539–555.

Ronzoni, P, Dogra, N, Omigbodun, O, Bella, T and Atitola, A 'Stigmatization of mental illness among Nigerian schoolchildren' (2009) *International Journal of Social Psychiatry* (Aug 2009; vol. 0: pp 0020764009341230v1)

Rousseau, C, Measham, T and Bathiche-Suidan, M 'DSM-IV, culture and child psychiatry' (2008) 17(2) *Canadian Academy of Child and Adolescent Psychiatry* 69–75.

Yeh, M, Hough, R, McCabe, K, Lau, A and Garland, A 'Parental beliefs about the causes of child problems: exploring racial/ethnic patterns' (2004) 43(5) *Journal of the American Academy of Child and Adolescent Psychiatry* 605–612.

PLENARY 4

CHILDREN'S MENTAL HEALTH PROBLEMS – NATURE, NATURE AND NURTURE, AND NURTURE

NATURE NURTURE: CHILDHOOD MENTAL HEALTH DISORDERS ISSUES RELEVANT TO DECISION MAKING IN THE COURTS

Dr Claire Sturge

Consultant Child and Adolescent Psychiatrist

SUMMARY OF PAPER

The legal profession would benefit from some insight into what is presently understood about the interactions between genes and the environment, and how this might contribute to understanding the relative contributions of each to a child's disturbance. While some specific genes have been discovered relating to certain disorders, in others, for example autism, a simple result has been elusive. Nevertheless there has been progression looking at the continuum of expression of certain traits: there are conditions with genetic pre-determination, those with no or minimal genetic determination and the 'in-betweens' where conditions are influenced by both genes and the environment.

'Genetic vulnerability' describes the existence of a certain genetic vulnerability. If and how someone presents with the disorder will depend on the gene-environment interaction. 'Resilience' can be seen as an intervening variable lessening the likelihood of the expression of some genes and some adverse environmental events. There is a complex interaction between genes and the environment which can be explained by reference to some common child and adolescent mental health conditions including conduct (antisocial) disorder, autism spectrum disorder, emotional disorders, attention deficit hyperactivity disorder, schizophrenia and bipolar disorder and mental retardation.

Genetics, epigenetics and gene-environment interaction effects are complex, but they are being increasingly understood. Developing an understanding of these issues will help the judiciary think about cases involving different types of disorders and give a sense of the relative importance of genetic or innate factors in the child's problems as opposed to the environmental ones (usually parenting and or abuse or neglect) and the way these influences may interact.

THE PAPER

Donald Debb, a psychologist was asked by a journalist: 'Which, nature or nurture, contributes more to personality?' He asked in response: 'Which contributes more to the area of a rectangle, its length or its width?'

INTRODUCTION

This is an enormous and rapidly evolving topic.

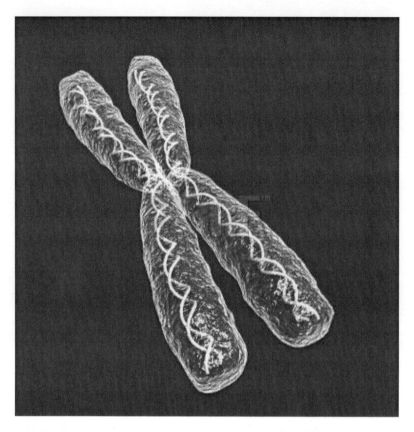

What can be of great relevance to the legal profession is some understanding of what is understood about the interactions between genes and the environment and how this might contribute to understanding the relative contributions of each to a child's disturbance.

There is no easy formula or answer but some conditions have a much greater genetic loading than others. In others, environmental factors play the key part.

I am no expert in this field but that may help in giving a simple overview. I have had what I say checked by those who are expert.

Heritability refers to the proportion of variability in a particular population that is attributable to genetic influences. A heritability of over 50% indicates that the risk of the disorder attributable to the individual's genetic make-up is greater than that attributable to their environment. But it is more complex than this because of the gene-environment interaction, ie factors that are more or less likely to lead to the gene being expressed (genotype) in the individual and factors that affect how the gene is expressed (phenotype).

Genetic defects affect synaptic activity and cortical networks.

In children, all this is of particular interest because:

- children are changing developmentally (including their neurodevelopment – of brain, neural pathways, brain anatomy, grey and white matter);

- they are developing in situations where their environments have a very strong influence on their development – family, social and community; and

- their developmental trajectory is a highly dynamic interaction with a constant interplay between their neurodevelopment and their environment in both directions, ie their development impacts on their environment which in turn affects their development. Their neurodevelopment has a genetic underpinning but this is moulded by the dynamic interactions.

Adulthood is in comparison a much more static time.

One stark example is how severe emotional trauma in early childhood can actually be shown to affect brain development and function. The consequences of this will depend on genetic and environmental factors (eg protective factors).

GENETIC STUDIES

Traditional studies relied on assuming heritability rates between monozygotic twins, dizygotic twins and siblings usually in a shared environment (living in the same family situation. Long ago there were a few twin studies where each twin was adopted into a different family). In the chart below, social communication difficulties are likely to be inherited as a Trait A whereas antisocial tendencies might be inherited as a Trait C.

Figure 1 illustrates how the highly inheritable Trait B shows 90% concordance (both twins affected) in monozygotic twins, with biological siblings (including dizygotic twins) showing 50% concordance but in adoptive siblings (biologically and genetically unrelated) there being only 20% concordance.

Figure 1

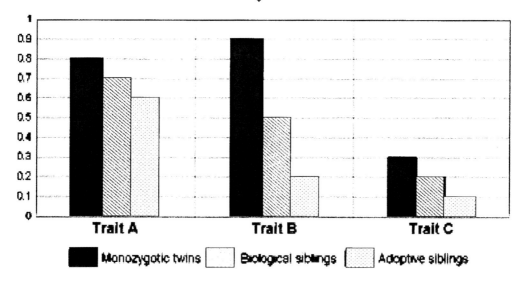

Since the unravelling of DNA (deoxyribonucleic acid), it has become possible to look more directly at genes and the race is on to identify the effects of each of the hundreds and hundreds of our genes and the genes responsible for different disorders.

But while some specific genes have been discovered relating directly to certain disorders in other disorders (eg autism), a simple result has been totally elusive. What has been learnt is that it is likely to be far more productive to look at the continuum of expression of certain traits rather than at disorders or syndromes. So in autism research is focusing on the genetic relationships between the ability across the general population to look at and recognise facial expressions and to recognise the 'other mindedness' of other people. Syndromes (as opposed to traits or symptoms) may well represent an interaction of particular genes in an individual.

GENETIC PRE-DETERMINATION

Dominant inherited conditions, some that are carried on the sex chromosomes and those conditions resulting from the co-existence of two recessive genes are the best examples of where genetics may wholly determine a disorder. In Huntingdon's Chorea this is a dominant gene, i e one parent has it and 50% of their offspring will have the disease too. In Sickle Cell Disease, Haemophilia, Cystic Fibrosis the gene is recessive so both parents need to be carriers for the child to have the disease. In Retts' Syndrome, the transmission involves sex-linked dominant inheritance. In these the genetic loading determines the disease irrespective of environment although environment will affect coping with the disease and quality of life.

Another interesting example is Turner's syndrome, a genetically determined syndrome where there is a missing sex chromosome ie XO. Such children are phenotypically girls (appearances are all female): IQ is somewhat limited, there is webbing of the neck and other unusual features. Recent research (I oversimplify this here) indicates that when the effect of the extra gene is derived from the father the child also has features of an autism spectrum disorder but not when it derives from the mother (Marco and Skuse 'Autism lessons from the X chromosome' (2006) 1(3) *Social Cognitive and Affective Neuroscience* 183–193).

I have chosen some better known examples, there are many others.

It is thought that the disastrous Huntington's Chorea gene survives because the disease usually does not present until after child-bearing age, i e evolution cannot eliminate it. Another example is sickle cell disease. The sickle cell gene is thought to have survived despite most people affected by sickle cell disease dying before they can have children because carriers of the gene (who do not become ill) are more likely to survive malaria than non-carriers (ie selective survival advantage in malaria endemic regions where sickle cell disease is most prevalent).

CONDITIONS WITH NO OR MINIMAL GENETIC DETERMINISM

Obviously this applies to acquired conditions – conditions acquired in utero or after birth. This would include injuries, infectious diseases, traumas and other insults to the brain or body.

Specific serious brain injuries will affect people in similar ways irrespective of their genetic phenotype – it over-rides other influences as it were.

But again there are lots of 'in-betweens'. Responses to trauma will vary very much according to the individual's general emotional and behavioural phenotype prior to the trauma and to previous experiences and life stressors. Thus, whether the individuals exposed to the same or the same level of trauma present with a post-traumatic stress disorder will depend on many factors (including resilience). In some people the full syndrome will be seen after a relatively minor trauma and in others huge traumas are coped with well. I am sure lawyers see this variation frequently in compensation cases.

GENE-ENVIRONMENT INTERACTION: THE IN-BETWEENS

I think this is best addressed by first looking at some issues as they relate to the nature nurture balance.

Figure 2

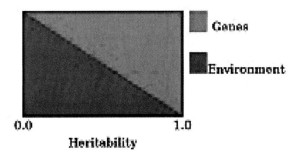

Genes and the environment both account for varying degrees of the expression of the genotype (the phenotype) and interact, ie the genes affect the environment and the environment the expression of the genes.

This is why people refer to genetic vulnerability: you may have a certain genetic vulnerability but if and how you present with a disorder will depend on the gene-environment interaction.

Figure 3

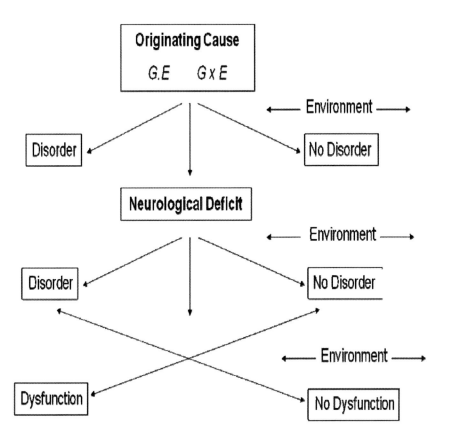

The complex interaction between genes and environment is relevant to all common childhood and adolescent mental health problems and disorders.

Resilience can be seen as an intervening variable lessening the likelihood of the expression of some genes and from some adverse environmental events. Resilience is not synonymous with a good outcome or an individual trait per se. It is a measure of a positive resultant of an interactive process between risk and protective factors (adapted from Rutter).

Some examples will illustrate this.

SOME COMMON CHILD AND ADOLESCENT MENTAL HEALTH CONDITIONS

Conduct (anti-social) disorder

This is not a unitary disorder. For example, where anti-social behaviour is seen at a young age (pre-adolescence) there is a completely different course to the disorder (more serious and long-lasting) than those that appear later.

In both those presenting in the younger years and those presenting later, environment plays the major part. There is also a genetic 'vulnerability' but the environment can modify this to a large extent, for example children adopted from a family with a high level of criminality into a stable, pro-social environment may never show any anti-social traits.

Environmental factors associated with conduct disorders are:

(i)   insecure and disorganised patterns of attachment behaviour which is mediated through the sensitivity of the parenting they receive;

(ii)   harsh and/inconsistent or explosive discipline;

(iii)   lack of clear rules and boundaries that are consistently enforced;

(iv)   low levels of warmth expressed towards the child;

(v)   low levels of supervision;

(vi)   abuse.

You may need little or even no genetic loading to develop a conduct disorder when there is a high level of adverse factors or there might be an interaction between these factors with, say, low IQ (which might have a genetic substrate) which increases the likelihood of anti-social behaviour.

A study by Jaffee et al showed that boys with anti-social fathers were less likely to become anti-social themselves if the father ceased to be part of their lives (Jaffee et al 'Life with (and without) father: the benefits of living with 2 biological parents depend on father's antisocial behaviour' (2002) 41 *Child Development* 1095–1103).

Figure 4 illustrates the complex interaction between what the child brings to his or her adoptive environment from the family of origin and how this interacts with the parenting style of the adoptive mother, ie even the child's environment is totally altered, genes and each environment influence outcome.

Figure 4

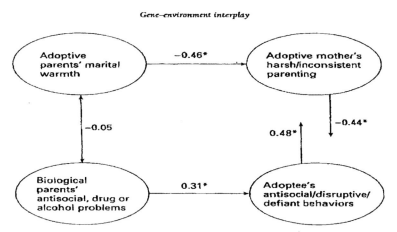

Gene–environment interplay

Effects of disorder in biological parent on disciplinary practices of adoptive mother – mediated by biological effects on child behaviour.
Source: based on Ge et al., 1996.

In contrast there is now some scientific evidence that in a subgroup of those with conduct disorder (or anti-social personality disorder) there is a very high heritability factor and some anatomical brain that distinguish people in this subgroup from other anti-social individuals.

Those in this subgroup:

- are callous and unemotional ('psychopathic');

- have histories dating back to early childhood (those who become anti-social for the first time in adolescence have a far better outlook).

Dr Vizard refers to these callous unemotional individuals (who include the dangerous personality disorders) as having a brain-based deficit (De Brito, SA et al 'Size matters: increased gray matter in boys with conduct problems and callous-unemotional traits' (2009) 132(4) *Brain* 843–852).

Promotive factors are now distinguished from risk factors in conduct disordered children. Factors we used to call risk factors, eg poor academic achievement, is not predictive but in those with high academic achievement there is less likelihood of ongoing offending (Farrington: Cambridge and Studies and The Pittsburgh Youth Study).

Temperament and personality

In children we talk about temperament rather than personality as personality is evolving whereas by the twenties it is largely fixed and disorders are defined as 'ingrained patterns of functioning'.

Temperament is largely inherited – can be seen as the early building block for later personality development.

Thomas, Chess and Birch showed that the most difficult temperament for parents to cope with was babies (and later toddlers and children) with low thresholds (react at a low threshold to stimuli – protesters) with high intensity (the response is not mild but intense) with low regularity (the body's internal set for regular functions such as sleep, elimination) and mood instability/hyperactivity.

However, with a good match between parent and child in terms of sensitivity to the child's needs these children can do well as if the difficult traits are channelled into constructive channels – such as banking!

The building blocks of personality, extraversion, neuroticism, conscientiousness, agreeableness and openness have a genetic basis and link both to temperament and personality.

Childhood maltreatment

The interplay between genetic endowment and environment is illustrated in the following figures:

Figure 5 illustrates how the combination of a genetic propensity for conduct problems and childhood maltreatment significantly increases the likelihood of anti-social problems.

Figure 5

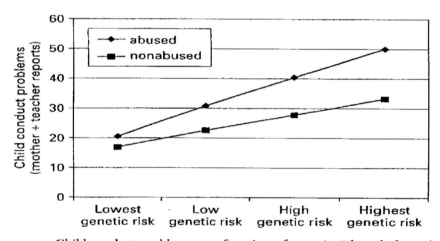

Child conduct problems as a function of genetic risk and physical maltreatment.
Source: from Jaffee et al., 2005.

Figure 6 illustrates how when children are maltreated certain genes moderate the development of depression.

Figure 7 is another example from a study by Jaffe links genetic risk with childhood maltreatment in the development of conduct problems.

Figure 8 illustrates how the genetically determined monoamine oxidase antagonists (MAOAs) interact with childhood maltreatment in the development of anti-social behaviour.

Attachment

An interesting study has recently identified a gene that is associated with developing disorganised attachments. But again if these children have a carer who is highly sensitive and

Figure 6

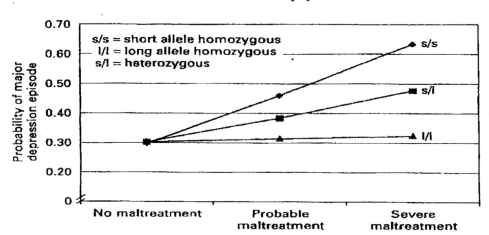

Effect of maltreatment in childhood on liability to depression moderated by 5-HTT gene.
Source: from Caspi et al., 2003. Copyright © 2003 by Science. Adapted by permission of Science.

Figure 7

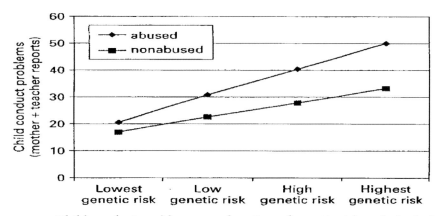

Child conduct problems as a function of genetic risk and physical maltreatment.
Source: from Jaffee et al., 2005.

responsive to need then a secure attachment can be formed. With suboptimal parent there are serious problems (Barry, RA, Kochanska, G and Philibert, RA 'G x E interaction in the organization of attachment: mothers' responsiveness as a moderator of children's genotypes' (2008) 49(12) *Journal of Child Psychology and Psychiatry* 1313–1320).

Figure 8

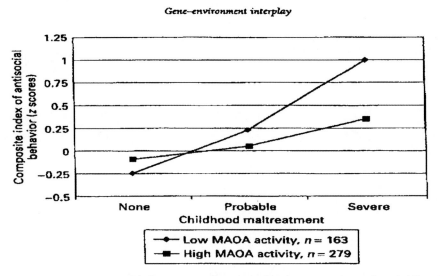

Antisocial behavior as a function of MAOA activity and a childhood history of maltreatment.
Source: from Caspi et al., 2002. Copyright © 2002 by Science. Adapted by permission of Science.

Autism spectrum disorder

This disorder, while highly heritable, probably has a variety of forms and, may lie along a continuum relating to an individual's ability to identify with others. Various gene markers have been identified but no causal gene or genes.

In this disorder it is highly likely that first degree relatives have lesser forms of the disorder – abnormalities on one or two of the triad in the disorder. So a close relative of someone with autism, ie a brother, may be a poor communicator or be rigid and unimaginative.

Emotional disorders

These are very much midway. There are clear genetic vulnerabilities but experiences that reinforce or diminish the emotional reactivity will affect the course. Here we also have the interaction with the parent (environment but partly determined by their genes) who because of their emotional disorder may reinforce and exacerbate the child's difficulties.

For example, where a child has a mother with panic attacks or obsessions he or she will have both some genetic predisposition and be affected by his or her mother's anxious reactions in their child rearing. Researchers refer to the child's impact on their environment and another form of evolving gene-environment interaction: the child with an anxiety disorder may destabilise the environment of their family and a vicious circle can develop.

Resilience or lack of it will determine the extent to which traumas affect the emotional well-being of a child.

Attention deficit hyperactivity disorder (ADHD)

There is a high level of genetic vulnerability – heritability of 30–70%. Such genetic vulnerability is relatively common in the population (unlike say a vulnerability to bipolar disorder): those vulnerable to milder problems may never show problems in a good environment but for those vulnerable to marked problems the environment will not fully protect them.

A significant proportion of children with the vulnerability will be growing up with one or more parents with ADHD adding to the complexity of the gene-environment interaction.

Schizophrenia and bipolar disorder

Both have a high genetic loading.

Figure 9 illustrates how with a genetic vulnerability to schizophreniform disorders (including schizophrenia) the risks of developing these serious disorders is greatly heightened by cannabis use.

Figure 9

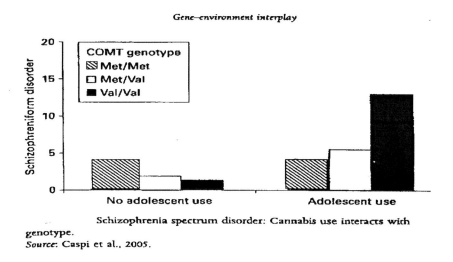

Gene–environment interplay

Schizophrenia spectrum disorder: Cannabis use interacts with genotype.
Source: Caspi et al., 2005.

Diagram illustrating the gene-environment interplay linking genes, cannabis and schizophrenia form illness. Those adolescents who use cannabis and had the double value catechol-O-methyltransferase (COMT) gene had a much higher risk for such disorders.

Bipolar disorder (formerly manic-depressive disorder) has quite a high heritability of about 60%.

Mental retardation

In some this is largely genetic (as in the general population where the pattern is one of regression to the mean) while in others (severe mental retardation) it is largely environmental.

Figure 10 illustrates how IQ is distributed in the general population and how it is distributed in the siblings of children with mild and severe mental retardation. The implication is that with mild mental retardation the influences (largely genetic but with some shared environmental influences) are similar to the influences in the general population whereas with severe mental retardation the distribution is very different as the very low IQ is usually the result of gross brain abnormalities (usually secondary rather than genetic).

Figure 10

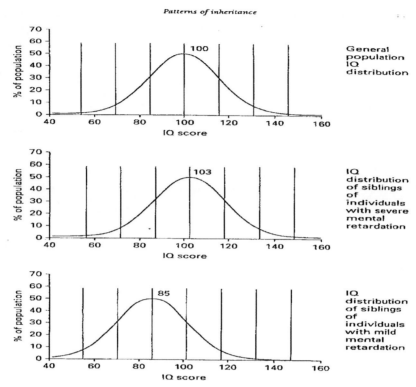

Schematic representation of findings on IQ distribution of siblings of individuals with either severe or mild mental retardation.
Source: from study by Nichols, 1984.

So

Let us consider when parenting or other environmental factors are likely to be the major determinant in a child's difficulties and when the environment. The following diagram is a very rough guide.

Childhood psychiatric disorder

Genes as the major player in determining outcome		In the middle		Environment as the major player in determining outcome
Autism Spectrum Disorders				Antisocial/conduct disorder
	ADHD			
			Disorganised attachment	
	Bipolar disorder – early onset			
		Anxiety disorders		
Temperament		Personality		

CLINICAL EXAMPLES

Compensation cases

(1) and (2): Two children a boy and a girl of 7 and 8 both of whom I saw in completely unrelated compensation cases about traumas 2 years previously.

The girl had been raped four times in four different rooms in a neighbour's house after being invited in: she was seriously injured.

The boy had been mauled by a Rottweiler and had some but not serious injuries.

The girl was thriving 2 years later, she was securely attached and had a very accepting and supportive family who got on with normalising her life and making her feel safe and loved.

The boy was in considerable difficulties. He had pre-existing anxieties as did his mother. He was by the time I saw him insecurely attached to his mother. He was having difficulty leaving the house, going to other children's houses, attending school.

The girl had no genetic vulnerabilities and a protective, emotionally healthy environment.

The boy had a genetic propensity for anxiety problems and lived in an anxious, albeit supportive, environment.

You know who got much the greater compensation.

(3) Four children: issue: did the local authority fail to remove them from their natural parents at the appropriate time?

These children are now aged 14, 16, 18 and 19. All born to the same mother and putatively the same father (the young people themselves believe they all have different fathers).

Placed in what became an adoptive placement when aged 4, 6, 8 and 9 respectively (all at the same time). This followed multiple fractures being found in the 6-year-old. The 8-year-old had a fracture and bruising 4 years previously.

Issue: how would their development have been different if all had been removed 4 years previously, ie when 4 years younger – just born, 2, 4 and 5?

Genetic factors: the mother had a mild learning disability and a dependent, borderline personality disorder. The putative father had an anti-social disorder. Likely that there are additional fathers of whom nothing is known.

Environmental factors: many adverse factors including quite extreme emotional and physical neglect.

The children:

The 18-year-old is most severely affected with anti-social problems and emotional disorders – depressed, out of the home. She has ADHD.

The 19-year-old dropped out of school, ran away from home, he has a one-year-old son and a partner with learning difficulties and three children of her own: his prospects are poor. History indicative of ADHD.

The 16-year-old has mild/moderate learning difficulties, language difficulties and an anxiety disorder.

The 14-year-old has many social problems/features of autism.

The answer?

IMPLICATIONS FOR LAWYERS AND JUDGES

Genetics, epigenetics and the gene-environment interactional effects are complex and understanding is increasing by the day. A rudimentary understanding of some of the issues will help the judiciary in understanding some of the opinions or arguments presented by experts about these matters. It will also contribute to the thinking about cases involving different types of disorder and give a sense of the relative importance of genetic or innate factors in the child's problems as opposed to the environmental ones (usually parenting and or abuse or neglect) and the ways the genetic and environmental influences might interact.

CONFERENCE PRESENTATION

At the conference Dr Sturge asked the delegates to consider (a) whether the courts will soon be seeking genetic testing (not DNA matching to establish paternity, but seeking individual genes in order to better weigh up the nature-nurture balance and the culpability of parenting), and (b) how soon we will all know our genetic profiles, with all the implications that has for abortion law, life choices and the financial implications (eg with respect to mortgages and life insurance).

GLOSSARY

Allele: An alternative form of a gene at a particular locus – such as the A, B, and O variations for the ABO blood group marker.

Autosome: Any chromosome other than the X or Y chromosomes. Humans have 22 pairs of autosomal chromosomes and one pair of sex chromosomes (XX in females and XY in males).

Chromosome: A structure mainly made up of chromatin that is present in the nucleus of cells and which contains DNA. Humans have 23 pairs of chromosomes.

Concordance: Presence of a particular trait or disorder in two family members, usually used in relation to twin pairs.

Correlation: A statistical measure of association, or resemblance, that ranges from +1.0 (indicating perfect association), through 0.0 (no association) to -1.0 (meaning complete disagreement or negative association).

Dizygotic: A twin pair that is non-identical (or fraternal) and therefore equivalent genetically to a pair of siblings.

DNA: Deoxyribonucleic acid; the double-standard molecule, in the form of a double helix that codes for genetic information.

Dominant inheritance: A pattern of inheritance in which the possession of just one particular mutant allele (ie heterozygote) is sufficient to cause the disorder.

Epigenetic: Changes that are heritable but that do not involve any change in DNA sequence.

Genome: The entire DNA of an organism as represented in one member of each chromosome pair.

Genotype: The genetic make-up of an individual; usually, however, a term restricted to the combination of alleles at a particular genetic locus.

Heterozygote: A person who has different alleles at a given locus on the two members of a chromosome pair.

Monozygotic: A twin pair that is genetically identical.

Phenotype: The manifestation of a trait or disorder that results from the effects of genes, either with or without environmental influences.

Sex chromosome: One of the two chromosomes (X and Y that specify genetic sex (XX in females, XY in males).

Shared environmental effect: Environmental influences that have the net effect of making siblings more alike. The term is often referred to as the 'common family environment' but this is misleading because it has no necessary connection with either the family or whether the environmental influence is family-wide.

Susceptibility gene: A gene that increases the likelihood that a person will develop a particular trait or disorder, but which does not determine the disorder on its own.

PARENTING SHORTCOMINGS THAT LEAD TO MENTAL HEALTH PROBLEMS FOR CHILDREN – ATTACHMENT ISSUES, ABUSE AND NEGLECT

Dr Danya Glaser

Consultant Child and Adolescent Psychiatrist

SUMMARY OF PAPER

There is ample evidence for the harm which parental maltreatment can cause to children's well-being and development. As has been outlined in the paper on gene-environment interaction, the effects on the child are a resultant of this interaction. The more innately vulnerable the child and the more intense and prolonged the maltreatment, the greater is the likely effect. This paper is concerned with disorders and difficulties with which children present and which are largely attributable to environmental influences, specifically parental interaction with the child. The first one to be considered is attachment, followed by attachment disorders. Lastly, there is a discussion of children's presentations which are due to child maltreatment, with a special emphasis on emotional abuse and emotional neglect.

THE PAPER

Attachment

Attachment is not synonymous with affection. It is one, albeit crucial, aspect of the child-parent relationship. Attachment is the affectional bond between the child and parents, caregivers and a limited number of other significant figures in the child's life. The complementary parental bond is termed 'caregiving'.

Attachment behaviour is the proximity-seeking by the child towards a caregiver at a time when the child feels threatened, frightened or distressed. Appropriate and sensitive caregiving consists of a response, which is timely, specific to the child's needs at that point, benign and not overwhelming or anxiety-provoking. Such a response leads to the child developing a *secure* attachment. It is also important for the formation of secure attachments, that the parent's response is, overall, consistent.

A child, whose caregiver responds to the child's attachment needs with anger or who ignores the child's needs, is likely to develop an insecure *avoidant* attachment pattern. Inconsistent and unpredictable responses lead to insecure *ambivalent* attachment. One process by which *disorganised* attachment develops is fear induced by a caregiver, to whom the child would expect to go for assuagement of his/her fear, leaving the child with no strategy to deal with their fear. Disorganised attachment is strongly associated with physical and emotional abuse and neglect.

Based on the child's experiences with particular caregivers during the first year of life, the child will have developed its attachment organisation, having formed secure, insecure or disorganised attachments with respect to his/her caregivers. The child will also develop 'internal working models', which are predictions about the child's nature and what the child can expect from the caregiving environment. Attachment patterns tend to remain stable over time, unless there is a change of caregiving, which might include a change of caregiver. New patterns can, therefore, develop and overlay the previous ones, which cannot, however, be erased.

Insecure and disorganised (as well as secure) attachments are measurable and specific. They are not, however, clinical disorders. The significance of attachment organisation is that it is a probabilistic indicator of mental health and quality of interpersonal relationships. *Secure* attachment is associated with positive affect, interpersonal flexibility and competence, and a capacity to reflect. Secure attachment buffers the intensity of the biological stress response in young children, with less elevation of cortisol secretion. By contrast, insecure *avoidant* attachment is associated with hostility, aggression and negative affect. Children whose attachment organisation is avoidant, tend to suppress their sense of fear, threat or distress, often appearing to be unaffected by significant stressors. Insecure *ambivalent* attachment is associated with anxiety. These children are often clingy and may show reluctance to separate from their caregivers.

However, *disorganised* attachment is of greatest concern, being strongly associated with aggression and poor interpersonal functioning, as well as possible later dissociation. Some children with disorganised attachment go on to develop either a compulsive controlling or caregiving pattern of interaction towards their caregivers, which is a form of role reversal. Alternatively, some children with disorganised attachment appear to have no adaptive strategy to deal with significant stress.

The child's attachment patterns are determined not by the child's temperament or genetic endowment, but by the nature of the caregiving which the child receives. The child's difficult temperament will undoubtedly pose a greater challenge to the parent's caregiving of the child but, with help, a parent can learn to respond sensitively and appropriately even to a 'difficult' child. Such children are, thus, quite capable of forming secure attachments.

A crucial aspect of a sensitive caregiving response to a child's alarm or distress is the regulation of the child's aroused affect. Repeated experiences of becoming calm again after upset are vital for the child's development of the capacity to calm themselves. Insensitive, hostile or neglectful caregiving responses do not lead only to insecure or disorganised attachment. Poor affect regulation, uncontrolled arousal and repeatedly 'flying off the handle' are often met with in children who have been significantly abused or neglected. Sensitive and responsive caregiving is dependent on the caregiver's capacity to 'read' the young child's mind, understand and empathise with what the child feels. In time, the child develops this capacity to 'mentalise', which counters the tendency to interpersonal aggression.

Attachment disorders

The term attachment disorder is applied to difficulties which some children, who have been subject to maltreatment in their early years, show. There is, however, a lack of clarity about the definitions, which differ between two classification systems.

The *disinhibited* form of attachment disorder is clear. It refers to children who, despite now having an attachment to permanent, non-maltreating, caregivers, will go off with anybody and show no appropriate social wariness to strangers. These children lacked a consistent attachment figure in their early life and experienced significant deprivation and neglect. They may not subsequently develop appropriate stranger wariness and remain socially indiscriminate even after living for some years with appropriate caregivers. They thus remain vulnerable in unfamiliar social settings.

The problematic variant is *reactive* or *inhibited* attachment disorder. This, too, follows significant maltreatment in early life. There is no consensus about the behavioural and emotional difficulties variously subsumed under this overall term. Difficulties include failure to seek and accept comforting when distressed. Some of the children are described as hypervigilant; aggressive to self and others; and lacking empathy, remorse or conscience. They are also described as having difficulty with affect regulation and modulating their angry responses (see earlier). Not all of the significant difficulties which these children show are directly related to the attachment-caregiving aspect of their early relationships, others being direct effects of early abuse and neglect, which affect brain development and neural pathways not related to attachment. At present, the term is best regarded as denoting an extremely, multiply-troubled, child whose difficulties are due to significant early deprivation, neglect and abuse.

While disinhibited attachment disorder is often enduring, children with the reactive/inhibited variant (whatever it may ultimately come to constitute) can show considerable, albeit slow, improvement with good caregiving and skilled therapeutic work.

One or both forms of attachment disorder may be found in the same child, but they are different developmental entities with different trajectories.

ABUSE AND NEGLECT

This section addresses some of the emotional and behavioural disorders and disturbances in children's functioning (other than attachment disorders) which are primarily attributable to the parenting and care which the children have received. Difficulties arise when the starting point for establishing significant harm is the child's presentation and functioning. While dysfunctional parenting and maltreatment cause many forms of harm, there may also be alternative or additional explanations for the child's difficulties. Overall, there are no specific post-abuse or post-neglect syndromes, even for sexual abuse. This section addresses some of the likely causal associations and mechanisms by which the psychological harm to the child is brought about.

All forms of child maltreatment, including neglect, are more or less stressful and some are actually frightening and traumatic.

Sexual abuse

The consequences of sexual abuse have been studied most thoroughly, even though it is by no means the most common form of child maltreatment. A frequent sequel of child sexual abuse is age-inappropriate sexualised behaviour. It includes intense preoccupation with, and coercion of other children in genital activities such as touching genitalia and sexual talk which, as more isolated phenomena, are not unusual at certain stages of a child's development. It also includes more unusual behaviour such as attempted or actual penetration of vagina or anus of another child and oral-genial contact. Explanations for age-inappropriate sexualised behaviour other than sexual abuse include significant exposure to sexual activity of others.

A significant proportion of sexually abused children suffer from post traumatic stress disorder. This leads to irritability, sleep disturbance with nightmares, fears and voidance of reminders of the abuse which may not be obvious to others and not readily explained by the child.

Other strong associations with sexual abuse include depression, substance abuse, and aggressive and anti-social behaviour, all of which may also, however, follow *physical abuse, neglect* and *emotional abuse.* Sexual abuse also leads to low self-esteem and feelings of shame, which may not, however, be directly expressed and which also follow other forms of maltreatment.

Emotional abuse

Emotional abuse and neglect lead to a wide range of difficulties in all domains of the child's functioning.

- In the *emotional* domain, children may be distressed, anxious, unhappy or depressed and may develop low self-esteem.

- They may show *behaviour* problems either oppositional/defiant or conduct disorders; they may seek attention in a maladaptive way; and they may show role reversal with age-inappropriate responsibility.

- They may present with developmental delay (for instance delayed language development) or educational underachievement. This may be due to poor school attendance.

- They experience difficulties in their peer relationships, being either withdrawn or isolated, or aggressive.

- Their physical functioning may be compromised with non-organic pains, soiling, and poor growth or failure to thrive.

Any of these difficulties could be attributable to, or exacerbated by causes other than emotional abuse.

The reason for the wide array of difficulties caused by emotional abuse is that emotional abuse is defined as persistent harmful parent-child interactions, which include both omission and commission (abuse and neglect) and which do not require physical contact with the child. Within this definition, many different forms of maltreatment can be subsumed. It is useful to place the various interactions into categories. Five categories have been constructed, each of which refers to a different aspect of a child's basic needs. Parent-child interactions within the respective categories affect the child's development adversely in different ways and call for different approaches to intervention and treatment. Harmful interactions within different categories may co-exist.

These interactions are observable, witnessed and reportable. Unlike sexual abuse, the debate is not usually about their actual existence but, rather, about the extent of their harmfulness to the child.

The categories are:

(i) **Emotional unavailability, unresponsiveness and neglect of the child**
    This category addresses the child's most basic need, to be recognised and acknowledged as a living individual. Emotional neglect is more common towards infants and young children and affects the child's emotional development. It is often associated with insecure attachment and deprives the young child of opportunities to develop regulation of their frustration and distress, leading some young children to become apparently detached or 'cut off' from others. It may also be accompanied by lack of stimulation, leading to children's developmental underachievement and delay. Many parents who neglect their children's emotional needs are troubled, depressed, abusing drugs or alcohol or otherwise preoccupied.

(ii) **Negative attributions to the child leading to rejection and harsh punishment**
    These parents have developed beliefs about their children's character as being bad or flawed in some way and which leads to hostility, scapegoating and rejection of the child. In this form of emotional abuse, the child is not valued or loved for who they are. In addition,

[handwritten margin note: array of caregers shoer vulnerability of chidren]

rejecting primary carers are less likely to help children to learn to deflect their attention from frustrating to less frustrating, or rewarding, stimuli, so that the children continue to focus on negative stimuli and respond with anger. Children who are persistently met with hostility develop a bad self view which becomes self-fulfilling by their behaviour.

(iii) Developmentally inappropriate and inconsistent interactions with the child
These include developmentally unrealistic expectation of the child, overprotection and inappropriate ways of disciplining. This may cause or exacerbate a child's behavioural difficulties. This category also includes exposure to disturbing or frightening experiences, in particular domestic violence. This is stressful and may actively traumatise the child. Exposure to domestic violence is associated with children's aggressive peer interactions. The ensuing anxiety may also interfere with children's attention to learning.

(iv) Failure to recognise the child's individuality and psychological boundary, and using the child for the fulfilment of the adult's needs
This includes using the child in marital/parental couple disputes. These children experience anxiety, confusion and the discomfort of divided loyalties which may be expressed through physical symptoms, difficulties with peer relationships and interference with learning.
In fabricated or induced illness, the underlying dynamic is the mother's (usually) need for her child to be recognised as ill when the child is not, or more ill than the child actually is. This is thus another manifestation of this form of emotional abuse. Fabricated or induced illness, as well as subjecting children to unnecessary and sometimes invasive and unpleasant medical investigations, procedures and treatment, also causes the child confusion and anxiety about their state of health, also reinforced by the use of aides such as wheelchairs. The majority of these children also miss out significantly on education and social interaction. There may also be other aspects of disturbed parent-child interaction.

(v) Failure to promote the child's social adaptation
Another need of children is to adapt to their social environment outside the immediate family. This may be disrupted both by parents who place the child in conflict between their own (possibly anti-social) values and those prevalent in society, by isolating the child and by failing to ensure that the child receives appropriate education. Harm to the child includes difficulties with peer relationship and educational underachievement.
In addition to the various forms of maltreatment, there are also some parental circumstances and difficulties which, while not constituting maltreatment in their own right, are recognised risk factors for the likelihood of maltreatment. They include domestic violence, mental health disorders, drug and alcohol abuse and a history of significant maltreatment in the parent's own childhood.
Lastly, there are circumstances in the family's environment which also pose risks to the family's well-being and for possible maltreatment. They include poverty, significantly unsuitable and unsafe housing, seriously troubled environment and unresolved issues of immigration and asylum.

CONCLUSIONS

In order to gain an understanding of a child's difficulties in the context of possible maltreatment, it is useful to place the various factors, information and evidence into four tiers:

0   Comprises of psycho-social factors outside the immediate family.

I   Comprises parental risk factors associated with maltreatment.

2   Comprises of harmful parent-child interaction which includes emotional, physical and sexual abuse, emotional neglect and neglect by lack of provision or supervision.

3   Comprises of difficulties and disorder in the child development and functioning, distinguishing between those which are primarily attributable to maltreatment and those for which are largely explained by the child's temperament and genetic endowment. However, even in the latter circumstances, genetic factors are to be regarded as vulnerability factors which might well be ameliorated by sensitive, responsive, non-aggressive and positive caregiving.

CONFERENCE PRESENTATION

In the course of her presentation Dr Glaser drew attention to the guidance issued by NICE on when to suspect child maltreatment (which includes a quick reference guide) which includes evidence based indicators of which children and which parent-child interactions should raise questions of adult-child maltreatment. The guidance includes mental health indicators in children.

The existence of parental risk factors is not synonymous with significant harm: adult mental health disorder is not synonymous with child maltreatment. The existence of domestic violence is not synonymous with child maltreatment, but exposure to domestic violence is undoubtedly so. The task is not only to prove that there is domestic violence but also that there is exposure to that violence. Dr Glaser suggested that the evidence of harmful interactions is in the verbal descriptions of the persistent interactions. Professionals (social workers or CAMHS workers) should describe the interactions that they witness. Descriptions of those interactions are the evidence of their existence.

Dr Glaser asked the conference to consider how the courts can better interpret the meaning of a child's disturbed mental health and attachment, how Family Law can more effectively respond to the evidence that early and enduring intervention can alter the trajectory of troubled emotional, behaviour and social development of young children, and whether there should be early identification of children likely to be genetically vulnerable.

PLENARY 5

INTERVENTION OPTIONS

THERAPEUTIC SUPPORT FOR PARENTS WITH MENTAL DISORDERS – FOCUS ON NEURODEVELOPMENTAL DISORDERS (LEARNING DISABILITIES, AUTISM, ADHD)

Dr Kiriakos Xenitidis
Consultant Psychiatrist,

Dr James Jeffs
Honorary Specialty Registrar

and

Dr Sally Cubbin
Locum Consultant Psychiatrist
Maudsley Adult ADHD Clinic

SUMMARY OF PAPER

General adult mental health services are becoming increasingly interested in child maltreatment and neglect issues: child risk screens are being introduced, as part of standardised hospital assessments, in part due to the publicity of a number of failed child protection cases.

Clinical and legal interest in the category of mental disorders collectively known as neuro-developmental disorders has emerged. This is a group of disorders, unified by the fact that they are childhood conditions that often persist into adulthood: learning disabilities, autism spectrum disorders and attention deficit hyperactivity disorder (ADHD). Each of these conditions may affect a person's capacity to parent, they tend to cluster together and the presence of one increases the possibility of either or both of the other two.

Therapeutic support is available by way of medical treatment and/or psychosocial interventions. Medical treatment is available for some conditions: in certain circumstances the response to treatment (symptom reduction and increased level of functioning) is impressive, resulting in clear improvement of parenting capacity. Where improvement is less obvious psychosocial intervention is crucial. This includes specific psychological treatments which are typically delivered by specially trained therapists.

Although there are a number of therapeutic approaches available, actual access can be difficult. Service provision criteria may vary by geographical area and there is generally a lack of clarity as to which mental health team should provide services for adults with autistic spectrum disorders and/or ADHD. At primary care level practice varies significantly in terms of clinical experience and knowledge base, interest, threshold for referral to a secondary service and resource availability.

THE PAPER

Child protection workers and mental health professionals often work together for the prevention of child maltreatment and neglect. From a mental health perspective, it has typically been the domain of child psychiatrists and other child mental health professionals.

However, a wide range of adult mental health specialists are at times concerned with the assessment of parenting capacity of their patient. From a clinical point of view typical examples include a General Adult Psychiatrist assessing a depressed single mother, a Forensic Psychologist treating a woman with a personality disorder and an offending history, the Peri-natal Psychiatrist planning to discharge from a Mother and Baby Inpatient Unit a woman with postnatal psychosis, a Learning Disabilities nurse teaching parenting skills to a couple with learning disabilities and an Addiction specialist treating a father with alcohol dependence.

The paramount importance of making child safety a primary consideration is a well-established philosophy in childcare services. It is being increasingly recognised in the adult mental health field. Alongside the standardised Risk Assessment procedures that NHS Trusts and other healthcare providers are required to consider, child protection issues and specific Child Risk Screens are being increasingly introduced. This increased interest is partly due to publicity of a number of failed child protection cases.

In addition to their clinical interest adult mental health professionals are frequently involved as expert witnesses in child protection cases including care proceedings. The tasks of the expert is multi-fold and may include:

(1)   comprehensive diagnostic evaluation of the parent;

(2)   assessment of the impact of the symptoms on the parenting capacity;

(3)   recommendation on therapeutic support that may:
      (a)   reduce the severity of symptoms;
      (b)   improve their parenting skills;

(4)   a prediction/prognosis.

The impact on parenting capacity of three main categories of mental disorder has been extensively studied. A number of papers have been published in both academic and professional journals. These categories include (a) *severe and enduring mental illness* (such as schizophrenia, mood disorders), (b) *substance misuse* (including drug and alcohol dependency syndrome) and (c) *personality disorders* (such as borderline, anti-social and organic personality disorders) and the association with Munchhausen Syndrome by Proxy. The identification of symptoms and the diagnosis of these conditions in parents or parents to be is relatively straightforward. Moreover treatment and support is available through community mental health teams, day centres, voluntary organisations etc.

In recent years, clinical and legal interest in another category of mental disorders, collectively called, neurodevelopmental disorders, has emerged. This category includes a group of mental conditions that are unified by the fact that they are childhood conditions that often persist into adulthood. The main representatives of this category of mental disorders are (a) *Learning Disabilities* (LD, Mental Retardation), (b) *Autism Spectrum Disorders* (Pervasive Developmental Disorders – PDD) and (c) *Attention Deficit Hyperactivity Disorder* (ADHD).

Learning Disability is defined as the combination of (a) significantly sub-average intellectual functioning associated with (b) significant deficits in adaptive skills, both of which are (c) arising in the developmental period. Intelligence is typically, but not invariably, measured by psychometric testing estimating IQ scores. An IQ score of 70 is widely accepted as the cut-off point for the diagnosis. Adults functioning intellectually in the 'borderline' area are often included in this category. According to the level of severity the condition is subdivided into Mild, Moderate, Severe and Profound Learning Disability. Parenting issues are almost exclusively likely to be relevant to adults with Mild and (less so) Moderate Learning Disability.

Autism Spectrum Disorder is characterised by (a) qualitative impairment of social interaction (eg facial expression, gaze, socio-emotional reciprocity), (b) qualitative impairments in communication (eg idiosyncratic use of language, non-verbal communication abnormalities) and (c) restricted/stereotyped patterns of behaviour, interests and activities (eg intense preoccupation with certain subjects, compulsive adherence to routines or rituals) (International Classification of Diseases 10th Edition ICD-10). The condition is often associated with Learning Disabilities, although High Functioning Autism and Asperger's Syndrome are becoming increasingly recognised both in clinical and legal contexts. Thus, adults with autism spectrum disorders encounter significant difficulties with expressing themselves and 'reading' other people's feelings.

The key features of *ADHD* are (a) inattention (eg difficulty in concentrating, and paying attention), (b) impulsivity (eg problems with self control) and (c) hyperactivity (eg restlessness, 'on the go' all the time) (American Psychiatric Association, 1994). The symptoms of ADHD result in impairment in several areas of the individual's life, including significant difficulties in organisation, time management, task completion, and emotional control. In addition, the patient may also have low self-esteem, mood swings, increased frustration, and academic or vocational failure.

Having briefly discussed the salient features of each of the main neurodevelopmental conditions and how they can affect the lives of adult sufferers, the critical relevance of each of these conditions individually on the parenting capacity becomes quite obvious. Cognitive abilities, intact attention, of ability to control oneself, social interaction and communication skills are at the heart of any parenting skills assessment. Moreover, the above conditions tend to cluster together and the presence of one increases the possibility of either or both of the other two, the so-called 'co-morbidity'.

In recent years there have been a number of documents published emphasising the importance of the assessment and support of parents who have a mental disorder. In 2002 The Royal College of Psychiatrists published the report; *Patients as Parents*, which attempted to highlight and clarify the responsibilities of mental healthcare staff in safeguarding children. This report makes it clear that most parents with mental health problems do not abuse their children. However, there is a link between parental mental health problems and 'adverse outcomes for children', but that 'in many cases the neglect of children's emotional needs is unintentional. The 1999 UK Department of Health report *Working Together to Safeguard Children* states that, 'Mental Illness in a parent or carer does not necessarily have an adverse impact on a child, but it is essential always to assess its implications for any children involved in the family'. The Joseph Rowntree Foundation report of 2003 criticises the National Service Framework for Mental Health for not adequately commenting on how parents with Mental Health Issues can be enabled as parents.

Accurate and detailed assessment of adults with parenting responsibilities who have a mental disorder should include an evaluation of: (a) the presence or absence but also the severity of each symptom, (b) the degree of impairment arising from these symptoms in the form of the impact on the person's life (work, family, social), (c) the support networks (formal and informal) that may be available and (d) treatment response in previous and current episodes.

In terms of therapeutic support available this can be divided into (a) medical treatment and (b) psychosocial interventions.

Specific medical treatment is available for some conditions, such as stimulant medication (eg Methylphenidate – 'Ritalin') for ADHD. Under certain circumstances the response to treatment in the sense of symptom reduction and increased level of functioning is impressive, resulting in a clear improvement of parenting capacity and reduction of risks to a child's safety. In other cases the improvement on medication is less obvious and the need to augment the therapeutic effect of medication with psychological interventions is crucial.

Psychosocial interventions are often necessary either in combination with medical treatment or alone. Such interventions include specific psychological treatments, such as Cognitive Behaviour Therapy, behaviour modification, psycho-education, family therapy, couple therapy, group therapy or individual psychotherapy. These are typically delivered by specially trained therapists, often clinical psychologists or nurses. Based on the principles of the above-mentioned psychological treatments short-term interventions aiming at a specific problem may by beneficial, such as anger management, anxiety management, social skills training, sex education etc. Finally techniques aiming at functional skills development (including parenting skills) may be delivered in a group or individual format by suitably trained nurses, occupational therapists or counsellors.

Although a number of therapeutic approaches may be available to adults with mental health problems and neurodevelopmental disorders, it is important to consider the context of therapy. Service provision criteria, especially in the area of neurodevelopmental disorders may vary by geographical area even in the same country. For example some Adult Community Learning Disabilities teams are 'stricter' than others, using a narrow definition of LD and therefore excluding people with borderline IQ or even mild LD. Furthermore there is generally a lack of clarity as to which mental health team (General Adult, LD, Forensic etc) should provide a service for adults with Autistic Spectrum Disorders and/or ADHD.

At a primary care level practice varies significantly in terms of clinical experience and knowledge base, interest, threshold of referral to a secondary service, and resource availability. Although primary care is key, it is likely that the majority of the adults with parenting issues arising in the context of mental disorders will have some involvement with the secondary and in some cases tertiary care services. Whilst the contribution of such assessment and therapeutic services are provided by or commissioned by the NHS a number of private and voluntary organisations offer relevant services on a community based or residential services; for example parenting/family assessments by St Michael's Fellowship and Risk Assessment and psychotherapy services by Respond.

In any case multidisciplinary working and interagency collaboration is essential for the success of any therapeutic programme. Inter-service collaboration has been highlighted repeatedly over numerous reports (*Working Together to Safeguard Children* 1999; Lord Laming Enquiry 2003).

CONFERENCE PRESENTATION

In his presentation Dr Xenitidis highlighted the importance of assessment (which must have a developmental perspective, looking at all the available records and interviewing the patient and their relatives) and then considered how the symptoms actually affect the person's ability to parent. Dr Xenitidis asked the delegates to consider ways of ensuring that treatment recommendations are actually implemented in the court process, and issues of treatment evaluation.

REFERENCES

Biederman et al 'Further evidence for family-genetic risk factors in ADHD' (1992) 49 *Archives of General Psychiatry* 728-738.

Department of Health *Working Together to Safeguard Children* (UK, 1999).

Department of Health *A National Service Framework for Mental Health* (UK, 1999) available at www.dh.gov.uk/prod_consum_dh/groups/dh_digitalassets/@dh/@en/documents/digitalasset/dh_4077209.pdf.

Patients as Parents. Addressing the Needs, Including the Safety, of Children Whose Parents Have Mental Illness (Royal College of Psychiatrists Council Report CR105, 2002).

Report of the Task Force on Supporting Disabled Adults in Their Parenting Role (Joseph Rowntree Foundation, 2003) available at www.jrf.org.uk/sites/files/jrf/1859351352.pdf.

THERAPEUTIC SUPPORT FOR CHILDREN AND YOUNG PEOPLE DURING PROCEEDINGS AND IN SHORT-TERM PLACEMENTS

David Lucey

Independent Clinical Child Psychologist, Yorkshire

SUMMARY OF PAPER

There is a conflict between parents, carers and professionals involved with children, who are likely to view therapy with the individual child as a key means of reducing any distress shown by children and to address any previously adverse experiences they may have suffered, and CAMHS clinicians who are concerned that they may be pressurised to offer individual therapy to children in circumstances where such an intervention may be contra-indicated. Distinguishing individual therapy from broader packages of therapeutic support can significantly reduce the potential for tension between these viewpoints.

Therapeutic support encompasses a wide range of interventions, including direct work with parents; group and family therapy; supervision of, and consultation to, non CAMHS professionals in their work with children; consultation to carers and training of carers in order to facilitate their psychological understanding of children.

CAMHS clinicians are often reluctant to offer children in private law proceedings individual therapy because they are concerned that the presentation of these children is best viewed as a normal response to abnormal circumstances. However, children may have psychological difficulties amenable to intervention independent of the dynamics within their family, and a small number of children may be involved in proceedings for several years. One mechanism to resolve these difficulties is to allow for access to CAMHS assessments to determine whether individual therapy would be appropriate and if so when. Another is to ensure that parents are aware from the outset that any clinician offering therapeutic support to the child will not prepare a report for the court, but would instead be willing to liaise with a CAFCASS practitioner or any independent expert who might be appointed by the court.

CAMHS clinicians have generally been reluctant to become involved with children still involved in public law proceedings. While most of this reluctance stems from doubts as to whether any meaningful therapy can take place when there is so much uncertainty as to the child's future, it can be compounded by a wariness of being caught up in the court process. One way of overcoming clinicians concerns about becoming involved in the court proceedings is to adopt a similar model to that suggested for private law proceedings. Where the court wants to hear directly from the clinician they must engage fully with the court and provide a summary of their involvement with the child.

Children who are 'in transition' can also benefit from a wide-ranging and flexible definition of 'therapeutic support', especially so given the evidence for increased risk of emotional and behavioural disturbance in children in such circumstances.

THE PAPER

I can fully sympathise with parents and carers of children and young people[1] in such circumstances and court and social care professionals involved with these children in their attempts to ensure all that is possible is done to reduce any distress shown by the children and to address previous adverse experiences they may have suffered. I can also recognise how parents, carers and professionals are likely to view therapy with the individual child as a key means of achieving these aims and therefore, are likely to be particularly concerned and frustrated if they perceive the child is being denied appropriate therapeutic support, especially so if they can perceive little merit in the reasons offered. Equally, as someone who has worked in Child and Adolescent Mental Health Services (CAMHS) for over 25 years I can also understand the concern of CAMHS clinicians that they may be pressured to offer individual therapy to children in circumstances where such an intervention may be contra-indicated.

However, the clarification of terms and concepts, with particular reference to drawing a distinction between individual therapy and broader packages of therapeutic support, driven by systemic models of practice[2] and the literature on factors that promote resilience in children,[3] can significantly reduce the potential for tension between these viewpoints and in my experience can lead to the provision of appropriate 'therapeutic support' services for these children, as indicated by an informal review of services offered by CAMHS for this population. Personal experience however, suggests that a minority of local CAMHS continue to adopt an inappropriately defensive attitude toward offering any type of service to children in such circumstances.

THERAPEUTIC SUPPORT

The term 'therapeutic support' would be understood by most CAMHS clinicians to encompass a wide range of interventions including therapy with individual children; direct work with parents; group and family therapy; supervision of, and consultation to, non CAMHS professionals in their work with children; consultation to carers and training of carers in order to facilitate their psychological understanding of children. Such an approach reflects not just the potential for individual therapy to help children, but how other therapeutic interventions, especially those drawing on 'systemic' approaches to understanding children's experiences and consequent effects on their presentation, can also help and how carers[4] and school staff, through their interactions with children, can promote children's resilience. However, if parents, carers, other childcare professionals and legal representatives view 'therapeutic support' as synonymous with therapy with individual children, or if they are aware of the other approaches that might be captured by that term, but they still view individual therapy as the intervention of choice, they are likely to be frustrated if CAMHS do not at least offer this to children as part of a broader package of 'therapeutic support'. My own experience is that where CAMHS have been proactive in explaining their model of understanding to colleagues a much more productive relationship between them and parents, carers and court and social care colleagues has developed.

---

[1]   Henceforth, the term 'children' will be used to encompass 'infants, children and young people' and the term 'child' used to mean 'infant, child and young person'.

[2]   Rushton, A and Minnis, H 'Residential and Foster Family Care' in M Rutter, D Bishop, D Pine, S Scott, J Stevenson, E Taylor and A Tharpur (eds) *Rutter's Child and Adolescent Psychiatry* (Oxford: Blackwell Publishing, 5th edn, 2008) 487–501.
      Golding, KS, Dent, HR, Nissim, R and Stott, L *Thinking Psychologically About Children who are Looked After and Adopted* (Chichester: Wiley, 2006).

[3]   Gilligan, R *Promoting Resilience: Supporting young people who are in care, adopted or in need* (London: BAAF, 2009).

[4]   Wilson, K 'Can Foster Carers Help Children Resolve Their Emotional and Behavioural Difficulties?' (2006) 11(4) *Clinical Child Psychology and Psychiatry* 495–512.

PRIVATE AND PUBLIC LAW PROCEEDINGS

The need for 'therapeutic support' can apply to children in both private and public law proceedings, with the very likely difference from the perspective of a CAMHS clinician that the child involved in private law proceedings will require that support to involve at least one parent (usually the one with whom the child resides), whilst the child involved in public law proceedings is much more likely during proceedings to be in local authority care, or possibly living with extended family members.

Services for children involved in private law proceedings

I can fully appreciate the concern of CAFCASS practitioners as to the compromised emotional well-being of many of the children they encounter in private law proceedings, as I can their wish that 'something must be done' for these children, which in my experience is usually synonymous with 'they require therapy'. However, CAMHS are often reluctant to offer individual therapy in such circumstances, usually based on a concern that the presentation of these children is best viewed as a normal response to abnormal circumstances, namely, likely tension and acrimony, if not outright hostility, between parents or other family members and that a systemic model of understanding children's presentations would strongly indicate that the most effective approach would be to address that aspect of the system (usually the discord between the parents) which appears to be the source of distress for the individual child.

However, it is possible to take such a view to an extreme and preclude all children who might be involved in private law proceedings from access to CAMHS. When confronted by clinicians arguing for such a position I have usually countered with the following. Many children involved in such proceedings may well have psychological difficulties amenable to intervention independent of the dynamics within their family that are likely to have led to the proceedings, for example, school related anxiety. Also, a small number of children can remain involved in proceedings for several years and therefore the rather simplistic injunction 'leave it until the court sorts things out between the parents', could leave some children without necessary support for years rather than weeks or months, which some clinicians erroneously believe would be the case.

Once alerted to these points many clinicians will concede and express their wish not to disadvantage any child because of circumstances beyond their control but will often relate personal experiences of seeing children and parents where they have assessed the child's problem as predominantly a reflection of the difficulties between parents but where one of the parents (usually the one with whom the child resides) has actively sought therapy in order to confirm their position that the child is showing signs of disturbance due to the nature of their relationship with the non-resident parent and who proceed (sometimes with the support of their legal representative) to pressure the clinician to provide a report for court confirming this position.

However, I am aware of a compromise which allows equitable access to CAMHS assessments for all children, whether they are involved in private law proceedings or not. This means no child is denied access to possible 'therapeutic support' because of their involvement in proceedings but allows for an assessment of the child and any contextual factors relating to their presentation to be undertaken. In some instances, where the concerns over the child are deemed to be primarily due to the difficulties within the parental relationship, this may lead to the conclusion that individual therapy with the child is contra-indicated at that time and if that is the case, this conclusion, along with the rationale for it and crucially what would need to change elsewhere in the child's life to either relieve the stress on the child and thereby remedy the concerns over his presentation or place him in a position where individual therapy would be indicated, should be clearly conveyed to the parents and where appropriate, allocated CAFCASS practitioner.

Another policy adopted in some CAMHS is to ensure such parents are aware from the outset that any clinician offering therapeutic support to their child (especially if this involves individual therapy with the child) will not prepare a report for court, but would instead, be willing to liaise with a CAFCASS practitioner or any independent expert who might be appointed by the court over their involvement with the child and if this was the case the clinician would obviously have to abide by accepted guidelines and protocols over the sharing of confidential information.

I appreciate the above approach does not provide the guarantee some parents, CAFCASS practitioners and courts might want that children involved in private law proceedings and showing significant signs of distress will be offered individual therapy. However, a commitment to offering such children the same level of access to a CAMHS assessment as any other child ensures equity in that respect, even if it does mean not all children will receive the hoped for individual therapy.

Services for children involved in public law proceedings

CAMHS clinicians have generally been reluctant to become involved with children still involved in such proceedings. Much of this reluctance stems from doubts as to whether any meaningful therapy with an individual child can take place at a time when there is so much uncertainty as to the child's future, but this is often compounded, in my experience, by clinicians' wariness of being caught up in the court process. While some of this wariness is undoubtedly due to concerns over confidentiality and whether the clinician's involvement in the court process might undermine the quality of their therapeutic relationship with the child, many clinicians fear the scrutiny of them, their professional qualifications and conduct, which they believe would be the case if they had to give evidence in court. This is likely further exacerbated by their level of ignorance around court proceedings, with not all CAMHS professions receiving training on court issues for children as part of their core professional training. As a result many clinicians are unlikely to draw a clear distinction between family and criminal proceedings but will have a general awareness of some of the recent issues and controversies around offering therapy to children who are potential witnesses in ongoing criminal proceedings. While this issue has to an extent been helpfully addressed by the CPS document on 'Provision of Therapy for Child Witnesses Prior to Criminal Trial',[5] this document is unlikely to be familiar to many CAMHS clinicians.

Given the nature of public law proceedings, with their focus on the child's development and account of past experiences, it is very likely for those children who do receive individual therapy during proceedings, the court will be interested in the progress of that therapy and what the child might have said to the clinician as far as it is relevant to questions of abuse and the identity of possible perpetrators and, as such, the court is likely to want to hear from clinicians offering such therapy.

One way of overcoming clinicians' concerns about such a development is to adopt a similar model to that suggested for private law proceedings, with the clinician involved with the child liaising either with the Children's Guardian or a jointly appointed court expert and for the court to be made aware of the views of the clinician through their reports. However, there will always be some cases where the court wishes to hear directly from the clinician offering therapy. In such cases, I believe it is essential for the clinician, presumably with the status of 'professional witness' rather than 'expert witness', to engage fully with the court and to provide a summary of their involvement with the child.

---

5   The Crown Prosecution Service *Provision of Therapy for Child Witnesses Prior to a Criminal Trial: Practice Guidance* (2001).

CHILDREN IN SHORT-TERM LOCAL AUTHORITY PLACEMENTS, POST COURT PROCEEDINGS

For such children, who might be viewed as 'in transition', many of the arguments outlined above in respect of doubts over offering individual therapy to children involved in proceedings would also hold from the perspective of CAMHS clinicians. However, children in short-term placements can also benefit from a wide-ranging and flexible definition of 'therapeutic support' being adopted by CAMHS; especially so, given the evidence for the increased risk of emotional and behavioural disturbance in children in such circumstances.[6] In Leeds, where I worked for 12 years, in recognition of this increased risk, we effectively operated a 'positive discrimination' model for all children actively involved with Social Care; including those in short-term placements post proceedings. We requested that Social Care prioritised referrals for 'therapeutic support' by CAMHS, who in turn, undertook to respond to those referrals quicker than standard waiting lists. Much of this work was and is undertaken by an excellent therapeutic social work team in Leeds[7] aided by general CAMHS clinicians, though in reality, a subset of CAMHS clinicians with a particular interest and expertise in working with children in such circumstances are most likely to respond to such requests.

From its inception it was recognised that for such an approach, which may mean offering types of support other than individual therapy with the child, to find favour with Social Care professionals, foster carers and residential staff, CAMHS needed to actively engage with such professionals and carers at all levels, including training and consultation events in order to familiarise them with this way of thinking about 'therapeutic support' and to reassure them that all referrals would be considered and the type of support needed assessed. The reality is that many children in such circumstances have been offered individual therapy as a result of this process, but for others this has not been deemed either appropriate at the time or necessary following a fuller assessment or that the children would commit to such an approach. In those cases, the thinking behind such a decision is clearly documented and conveyed to those caring for the child either directly or through Social Care professionals with responsibility for the child and in nearly all cases continuing support for carers and more broad consultation to professional system is made available with the usual undertaking that during this process if circumstances change for the child then the question of individual therapy can always be revisited.

NATIONAL DEVELOPMENTS IN THE PROVISION OF SUCH SERVICES

An informal (internet) review of other services provided by CAMHS for children who are 'looked after' suggests that in many parts of England and Wales at least, recent CAMHS

---

[6] McGann, JB, James, A, Wilson, S and Dunn, G 'Prevalence of Psychiatric Disorders in Young People in the Care System' (1996) 13(7071) *British Medical Journal* 1529–1530.
Kelly, C, Allan, S, Roscoe, P and Herrick, E 'The Mental Health Needs of Looked After Children: An Integrated Multi-Agency Model of Care' (2003) 8(3) *Clinical Child Psychology and Psychiatry* 323–335.
Mount, J, Lister, A and Bennun, I 'Identifying the Mental Health Needs of Looked After Young People' (2004) 9(3) *Clinical Child Psychology and Psychiatry* 363–382.
Milburn, NL, Lynch, M and Jackson, J 'Early Identification of Mental Health Needs for Children in Care' (2008) 13(1) *Clinical Child Psychology and Psychiatry* 31–48.
[7] Seneviratna, C 'The Fostering Surgery: Therapeutic Support for Foster Carers in Leeds' (2007 at www.communitycare.co.uk/Articles/2007/11/28/106615/the-fostering-surgery-therapeutic-support-for-foster-carers-in-leeds.htm.

modernisation monies have been used to develop delegated teams to work with such children.[8] Most of these services highlight the raised levels of emotional and behavioural disturbance among these children and how CAMHS have not always provided sufficiently flexible services to 'looked after' children. As a result, these new services actively promote their flexibility, usually adopting a wide-ranging model of what constitutes 'therapeutic support' (including some potential for direct individual work), and many are explicit in not excluding children from their service who might be involved in (public law) proceedings or are in placements where there is no guarantee of permanency.

CONCLUSION

From the point of view of those in a position to offer individual therapy to children during public law proceedings or in short-term placements post proceedings (most often CAMHS clinicians) there is much merit in the argument that during periods of transition or where doubts over permanency are of central importance to the child, it may not be possible to embark upon individual therapy with the aim of providing the child with the means and structure to process past abusive or neglectful events. However, in such circumstances the well-being of children can also be promoted by other forms of 'therapeutic support', including consultation to carers and more general training of carers in understanding the nature of psychological presentations. If such a model is adopted, the understandable concerns that some children in these circumstances are being 'sold short' by an apparent denial of 'direct therapy' should be less. Equally, CAMHS clinicians and the services within which they work should be aware of the need to provide broad based 'therapeutic support' to this group of children and it is unacceptable for such services to adopt an overly defensive position when considering their involvement which such children, particularly one that may be driven by personal and professional concerns about becoming involved in and subjected to the scrutiny of court processes. As such, CAMHS should offer open access to all children in such circumstances, but it is appropriate that they retain responsibility for their own clinical decision-making in terms of what aspect of their service might be most helpful to the child at that particular time.

CONFERENCE PRESENTATION

At the conference Dr Lucey reiterated that provision for children during proceedings was a vexed issue, and that he was used to expressions of frustration from the judiciary. Cafcass officers are concerned that they are caught in a Catch 22: there can be no stable placement until the child's presentation is stable, which needs intervention, but there can be no intervention until the child's presentation is stable. CAMHS are concerned about the lack of certainty for the child, and the need for sufficiently supportive circumstances within which to begin treatment. There is however a potential for compromise, by focusing on emotional wellbeing. This is done by ensuring that children are not discriminated against for an assessment because of the circumstances they find themselves in, by offering therapeutic support that may not look like or be individual therapy but that still supports the child, and by engaging with foster carers who have real potential to bring about change in the child's life.

---

[8] Arcelus, J, Bellerby, T and Vostanis, P 'A Mental-Health Service for Young People in the Care of the Local Authority' (1999) 4(2) *Clinical Child Psychology and Psychiatry* 233–246.

Richardson, J and Lelliott, P 'Mental Health of Looked After Children' with Invited commentary by Vostanis, P (2003) 9 *Advances in Psychiatric Treatment* 249–251.

ENTRENCHED PARENTAL POSITIONS POST-SEPARATION – DO THEY AMOUNT TO A MENTAL HEALTH DISORDER AND HOW CAN THEY BE TREATED?

Eia Asen

Clinical Director, Marlborough Family Service

SUMMARY OF PAPER

The 'therapeutic assessment' protocol has been developed to help 'entrenched' parents, who engage in seemingly 'mad' battles over issues concerning contact and residence. Neither parent's presentation fits the criteria for making diagnosis of mental illness or disorder, but the continuing entrenched parental positions cause significant emotional harm to dependent children. The lives of children are impoverished because their parents are almost exclusively preoccupied with their own grievances; the children are deprived of a good and secure relationship with both parents.

The concept of 'entrenched' parents must be carefully distinguished from that of the concept of 'parental alienation syndrome' which is not recognised as a disorder by medical or legal professionals and does not stand up to scientific scrutiny.

The programme is a mixture of assessment and therapy. Assessment is used to understand the history of each person's current predicament and identify factors that maintain and feed the harmful dynamics; treatment aims to change the dynamics. Assessment reveals a number of common 'themes' which are at the heart of many seemingly intractable contact disputes. 'Therapeutic assessment' is carried out over a period of no more than 3 months, while court proceedings are ongoing and whilst the court can adopt a 'cajoling' approach to encourage therapeutic input.

THE PAPER

SANITY, MADNESS AND THE EXPERT WITNESS

Where sanity ends and madness starts has been a long and largely unresolved debate. Each culture and age has got its own definitions regarding what can be considered as 'normal' and not. Whilst we are able to diagnose a large number of mental health disorders, there is also plenty of behaviour on the border between sanity and madness which is worrying but not sufficiently 'pathological' to warrant an official diagnostic label. One such scenario is 'entrenched parental positions post-separation' which usually manifests itself in seemingly 'mad' battles between the parents over issues concerning contact and residence. The ferocity with which these battles are fought makes one seriously consider whether or not each or both partners can be regarded as 'normal'. In such situations expert witnesses, usually psychiatrists or psychologists, are asked to formally assess each parent and they frequently find that neither parent's presentation fits the criteria for making the diagnosis of mental illness or disorder. This is in the face of each parent declaring the other as 'sick' or 'crazy' and viewing themselves entirely as the victim of their ex-partner's alleged insanity. Even though some of the behaviours displayed by each or both parents may at times be hugely destructive and irrational, clinicians will nevertheless point out that these do not meet the criteria required to make a diagnosis of borderline personality disorder, above all because these behaviours and 'mental states' are situation specific and not pervasive. Yet the children caught up in the parental crossfire between their parents often suffer most, not unlike the innocent victims of a civil war.

It is of course also the case that there are entrenched parental positions post-separation which are related to existing mental health disorder(s) in one or both parents (Asen & Schuff 2004). Delusional ideas or severe depression in one or both parents can contribute to entrenched positions, but in this paper I shall *only* concentrate on those cases where *no* formal diagnosis of mental health disorder in either parent can be made, but where the continuing entrenched parental positions cause significant emotional harm to dependent children. Psychiatrists (be they child and adolescent, adult or forensic psychiatrists or psychotherapists) and psychologists are instructed in these cases to determine what is in the best interest of the child and to address contact issues. It is generally accepted that contact with the non-resident parent is in a child's best interests by virtue of the harm that would be caused to the child if contact were to be denied. It is also accepted that a severing of the ties between a parent and a child can only be justified in the most exceptional circumstances. If therefore it is found that a parent, without 'good reason', wishes to obstruct contact or eliminate the other parent from the life of a child(ren), then everything should be tried to re-establish contact and prevent long-term harm to the child(ren). When one parent refuses to allow their child to have contact with the other parent, there can be a whole spectrum of reasons, from a parent exercising 'self-serving obduracy and recalcitrance' and hostility or opposition to contact, to a parent 'who refuses contact for subjectively good but objectively unjustified reason', as a result of having genuine and deeply rooted fears which may be irrational (Pressdee et al 2006). How then do these (unfortunately termed) 'implacable hostility' scenarios arise and how are dependent children affected?

ENTRENCHED PARENTAL POSITIONS AND THEIR EFFECTS ON CHILDREN

Children caught up in entrenched parental positions usually suffer severe emotional abuse as the result of:

- being deprived of developing a good and secure relationship with *both* parents;

- being used to fulfilling one or both parents' own needs;

- being exposed to persistent harmful parent-child interactions;

- being exposed to frightening experiences, including domestic violence between the parents, be that physical or emotional.

In this scenario children often suffer not only emotionally, but also materially and socially. They find that their lives are impoverished because their parents are almost exclusively preoccupied with their own grievances. This process of attrition almost always also affects the parents adversely and they tend to present with symptoms of anxiety, low mood and volatile affect, irritability and anger. These symptoms, whilst not reaching the threshold for the making of a formal diagnosis of mental illness or disorder, nevertheless do affect the children who are exposed to their parents' fluctuating feeling states. They experience their parents' unpredictability, seeming helplessness and at times dramatic behaviours. This further burdens dependent children who may take on a caring or 'confidante' role, entirely inappropriate to their age and developmental stage.

One of the most common features of children who have been caught up in entrenched parental positions is that they side with one of the parents against the other. This tends to be the result of a whole range of factors and cannot usually be merely attributed to one parent 'brainwashing' the child and/or the parent continuously promoting a negative picture of the non-resident parent. However, estranging or 'alienating' a child from the other parent is not all that uncommon, so much so that the term Parental Alienation Syndrome (PAS) was introduced more than two decades ago (Gardner 1985, Gardner 2001). This alleged 'syndrome' seemed to describe accurately how one parent deliberately, inadvertently or unconsciously attempts to alienate a child from the other parent, with the result that the child, on an ongoing basis, criticises and vilifies one parent without seeming justification. Gardner (1985) saw this above all as being the result of systematic indoctrination by the other parent, leading the child to make his own attempts to deprecate the target parent. However, the concept of PAS is not recognised as a disorder by the medical or legal professions and it does not stand up to scientific scrutiny. Furthermore, it is a rather linear and unsystemic way of viewing things, as blame is primarily assigned to one person (the 'alienating parent') whereas the behaviour should be viewed as being connected to the dynamics between the parental couple, as well as to the child's relationship with each parent before and after the separation and to the likely feelings of loss (Asen et al 1989). With one parent gone, a child's fear is that s/he will be abandoned by the other – and this may to some extent account for why the child appears to say whatever the resident parent wishes to hear. However, all clinicians involved in residence and contact disputes are likely to have come across the scenario where a child literally despises the other parent, appears to have no feelings of empathy for that parent whilst always siding with the favoured parent in conflicts and using identical language to that parent to refer to the 'enemy'. Typically this child will claim that the decision to reject the other parent is entirely their own and this denigration does not just concern the allegedly 'bad' parent but also members of his extended family and friends.

ASSESSING ENTRENCHED PARENTAL POSITIONS

It is established medical practice that any treatment given requires a clear diagnosis for the condition to be treated, or the identification of the particular need. In 'entrenched parental positions' (clearly not a disorder per se but a harmful scenario) the presenting problem is usually that the child(ren) are suffering emotional harm as the result of being exposed to the parental battles (Sturge & Glaser 2000). Work consists of a mixture of assessment and therapy. The purpose of assessment is to understand the history ('aetiology') and each person's current predicament and also to identify factors that maintain and feed the harmful dynamics. Treatment then aims to change the dynamics. However, there is considerable overlap between assessment and treatment, since in order to assess the parents' and the family's ability to change, clinicians will need to make therapeutic interventions to see whether there is potential for change. Such 'therapeutic assessments' (Asen 2007) can be carried out over a period of no more than 3 months whilst court proceedings are ongoing and whilst the court can adopt a 'cajoling' approach to encourage therapeutic input. The aims of therapeutic assessments are to improve the situation for children and to find better solutions for contact issues. This involves making recommendations to the court with regard to type, frequency, duration and location of contact, and handover issues.

Therapeutic assessment work generally starts without the children and consists of meeting initially with each parent individually, followed by parental couple sessions, with the children being invited towards the end of the scheduled work to participate in joint meetings with their parents. If the children also require assessment in their own right, then this will be done separately. In order to rule out the presence of any mental illness or disorder, the first individual meetings with each parent will need to include the examination of their mental states (Asen 2006), unless recent formal assessments are already available. In these individual sessions each parent is invited to tell their 'story' and typically they will want to list all the allegedly destructive acts the other parent has committed and continues to do so ('she manipulates the children and tells them to lie so that I have little chance to be granted contact with my child'; 'he arranges all these exciting activities for the children on the days they are meant to have contact with me – it's just plain obvious that they just wouldn't want to come and see me'; 'she says that she is not stopping the children seeing me and they suddenly started making excuses – and they send the gifts back'; 'he tells their school that I am not allowed to see any reports'). Even though the clinician is likely to have already read very detailed accounts of allegations and counter-allegations, as contained in the (usually very extensive) court bundles which arrive with the Letter of Instruction, it is nevertheless important that each parent feels that s/he is being listened to and heard. The list of allegations and accusations against the ex-partner may be long and repetitive and if asked to look at their own contribution to the current entrenched position, each parent will almost inevitably continue to apportion most of the blame to the other party. In the first session it is usually not wise to challenge this stance, but this happens in subsequent meetings.

During the course of the assessment a number of common 'themes' emerge which are at the heart of many seemingly intractable contact disputes and these are summarised below:

- *'Clean start'*: Here one of the parents has discovered and embraced a newly found independence and simply wants the other parent to disappear. If there is a new partner, the parent may want to prove to him that he is the one and only man in her life and ready to take on the role of 'father'. Similarly, a father may start a new involvement, or have difficulties with the existing one, and simply does not want the children to tell their mother about his affairs. A bit later he may wish to introduce his new partner as 'Mum' and, in his view, all connections with the past need to be severed for that to work.

- *'Old couple business'*: The children are used to punish the ex-partner for his/her alleged sins of the past. Unresolved couple issues between the parents lead to the children (and contact) being used as weapons. Not being able to let go, for example, due to remaining feelings of rejection and being let down, is a typical scenario. Jealousy that the parent gives more love and presents to the children than s/he ever gave to him/her, is another common issue. This might get mixed up with envy of the other parent if s/he is materially better off since the separation. If one parent is still in love with their ex-partner, then the children can be used to penalise her for having left. Here a strong urge for revenge and intense feelings of rivalry can lead to the making of deliberately malicious and untrue allegations, which often take the form of accusing the other parent of sexually abusing the child(ren).

- *'Hopeless parent'*: One parent is very critical of the other's parenting capacity. There is often a real or invented (hi-)story of the other parent never having been interested in the child(ren) before and having no actual experience of parenting at all. There can be claims that the other (non-resident) parent, due to an inability to concentrate or be vigilant, is poor at supervising the children, so that there is a high risk that they will suffer physical harm or be neglected. Poor parenting capacity is often connected with one of the parents having had a deprived childhood and not having experienced a good parental role model.

- *'Empty life'*: The resident parent is socially isolated, with no significant network of friends or any family support. This parent may regard the children as the only family s/he has and an enmeshed relationship with the child(ren) can develop, with an increasing inability to tolerate that the child(ren) share their love with the other parent. The parent is emotionally dependent upon the child and regards any affection the child shows for the other parent as depriving him/herself. In addition, court battles, frequent confrontations with the ex-partner, getting helpers drawn in – all these can 'fill in' an otherwise empty and unfulfilled life.

- *'Control games'*: Contact is used by both parents to regulate their own relationship, with attempts to also control the relationship between children and their parents ('if you don't behave then you can't see Mummy'). This is often the case when ex-partners appear to be 'addicted' to litigation and the protraction of contact battles. This seems important for both parents – despite their protestations – as it permits the continuation of the (highly dysfunctional) relationship between the parents and maintaining the status quo. This helps parents not having to make any decisions about having to commit themselves to other new relationships.

- *'Projected personal experiences'*: Parents who themselves have to deal with intense traumatic experiences dating back many years, including to their childhood and prior to meeting the other parent, can re-emerge post-separation. The feelings evoked can be so intense that a parent may no longer be able to keep apart their own and the child's reality and feelings. A mother who has suffered sexual abuse as a child but was unable to confide this to her own mother, may 'see' a similar situation happening with her own child. These projections can be very powerful and have delusional quality in that they cannot be corrected even by frequent medical examinations of the child which show that the feared abuse has not taken place. The mother will want to 'protect' the child by keeping the other parent away.

- *'Financial matters'*: Post-separation financial issues can feed into entrenched parental positions. These concern each parent's own financial situation, the dividing of assets, child support, welfare money and so on. Financial issues need to be sorted out separately and these are not discussed in the work as described in this paper. In fact, at times therapeutic work needs to be suspended until financial issues are settled, as otherwise children find themselves heavily drawn into financial negotiations and being used as bargaining pawns, particularly if a parent sees the children as a way of obtaining a house and other benefits.

- *'Beliefs and cultural issues'*: When each parent has quite different belief systems, cultural assumptions and practices from the other parent, this can cause stalemate situations, particularly if one parent (or both parents) does not want the child(ren) to adopt the other parent's way of life.

In many cases there is more than one of these dynamics present. It is part of the assessment to establish which of these maintain the current entrenchment and this 'diagnosis' helps to inform treatment.

PRINCIPLES OF TREATING ENTRENCHED PARENTAL POSITIONS

Therapeutic assessments start generally with two or three individual sessions with each parent. As already described, the first session is for the parent to explain the situation as they see it, to feel that the clinician is interested in and able to listen to their respective accounts – and for the clinician to understand the themes and dynamics. The second session – and any subsequent ones – could easily be 'more of the same' as parents in entrenched positions have a seemingly endless supply of horror stories and incidents. In practice, it is useful to start the second session by stating:

> 'Last time you told me how you see the issues and about some of the dreadful things that have happened and continue to happen. I have also read the court bundles carefully and there is a lot of information there. I am sure we could spend all day today just me listening to what you think went

wrong in the past. The problem is that the past can not be changed. This is why I suggest that we look at what each of you can do to change the present and future. So let's start with you – what can you do differently for things to change? I will stop you whenever you go back in time and I will re-focus the conversation onto what can be done differently today or tomorrow or some other time in the future. Of course I believe that the past is important and that it, at least in part, explains why we have got to where we are now. But looking back too much can stop us from looking forward.'

This new framework is likely to be initially resisted by the parent who will continue to seek to blame the other parent for most of what has gone wrong in the past. The clinician needs to be very firm and continuously re-focus:

'I fully understand what you are saying – but how is that going to help to change things for your child(ren)? What can you do to change this? Let us explore that now!'

And at a later stage:

'Give up all hope that you can't change him – the bad news is: you can only change yourself – and even that may be a very hard task . . .'

Focusing on the predicament of the child(ren) also helps to get away from chronic partner blaming:

'What do you think is it like for the child(ren) to see their father like that? What do you think they make of you when you cry? Do you think your son knows about how you feel about contact with his mother? How would you like him to feel? What can you do to help him feel better? When you and your partner have these loud arguments, what do you think is the effect of this on your child?'

Each parent's own past issues and how these are impacting on the present parenting need to be explored:

'Tell me about what sort of mother your mother was – and what sort of father your father was? What did your mother do really well? What not? What did you decide to do yourself as a mother? What did you want to do differently?'

The possibility of repeating family of origin 'scripts' has to be explored, as well as identifying how such scripts have been or would need to be rewritten (Asen 2007). This addresses the issue of being able to reflect – another area that can benefit from therapeutic intervention. This not only concerns the ability to develop understanding of and insight into any personal shortcomings, but it also concerns the ability to place oneself in the position of one's own child(ren). The ability to see the world through the child's eyes, to have or develop empathy with the child's predicament – all these are areas that need to be examined:

'Imagine that you are your 3-year-old daughter looking at you: what might she say is the one thing she'd worry about you most?'

In these individual sessions common themes emerge and they provide some explanation as to why the entrenchment continues. Three individual sessions with each parent prior to convening joint couple sessions tends to be a good average number. It may also be helpful to do a 'dry run' or rehearsal with each parent separately for the first parental couple session, considering likely emerging interactions and scenarios. This might be achieved via questions, such as:

'If he was here and heard you talk like this . . . what might he say? How might he respond? Do you like him to respond this way? No? So what could you do differently for him to respond differently? How might you avoid becoming again entrenched in a useless fight?'

The actual parental couple sessions need to be tightly chaired, with the clinician being initially very much in the driving seat. It helps to draw up an agenda of the issues to be discussed and each party is invited to nominate some items. Agreement is then reached with which item to start and it is the clinician's task to keep the focus only on the present and future and on concrete issues. It may also be useful to construct some 'do-able' tasks which can be carried out between sessions by each parent. Children should only be brought into the therapeutic assessment work once there has been some progress in the parental couple relationship. Prior to a meeting involving the children, both parents need to be in agreement with what they are going to tell the children. The experience for children of having their previously warring parents peacefully in the same room, supporting each other and agreeing on a joint plan forward, is of course novel and very positive – and a sign that their parents no longer occupy entrenched positions.

CONFERENCE PRESENTATION

In his presentation Dr Asen outlined how the programme works. The assessment starts with two to three individual sessions with each parent where common themes emerge, providing some explanation as to why the entrenchment continues. There follows a tightly chaired parental couple session, with children brought into the therapeutic assessment work once there has been some progress between the parents. A typical therapeutic assessment comprises 18 (hour-long) sessions over 3 months: three individual sessions with each parent, five parental couple sessions, two individual sessions with the child, three parent-child sessions and two family sessions.

Dr Asen asked the delegates to consider: (a) how the process and outcome of this approach could be researched and evaluated; (b) whether it is acceptable and/or desirable to merge the roles of expert witness and therapist; and (c) what where the advantages and disadvantages of 'coercing' parents to seek therapeutic help.

REFERENCES

Asen, E et al 'A Systems Approach to Child Abuse: Management and Treatment Issues' (1989) 13 *Child Abuse and Neglect* 45–57.

Asen, E 'Assessing Parents Considered to Pose Serious Risks to their Children: the Marlborough Approach' (2006) 18 *Nyas* 178–188.

Asen, E 'Therapeutic Assessments: Assessing the Ability to Change' in C Thorpe and J Trowell (eds) *Re-rooted Lives: Interdisciplinary Work with the Family Justice System* (Bristol: Jordan Publishing Ltd, 2007).

Asen, E and Schuff, H 'Disturbed Parents and Disturbed Families: Assessment and Treatment Issues' in M Goepfert, J Webster and MV Seeman (eds) *Disturbed and Mentally Ill Parents and their Children* (Cambridge: Cambridge University Press, 2004).

Gardner, RA 'Recent Trends in Divorce and Custody Litigation' (1985) 29 *The Academy Forum* 3–7 (New York: The American Academy of Psychoanalysis).

Gardner, RA (2001) 'Parental Alienation Syndrome (PAS): Sixteen Years Later' (2001) 45 *Academy Forum* 10–12.

Pressdee, P, Vater, J, Judd, F and Baker, J *Contact: The New Deal* (Bristol: Jordan Family Law, 2006).

Sturge, C and Glaser, D 'Contact and Domestic Violence – the Experts' Court Report' (2000) *Family Law.*

PLENARY 6

RESPONSIBILITIES IN RELATION TO SERVICES TO CHILDREN AND PARENTS

SUPPORTING THE FUTURE OR 'TOO LITTLE TOO LATE?' – A JUDICIAL PERSPECTIVE

Angela Nield

Circuit Judge, Manchester

SUMMARY OF PAPER

In order to address the question of whether and in what circumstances a judge can refuse to endorse a care plan where support services for parents with care of (or contact with) children are not sufficiently clear it is necessary to consider the timing and quality of information available to the court.

The timing of information provision is as much an issue during proceedings as it is at the end of proceedings (and indeed is relevant pre-proceedings). Whilst the Public Law Outline and Family Justice Council paper on Parents Who Lack Capacity to Conduct Public Law Proceedings advocate early coordination of multi-agency information, the luxury of early assessment pre-proceedings is rare, and all too often it is the court process of assessment that is relied upon.

Of particular concern is gaining sufficiently detailed information about the complexities of support available within the community to parents. The focus of each professional involved with a family is on their own individual perception of a 'successful outcome' to the care planning process. Moreover, there appears to be a lack of interdisciplinary coordination of information across the relevant bodies (mental health services, CAMHS and social work teams), perhaps as a result of a 'clash of cultures' with each organisation having its own rules and regulations, and different focus of concern.

It is arguably very simple for a court to refuse to endorse a care plan where there is insufficient assurance or clarity of support from social services or mental health services for the parent with care of or contact with their child: it is difficult to see how a care plan can be regarded as choate where key elements of a package of support are missing. However, this becomes yet more complicated where it is the nature and complexities of the mental health issues themselves that cause difficulties: how can a care plan for an issue itself characterised by an uncertain prognosis become choate? The court can refuse to approve a care plan, can adjourn the care proceedings and invite the local authority to reconsider the plan, and where the local authority has failed to discharge its parental responsibility and this results in parents' Article 8 rights being violated an action may lie by way of free-standing application under the Human Rights Act 1998 or by judicial review.

THE PAPER

I am charged with offering a judicial perspective upon the important and worrying theme of this conference, and I am asked to consider whether and in what circumstances a judge or magistrate can refuse to endorse a care plan where support services for parents with care of (or contact to) children are not sufficiently clear. This would include support from Social Services, Community Mental Health or other statutory service.

However, I feel very strongly that to offer a proper judicial perspective upon the anxious issues raised by the theme of this conference, I need to broaden that question to consider other matters which impact significantly upon the quality of information which is available to the court not only at the stage when the court would be considering endorsing the care plan, but at earlier stages, when equally crucial case management decisions are being taken.

I thus propose to raise two separate issues for discussion:

(a)   the quality and timing of material to inform care planning at interim stages, and the need for early multidisciplinary coordination; and

(b)   the legal position and how it may be affected by the inherent uncertainties of mental health issues.

To avoid detailed exposition of the law in this area I have attempted to summarise the position in relation to care plans and their endorsement by the court in Appendix 1 to this paper. To those lawyers present, particularly those whose cases I have chosen to summarise, I apologise in advance that this is material very familiar to you and no doubt not improved by my rather brief analysis. To others I hope that it offers a relatively simple overview.

In Appendix 2 I have provided a case scenario which in my view has elements of each of the areas of concern I have proposed for discussion.

I would invite those reading this paper, if they would, to consider the Appendices attached at this stage, in order to make more sense of what follows.

INTRODUCTION

Despite the notable increase over the last 12 months in care proceedings nationally, the figures that we see of cases involving parents with significant mental health issues (particularly if we leave aside from those figures, parents with learning difficulties and/or personality problems) do not correlate with the figures for incidence of mental health problems in the population as a whole.

It seems to me that what we see, having taken account of the obvious numbers of those affected who do not have the care of children, is the percentage of that group where the issues are most severe, and often complicated by the presence of other factors, such as lack of support structures, drug and alcohol abuse, and domestic violence.

It is not uncommon to find that an analysis of the psychiatric history of parents presenting with mental health difficulties reveals a complex picture whereby their diagnosis and prognosis are both complicated by the influence that, for instance, substance abuse has had upon their presentation.

In short, there are relatively few cases where the mental health of the parent alone, is going to determine the care plan for the children, or indeed, be the exclusive arbiter of the detail of the package of support provided under the terms of a care plan

(a) The quality and timing of information to assist care planning

I wish to emphasise that the question of information as to the provision of appropriate support for parents is as much an issue during proceedings as it is at the conclusion of proceedings, indeed it is relevant at pre-proceedings stage also.

I commend to all, the excellent work of the Safeguarding Committee of the Family Justice Council and their paper[1] on parents who lack capacity to conduct public law proceedings which deals substantially with the difficult question of the role of the Official Solicitor as litigation friend – an entire topic in itself which I have not touched upon here.

I also strongly advise any practitioner involved in a case concerning the mental capacity of parents to read the detailed and informed practice judgment in the case of *RP v Nottingham City Council*.[2]

Both the paper and the case mentioned above refer to the fact that the PLO,[3] of course, advocates early coordination of multi-agency information. It requires, in a significant number of cases, work to be undertaken with parents to avert the threat of proceedings and where proceedings are necessary, invites the Local Authority to file:

> 'a summary of any concerns which [they] may have about the mental capacity of an adult to care for the child or prepare for the proceedings.'

This arguably presupposes some form of early assessment pre-proceedings where mental health issues are suspected and I endorse the Safeguarding Committee's recommendations which include jointly agreed referral and assessment procedures between Children's Social Care Services and Adult Learning Disability teams/Mental Health Services and any other partner agencies (eg maternity services).

This would mean that in a significant number of cases where early decisions of such magnitude as separation of mother and child at birth are taken, those decisions are as informed as possible.

Sadly, the luxury of such information is rare, and we are left to fall back upon the court process of assessment.

Additionally, the structure of the way in which we conduct proceedings is sometimes unhelpful – early independent expert intervention is arguably crucial – if possible at CMC[4] stage in advising as to which expert input would best assist the court, and how to focus assessments. This is an area considered for some time by the Experts' subcommittee of the Manchester Family Justice Council. The possibility of this happening in a climate where resources are scarce and experts overburdened is remote, but much expense and heartache may well be spared by early intervention and early interdisciplinary coordination where possible.

One of the matters which regularly causes me particular concern, at the time when I am asked to assess the adequacy of a support package for parents, is gaining sufficient detailed information about the complexities of support available within the community (or indeed that which should be provided as of right, to parents under the Mental Health Act legislation). I mention also the difficult area of children with mental health problems, whether detained or otherwise. I have been indebted to one of the authors of an article in the May 2009 edition of *Family Law*,[5] who has greatly assisted me in my preparation for this paper and have been astounded at the complexities of both legislation and practice.

The coming into effect of the Mental Capacity Act 2005, on 1 October 2007, has assisted to a degree with its accompanying Code of Practice, statutorily defining capacity, a very relevant

---

[1]   To be provided with conference documentation.
[2]   [2008] EWCA Civ 462.
[3]   Public Law Outline.
[4]   Case Management Conference.
[5]   Jonathan Butler and Helen Wilson 'Mental Health Law for Family Lawyers: An Overview'.

issue when considering parents with mental health difficulties which preclude them from being represented independently of the Official Solicitor.

In the case which is described in Appendix 2 to this paper, it is clear that the focus of each of the professionals was very much upon their own individual perception of a 'successful outcome' to the care planning process.

(i)   The consultant psychiatrist heading the psychiatric mother and baby unit at the X Hospital, stabilised the mother's psychotic symptoms sufficiently to make a place at a mother and baby assessment unit a viable proposition *in itself* – it was not her role to consider a long-term care plan.

(ii) The Local Authority, seemed to feel compelled for understandable reasons, to follow this interim course of action – however, how far into the future they were looking remained uncertain – I was most anxious about how the placement could be supported and monitored in the long term, and at what cost?

(iii) What was missing from this crucial early case planning was information from the independent expert. In this case the provision of early information may arguably have meant that the interim care plan for assessment in the mother and baby unit may never have been put forward. Alternatively, if it had, it would have had a much more careful focus.

(b) The ability of the court to refuse to endorse a final care order where there is insufficient assurance or clarity of support from social services or mental health service, for a parent with care of, or contact to, their child

It is arguably very simple for a court to refuse to endorse a care plan in such circumstances when it is difficult to see how a care plan could be regarded as choate if key elements of a package of support are missing. This proposition is supported by the requirements of the detail and content of care plans as outlined by LAC (99) 29, and the requirement that detail of the support to be provided to the placement is fully outlined in the care plan (once again – see Appendix 1).

The more difficult question may arise when the uncertainties stem not from the support package, but from the nature and complexities of the mental health issues themselves; in short when does a care plan for an issue itself characterised by an uncertain prognosis, become choate?

It is in some ways easier to delay the approval of a care plan where the child herself has mental health needs and where services remain uncertain. In these cases, the threat of appearing before the court and justifying a decision as to the provision of services often concentrates minds. More pertinently, perhaps, the input into the care planning process of all professionals who will provide the child's support network for the future is of vital importance.

What is the situation where a care plan can be regarded as choate, viewed from the point of view of identification of 'solutions' for all the issues of concern, but where the detail of the services to be provided is either unclear, or the services proposed are not the 'best available' in all the circumstances?

It seems clear that a court may also consider inviting a local authority to adjourn a care plan and to reconsider it. This arises from the quasi-inquisitorial role of the court and the expectation that the differing but complementary roles of the judge/magistrate, and the local authority, should work together to achieve the best interests of the child.

If a local authority can be invited to consider a complete change in its care plan, why not to consider the provision of proper support for a care plan which is agreed by all to be in the best interests of the child? The more difficult issue may be when resources are recommended which are not readily available, where some element of creative compromise may well be needed to ensure that the best available alternative is in place.

In the case example in Appendix 2, I would have been more than prepared to adjourn approval of a final care plan to ensure the fullest package of support available to make that care plan work. My experience of the Children's Guardians in the area in which I sit is that they would be equally assiduous in their concern to ensure the best support available for the child before they, and the court, relinquished their respective roles.

It may be that there are cases where the local authority argue, with some force, that an element of support which is missing from the care plan can not be properly determined until some stage in the future. This may arise, for instance, because a child needs input from CAMHS[6] which CAMHS indicate can not be commenced until his or her final placement is identified. In such cases, the court may have to acknowledge that a stage has been reached where responsibility for a care plan must pass to the local authority.

The case of *Re S (Children: Care Plan); Re W (Children: Care Plan)*[7] offers a possible remedy to parents post final order, where a local authority has failed to discharge its parental responsibility under the terms of a care plan approved by the court. Where this results in parents' Article 8 rights being violated, an action may lie by way of a freestanding application under the Human Rights Act 1998 or by judicial review.

I refer again to the legal overview in Appendix 1 to the impact of the Human Right Act 1998 and to the provisions of s 118 of the Adoption and Children Act 2002 and the role of the Independent Reviewing Officer in relation to the monitoring of support services under a care plan.

I am the first to acknowledge that none of the remedies post care order mentioned in the foregoing paragraphs are either common applications or simple ones, and I recognise that the best and quickest method of ensuring an appropriate support package in cases where that support may well be crucial to the success or otherwise of an often high risk care plan, is when the proceedings are still before the court, and prior to endorsement of the final care order.

Conclusion

Whilst the courts can very easily dig in their heels to insist upon support, which they know is available, being confirmed before finalising a care plan, what causes me increasing concern is the extent of what we do not know about other available services. There appears to be a lack of interdisciplinary coordination of information across the relevant bodies including mental health services, CAMHS and social work teams. Mental Health Services and the NHS, as well as social services, all recognise and work with the concept of 'care plans' within their own professions.

Unfortunately, they are often less able to coordinate plans with multidisciplinary input, which seems to me to be essential if a court is to properly understand what can and cannot be expected to be available by way of support. All too often, I am told that other agencies can not or will not provide information within timescales directed by the court or, more worryingly, will not allow

---

6   Child and Adolescent Mental Health Services.
7   [2002] UKHL 10, [2002] 2 AC 291.

social workers access to important meetings such as discharge meetings where parents are detained under the Mental Health Act, even where there are public law proceedings ongoing.

I am convinced that this is not a case of any wilful determination to sabotage the court process; it is in my view rather a clash of cultures each with their own rules and regulations and perhaps different focuses of concern, unwilling to bend to other processes.

There are of course other issues which contribute to problems for parents, not least the impact of what appears to be regularly identified as a failure to diagnose mental health conditions for a number of years, or equally an incorrect diagnosis both of which problems lead to either no treatment, or incorrect treatment over a lengthy period. This can leave the process of intervention and support, when concerns are identified, so lengthy and difficult that often timescales are out with those of the child.

In saying this I do recognise the difficulty and reluctance to identify and 'label' a young person with what is sadly still the 'stigma' of a mental health diagnosis.

CONFERENCE PRESENTATION

In her presentation HHJ Nield noted that it was very rare for cases to come before her only involving issues of mental health difficulties: usually there was also some other matter (such as drugs or alcohol). Whilst the court had the power to refuse to finalise the care plan, this was often too late: there needs to be early coordination of multi-agency intervention from the very first time the matter comes before the court. Despite the court ordering expert assessment as quickly as possible it often came too late.

APPENDIX 1 – THE LEGAL POSITION

Statute

Adoption and Children Act 2002, s 121 (Care plans)

(1) In section 31 of the 1989 Act (care and supervision orders), after subsection (3) there is inserted—

'(3A) No care order may be made with respect to a child until the court has considered a section 31A plan.'

(2) After that section there is inserted—

'31A Care orders: care plans

(1) Where an application is made on which a care order might be made with respect to a child, the appropriate local authority must, within such time as the court may direct, prepare a plan ("a care plan") for the future care of the child.

(2) While the application is pending, the authority must keep any care plan prepared by them under review and, if they are of the opinion some change is required, revise the plan, or make a new plan, accordingly.

(3) A care plan must give any prescribed information and do so in the prescribed manner.

(4) For the purposes of this section, the appropriate local authority, in relation to a child in respect of whom a care order might be made, is the local authority proposed to be designated in the order.

(5) In section 31(3A) and this section, references to a care order do not include an interim care order.

(6) A plan prepared, or treated as prepared, under this section is referred to in this Act as a "a section 31A plan".'

(3) If—

(a)   before subsection (2) comes into force, a care order has been made in respect of a child and a plan for the future care of the child has been prepared in connection with the making of the order by the local authority designated in the order, and

(b)   on the day on which that subsection comes into force the order is in force, or would be in force but for section 29(1) of this Act, the plan is to have effect as if made under section 31A of the 1989 Act.

Failure to implement a care plan can now met with litigation by the legal and special casework team of CAFCASS. Section 118 of the Adoption and Children Act 2002 requires a local authority to appoint an independent reviewing officer (IRO) to monitor the functions of the local authority in relation to the review of looked after children's cases.

From September 2004 the IROs have had the power to refer cases that they are unable to solve to CAFCASS who may start proceedings against the local authority.

CAFCASS is empowered by statutory instrument to bring civil actions against a local authority with the following options:

(a)   Judicial review proceedings

(b)   Compensation claim

(c)   Freestanding Human Rights application.

Children Act 1989

The Act gives the court the power when making an interim care order or interim supervision order to give any directions it considers appropriate about medical or psychiatric examination or other necessary assessment of the child. However, if the child is of sufficient understanding he may refuse to submit to the examination or assessment (s 38(6)).

The court's powers under this provision are limited to a process that can properly be characterised as 'assessment' rather than 'treatment'. Any proposed assessment must be necessary to enable the court to discharge properly its function of deciding whether or not to make a care or supervision order. The court may also direct that no examination or assessment shall take place or make any it subject to its specific approval (s 38(7)).

Directions can be given when the order is made or at any other time while it is in force and can be varied on an application made by any party to the proceedings in which the directions were given. *In Re G (Interim Care Order: Residential Assessment)*[8] the House of Lords held that the court hearing care proceedings had no powers to order the local authority to provide specific services for anyone – that was a matter for the authority. The purpose of s 38(6) and (7) was to enable the court to obtain the information it needed.

The court has similar directions powers when making a child assessment order (s 43(6)(b)) and emergency protection order (s 44(6)(b); see Chapter 4). The court's powers are more limited when a final supervision order is made and it does not have power to give any directions when making a final care order as thereafter decisions on examinations and assessment fall within the scope of local authority's parental responsibility. However, the court will have considered the local authority's care plan, prior to making a care order, and will expect that its key elements will be implemented, unless the child's circumstances change markedly.

Human Rights Act 1998[9]

The Human Rights Act 1998 provides the county court or High Court a power to review the operation of a care order and care plan after a final care order has been made:

- Section 6(1) makes it unlawful for a public Authority to act in any way which is incompatible with the ECHR.

- Section 7(1)(b) allows a person claiming that a local authority has so acted to rely on Convention rights.

Such a challenge post care order should ideally be heard in the Family Division and if possible by a judge with Administrative Court experience.

---

[8]   [2006] 1 FLR 601.
[9]   Sections 6 and 7.

Where proceedings are pending there is no requirement for separate Human Rights Act proceedings – the remedy under s 7(1)(b) is available within the proceedings themselves and can be dealt with by the court dealing with the care proceedings.

Local Authority Circular

LAC (99) 29 'Care Plans and Care Proceedings under the Children Act 1989'

LAC (99) 29[10] provides detailed guidance on the appropriate contents of a care plan within care proceedings and provides that a care plan should be structured in five sections.

Of particular relevance to our theme:

- Section 2 – The child's needs – including how those needs might be met;

- Section 3 – The views of others' – including the child's parents;

- Section 4 – Other services to be provided to the child and/or his family either by the local authority or other agencies:
  - support in the placement;
  - specific detail of the parent's role in day-to-day arrangements.

Case-law

Case-law makes it clear that when deciding whether to make a care order, the court should normally have before it a care plan which is sufficiently firm and particularised for all concerned to have a reasonably clear picture of the likely way ahead for the foreseeable future. In other words, the care plan must as a starting point be 'choate':

> 'Since in each case the evidence which requires to be called in to satisfy the court as to the efficacy of the care plan will vary in substance and in degree, it is a matter for the good sense of the tribunal and the advocates appearing before it to see that a proper balance is struck between the need to satisfy the court about the appropriateness of the care plan on the one hand and the avoidance, on the other, of over zealous investigation into matters which are properly within the administrative discretion of the local authority.'

Re S (Minors) (Care Order: Implementation of Care Plan); Re W (Minors) (Care Order: Adequacy of Care Plan)[11] (hereafter *Re S; Re W*).

This case was carefully considered, together with a line of other authorities on the point leading up to that decision, in the case of *Re S and W (Care Proceedings)*[12] when in delivering the judgment of the court Wall LJ provided a detailed exposition of the case-law pertinent to the powers of the court when faced with final care orders which it was unwilling to endorse.

He emphasised the duty of the court to rigorously scrutinise the care plan and to refuse to make a care order if it does not think the plan is in the child's best interests.

---

[10]   Children Act Guidance and Regulations (2008) Vol 1 para 3.18.
[11]   [2002] 1 FLR 815.
[12]   [2007] 2 FLR 275.

The judgment in *Re S and W (Care Proceedings)* drew distinction between a number of different circumstances – clearly the court has a power to adjourn where a care plan is not choate; two further situations were identified which addressed the graveman of the facts before the court:

(a)   In that case, the care plan was choate, but the appeal centered around whether or not the judge at first instance had appropriately adjourned the proceedings to invite the local authority to reconsider a care plan which he regarded not to be in the best interests of the child. This was a course of action which the court of appeal upheld as perfectly justified:

> 'Care proceedings are only quasi-adversarial. There is a powerful inquisitorial element. But above all, they are proceedings in which the court and the local authority should both be striving to achieve an order which is in the best interests of the child. There needs to be mutual respect and understanding for the different role and perspective which each has in the process . . .'

(b)   A distinction was drawn between this situation and the situation where the judge had reached the 'point of no return' and here the court referred to the case of *Re S and D (Child Case: Powers of the Court)*[13] an appeal where the judge was literally faced with the 'lesser of two evils' having invited the local authority to review their stance and position and they actively chose not to do so. In that case, Balcombe LJ highlighted the dilemma facing a judge, knowing that were he to make care orders the local authority would implement a care plan which he felt was manifestly not in the child's best interests, but alternatively the choice was to make no order leaving the child in the care of an irresponsible, and indeed wholly inappropriate parent. Whilst identifying this to be a most unfortunate position, the Court of Appeal was clear that these were the stark options open to the judge.

---

[13]   [1995] 2 FLR 456.

APPENDIX 2 – CASE EXAMPLE

N was a 5-month-old child the subject of care proceedings brought by W Borough Council.

N's mother P reported mental health problems from early adolescence characterised by hearing voices, para-social behaviour and alcohol abuse. She was admitted to mental health hospitals and detained under the Mental Health Act on more than one occasion

She gave birth to her first child C at 19 years of age. A residential assessment in a mother and baby unit concluded that she was not able to safely care for C who was placed for adoption.

Psychometric assessment at this time identified that P functioned within the borderline subnormal level of intelligence, and she was thought to suffer from a borderline personality disorder.

She led an itinerant lifestyle, and was treated for a period of about 10 years by many different GPs.

She developed a relationship with N's father L in about 2000. He had been drug dependent until shortly before N's birth receiving professional input to address the chronic difficulty.

The couple's relationship had been characterised by geographical instability, behavioural volatility and substance misuse.

Nevertheless, the relationship was identified to be mutually supportive and enduring, and N was the result of a planned pregnancy.

The mother discontinued her long-term medication upon discovery of her pregnancy and when she was approximately 5 months pregnant she began to hear voices again and her behaviour became disturbed.

Following N's birth mother and child were transferred to the Regional Mother and Baby Unit at the X hospital. At the commencement of proceedings the specialist who headed the unit felt that the mother could be admitted to a mother and baby unit outside the hospital with her partner and child, for further assessment.

An independent psychiatric assessment of the mother was commissioned within the proceedings from Dr W a consultant psychiatrist which assessment ran concurrently with the mother and baby unit assessment. The local authority were persuaded by the court to maintain the placement pending the outcome of the assessment.

The assessment in the mother and baby unit was not without its problems. The mother's mental health had fluctuated significantly, but when well she was able to care for the child and reacted warmly and appropriately to him.

There had been significant concern about L's ability to recognise the significance of his drug use or to be honest about his dependence. He found the regime at the mother and baby unit very restrictive and difficult and there were a number of reported confrontations with staff.

When the father was on 'an even keel' the parents' care of N was undoubtedly good, and L would offer support to P when prompted.

The couple were identified as socially isolated and unable or unwilling to make social contact with others within the unit.

When she saw the independent psychiatrist the mother reported that the voices she had been hearing had now gone. She was clear in her belief that she could care for her child and that all she needed was her medication.

She believed that her assessment by the mother and baby unit was a positive one, and hoped for a rehabilitation home of their baby.

The report of the consultant psychiatrist was filed some days before the matter came before the court, to make its determination.

The report made stark reading. P had, according to the expert, been suffering from undertreated schizophrenia for over 10 years, and had only very recently begun to receive appropriate medication and support.

Had she received her diagnosis of schizophrenia following the birth of her first child (instead of a diagnosis of Borderline Personality Disorder) she would have been eligible for follow up from severe mental illness services, and her difficulties which were particularly pronounced during 2002–06 could have qualified her for an assertive outreach approach (a community based mental health team would have supervised her compliance with medication and tried harm reduction strategies to reduce alcohol misuse). The 11-year period of insufficient treatment would have negatively impacted on P's progress, poor outcome in schizophrenia being related to long duration of untreated psychosis and persistence of aggravating features such as alcohol misuse and homelessness or itinerancy.

Although it was clear that she had improved her capacity to care since the birth of her first child some 9 years previously, she remained in a highly supported setting where supervision and monitoring including of her partner, was essentially the only means of optimising support for her.

Set in the context of a severe relapsing illness complicated by both substance misuse and an unreliable (although committed) relationship with her partner, the psychiatrist was not confident that she could continue to meet her son's developing emotional and physical needs throughout his childhood.

This, coupled with only tentative positives emerging from the assessment of the mother and baby unit led to the local authority taking a decision that it could not maintain the family unit and that N should be removed from his parents' care. At an inevitably distressing interim hearing the parents eventually conceded the position and agreed to a placement of their child in foster care.

Although they indicated an intention to challenge the evidence at the final hearing some weeks later, they did not do so, and N was made the subject of care and placement orders without opposition from them.

I feel that a number of significant issues arise for discussion from this distressing case:

(1) Should the court have approved the recommended placement in the mother and baby unit in the first place?

(2) Is there any reason to doubt that earlier interdisciplinary intervention at the planning stage would have benefited the court in its decision-making process? How could this have been achieved?

(3) If there had been a positive assessment from both mother and baby unit and the psychiatrist but which nevertheless highlighted a high level of support was needed to ensure the child's placement with his parents, what could the court have done if:

(i) the local authority put forward a plan of permanent alternative care as resource issues prevented them from implementing such support; or

(ii) the local authority put forward a plan which proposed a placement with a package of support which did not meet the clear recommendations of the independent psychiatrist?

(4) If the local authority care plan rather than one of permanent alternative placement had been for placement with a maternal aunt and uncle under a Special Guardianship Order, with contact to the parents once every month, but with no proposals as to how the parents were to be offered support from Community and/or Mental Health services to ensure that contact was effectively exercised, could and should the court consider adjourning the final hearing?

RECLAIMING SOCIAL WORK – KEEPING FAMILIES TOGETHER

Isabelle Trowler

and

Steve Goodman
London Borough of Hackney

SUMMARY OF PAPER

'Reclaiming Social Work' is designed to reclaim social work from being an over-bureaucratised profession lacking confidence, expertise and gravitas. Small-scale incremental changes will not work; what is required is a whole systems approach to create fundamental and sustainable change.

There needs to be a change to the way of thinking about what is happening and why, and developing different ways of working with families to create positive and sustainable change. To achieve this, the '7S' framework has been used to help Hackney undertake a whole system change to their children's social care services.

- *Shared values: Primarily interested in keeping children safely together with their families wherever possible. When the state needs to intervene in families it should do so speedily, with depth and decisiveness.*

- *Strategy: A 3–5 year change agenda.*

- *Structure: Small Social Work Units as a way of supporting families towards change using prescriptive methodologies for interventions.*

- *Systems: Simplified so that they are relevant, intelligent, flexible and useful to practitioners. Designed to facilitate effective working with families.*

- *Style: Collaborative and respectful working, inviting the family and all members of the system to join in finding a solution to the presenting difficulties.*

- *Staff: Large scale change in staff, with all candidates undertaking verbal reasoning and written assessments before interview. Designed to attract high quality practitioners.*

- *Skills: A programme for staff which compensates for the gaps in the curriculum in social work training and builds their expertise in the chosen methodologies.*

After 3 years Reclaiming Social Work has created a critical mass of highly intelligent, thoughtful and committed practitioners. Early findings indicate that Reclaiming Social Work has an overall positive effect on the management of risk, the quality of care and the response to families.

THE PAPER

INTRODUCTION

In 2007, we decided to embark on designing a whole systems change to the way in which children's statutory social work in England is practised and managed. Having established strong political and staff support, the change programme, now nationally recognised as 'Reclaiming Social Work', is well under way and is in its second year of evaluation by Professor Eileen Munroe at the London School of Economics (LSE). This paper highlights the key elements of 'Reclaiming', emphasising its use of a systemic approach to practice. It offers the early findings of what we have learnt so far and what there is left to do. Overall it describes the intellectual journey of Reclaiming to date whose vision and approach has caught the imagination of social workers keen to get back to doing professional social work.

A CASUAL CULTURE – THE PROBLEM WITH SOCIAL WORK

Having practised, managed and led statutory social work services for a number of years, we believe that social work as a profession has lost its way, lacks confidence, expertise and gravitas and is over-bureaucratised. Nationally, local authorities and most importantly children and families, have to grapple with the consequences of this.

The intellectual ability of students accepted onto social work degree courses is in general not high enough and many do not have the requisite academic or personal qualities needed to do the job of statutory children's social work. Over the last decade and in an attempt to manage this widespread skills deficit a national system of performance management and centralised bureaucracy has emerged with many unintended consequences. The focus on risk assessment and management has been lost amongst a more generic, holistic approach to need. With greater reliance on a procedural approach to professional practice, and ICT systems' solutions, a workforce incapable of professional, creative and independent thinking has emerged. The profession suffers from a conveyer-belt, risk-averse mentality to the inevitable detriment of the children and families it seeks to serve. As practitioners are further and further removed from any sense of their own responsibility, capability to effect positive change, or sense of professional pride, a dangerous casualness emerges, where even automated tasks are often done badly.

We have stated from the start that it is our intention to reclaim social work and change what it has become. We have written extensively about what Reclaiming Social Work means and whilst an important structural change has helped mark a fundamental different way of working, we are clear that the real challenge is to change the professional culture described above. This means creating very different ways of thinking about what is happening in families and why, and different ways of working directly with families to create positive and sustainable change. This requires a very different skill set than is currently encouraged amongst employers and developed through qualifying courses. It also requires social workers to share our vision of when the state needs to take a coercive role in the protection of children and how that should be done. Reclaiming Social Work is very much about the statutory function of children's social work, ie child protection. When our professional and expert analysis tells us we need to act, we need to do that swiftly, and with exceptional skill.

THE 7S FRAMEWORK[1]

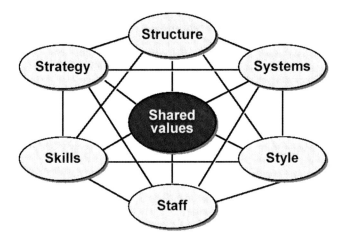

The 7S framework helps conceptualise all the different components that need attention if a whole systems change has a chance of being successful. All local authority children's social care services have undergone change programmes to address specific practice or management deficits, with varying success. We think that the small scale, incremental changes currently promoted by the Council for Workforce Development will not work. With such significant and entrenched problems within a profession nothing less than a whole systems approach is likely to create fundamental and sustainable change. The 7S framework simply shows the key interdependent elements present within organisations, and has provided us with a road map for our change management.

Our shared values

Critical to the success of Reclaiming Social Work is establishing a shared value base from which to work. In the often stressful, high risk and highly active environment that is children's social care it is all too easy to lose sight of our purpose and our values. This is often illustrated by a tendency to behave in punitive, risk averse ways towards some of the most vulnerable children and families in our society.

We have written extensively about this elsewhere[2] but fundamentally Reclaiming is primarily interested in keeping children safely together with their families wherever possible; that the role of the state in families' lives should be a limited one and when that role needs to be executed it is done speedily, with depth and decisiveness. Reclaiming is underpinned by a perspective on social disadvantage and discrimination and articulates the major impact this has on every aspect of life. Too often in the past it is possible to see how professional stories that are built around families and their children have lacked substance; often a result of value-laden assessments and judgments being made. Our judgments made about families must always be made within a context of emotional intelligence and empathy. Whilst holding the safety of the child in mind, we must work in partnership with parents (an often forgotten concept embedded in the Children Act 1989 although currently being resurrected by the Public Law Outline). In our work with families we need to stop, listen and think about what has been said and the meaning this has for the child's welfare. We want to see practitioners proud of the work they do and willing to take

---

[1]   Thomas J Peters and Robert H Waterman *In Search of Excellence* (1982).
[2]   Isabelle Trowler and Steve Goodman *The Way We Want To Do Things* (2007).

responsibility for their work and owning the impact they have on families' futures. Social workers are very powerful professionals and threatening to families by their very presence. Reclaiming seeks practitioners that hold confidence in the positions they take and have the courage and integrity to admit that sometimes they are wrong.

Our strategy

Reclaiming has always been described as a change agenda of 3 to 5 years. There are no quick fixes. The strategy in one sense is simple – we need the right people in the organisation who have a high level of skill and who are interested and able to design and deliver interventions that work. We are very prescriptive about methodology and equip our staff with a toolbox of evidence-based interventions through provision of extensive and high quality training (see 'Our skills') and offer extensive opportunity to be reflective and thoughtful about the intention and impact of current practice. As we have steadily reduced the numbers of looked after children we have been able to deliver on efficiency savings for the authority as well as invest more money into preventative services, keeping more families together. We encourage a sense of responsibility and shared risk decision making and as leaders are very involved in day-to-day practice, and visible and engaged in the minutiae of day-to-day life in our organisation. Our leadership voices are strong and unequivocal in our search and wish for a social work service of which we are proud.

Our structure – the Social Work Unit

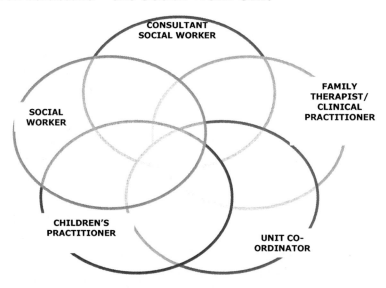

Hackney is the first children's statutory social care service in the country to introduce small multidisciplinary Social Work Units (SWUs) as a way of supporting families towards change using prescriptive methodologies for interventions. Having a range of professionals available in the Units means we are able to provide a service for young people and their families using the expertise of different perspectives, with direct lines of communication to more specialist services within the Borough if such a need is identified.

Each of the 48 new units is led by a Consultant Social Worker, who has working alongside them another Social Worker, a Children's Practitioner, a Unit Coordinator and a Clinician (a Systemic Family Therapist or a Clinical Practitioner in training to be so). The Units discuss all their children's cases on a weekly basis agreeing tasks with the Consultant Social Worker who has overall case responsibility. The thinking and striving on behalf of an individual child or family is held in mind within the Social Work Unit, a focus shared by its five members, each of whom will know and have a duty of care to that particular child or family. In this way families are helped to discover their own competencies and resources, and have a positive experience of their own abilities of implementing change. The model encourages greater continuity of care for families with no child reliant solely on one member of staff for their support.

Our systems

This refers to the procedures, processes and routines that characterise how the work should be done: childcare decision making; financial systems; recruitment and performance appraisal systems; information systems. In essence we are trying to simplify our systems so that they are relevant, intelligent, flexible and useful to practitioners. Anything which an organisation creates should only be done to facilitate effective working with families. Anything which exists which hampers effective practice should be quickly changed or stopped altogether. We have limited procedures preferring to encourage practitioners to think through what they want to do and why, and then do it, rather than do it because the procedure says so. Hackney has the advantage of the London Child Protection Procedures, which in the main serve practitioners and families well. We are strong opponents of the Integrated Children's System believing it to encourage fragmented thinking with no capacity to tell the story of the child and his or her family. We have made significant changes to the exemplars and are in the process of commissioning a family focused system for recording. We have to undo years of unnecessary red tape and replace this with systems fit for purpose.

Our style

Our style of practice is fundamentally connected with collaborative and respectful working, inviting the family and all the members of the system (including the professionals and others in the child's wider system – from family, to school, to other services) to join in finding a solution to the presenting difficulty. In this way professionals are not seen to have all the answers, but instead look to the family's own understanding and particular knowledge of what is not working, and help them to identify their own skills to create a way forward. By privileging the voices of parents/carers and children and those involved in their lives, we can provide a context in which families gain enough confidence to rely on their own strengths and resiliencies, and to play a greater role in finding a solution. We know that in general many family systems are self-regulating and can manage most difficulties on their own, or with minimal support. This is the everyday resilience by which most families survive the challenges they encounter over time. Where our intervention is required, however brief, SWUs must question some of the problem-saturated descriptions, which tend to accompany referrals as a way of liberating professional energy and attention.

The driver for decisions on who does what within the Units and across the organisation should be the interests of children and families and not dictated by procedural and/or service specifications. The latter are there to guide, not to bind us.

Our staff

Our staff are without doubt our most valuable resource and getting the right people in permanent employment our greatest challenge. The change agenda has seen over 150 staff leave our employment and a similar number arrive. All candidates now undertake verbal reasoning and written assessments before being considered for interview and to reflect how seriously we take this process all social workers are interviewed by a selection panel chaired by one of us. There is significant success in attracting staff of the highest calibre. Most of the Unit posts are relatively easy to fill with the exception of the Consultant role. Despite receiving over 400 applications from mostly London-based experienced social workers only 30 have been recruited. This is reflective not only of the rigour of the recruitment process and the standards we have set ourselves but provides an indicator of the level of competency at a senior practitioner level within the current labour market. It is also a sad reflection on UK social work training that many of our Consultants were trained abroad.

Our skills

Reclaiming has had to develop a programme for staff, which compensates for the gaps in the curriculum in social work training and supports staff more generally to think and behave differently in their professional worlds. We have developed strong partnerships with a number of academics and have commissioned extensive additional skills training including Systemic Family Therapy with the Institute of Family Therapy (20 practitioners have already completed their first year with the whole of that cohort now moving on to the intermediate year; another 25 practitioners begin their first year soon, and a smaller number are moving into their third and fourth qualifying years) and extensive courses in Social Learning Theory commissioned from De Montfort University. We have 15 social work trainees at any one time and are working with the University of Kent to develop a post qualifying Masters in Social Work (we do not currently support post qualifying training for staff other than that required for GSCC registration). This is a huge investment but we already have evidence that this expansive approach to staff development is motivating and intellectually stimulating for a group of highly intelligent and committed practitioners who want to get it right for the families they work with.

THE ROLE OF CLINICAL PRACTICE IN SOCIAL WORK[3]

In 2000–01 money was first allocated in the CAMHS budget to fund a therapeutic service specifically for Looked After Children (LAC). By 2002 Looked After Children's Therapy Service was operational. What separated the LAC Therapy model from other models was the speed, inclusiveness, and creativity of intervention. Whilst the child was coming as the bearer of the problem, slowly there developed the realisation that working with and supporting a child in isolation from his domestic/educational system rarely produced useful results, and the children themselves informed us of this fact. Our young clients brought their personal stories of experienced difficulties embedded within larger narratives of living in foster care, with often moving accounts of relationships with absent parents, or with their foster carers or other children in the placement. Our staff came to understand *the inevitability of engagement with those others within the system of the child*. Failure to include in a holistic fashion the system of concern minimised meaningful and sustainable change, and frustrated the child's efforts in making sense of his or her life experiences.

Whilst the therapeutic referrals continued to name the child or young person(s) whose symptoms had alerted professionals that something was amiss, there was for us a deep-felt and overwhelming recognition of *the complexity of all human systems*, and a belief that trying to change a child without effecting symmetrical changes in the environment of the child's daily life was not a solution. Thus we came to embrace all aspects and individuals within the child's particular sphere – from foster carers to social workers, from teachers to GPs, in seeking change. Professionals began to think very differently about the children and their families, and to specify more targeted interventions, which were really needed. Within the ambit of this expanded insightfulness we were enabled to see *not problem families, but problem systems*.

---

[3]   Debra Philip *Reclaiming Social Work, The Clinical Manual* (2008).

By 2006 a new Therapeutic Intervention Service was born, and staff were recruited who were Family Therapists or Clinicians dedicated to systemic working; not only with LAC, but with an expanded remit to respond to all referrals coming into Children's Social Care Duty and Assessment Teams. Clinicians provided rapid responses going out to see families with the relevant Social Worker within the hour when necessary and supporting the family through its initial crisis. This approach was instrumental is starting to see a steady decline in the numbers of LAC coming into the system. This innovative method of embedding Clinicians directly within Social Work teams served to pave the way for the current Social Work Unit Model.

The Clinical Service within Children's Social Care is best described as a CAMHS Tier 2 service. The clinical staff in the SWUs thus have a responsibility to provide a high quality child and adolescent mental health service to all the children, young people and families who require such an intervention. The Clinicians in the SWUs need to be able to screen all referrals in which a mental health component is identified. On this basis they will offer an initial clinical judgment concerning mental health risk if required. Consultation and guidance from the relevant Clinical Manager is available as and when required. An adult psychiatrist also based in the children social work service offers consultation as and when needed. These consultations are available to all Consultant Social Workers. In accordance with the defined function of a Tier 2 CAMHS service the Clinicians in SWUs have the task of intervening at an early point to prevent mental health deterioration in children, young people and their families.

THE LEARNING SO FAR

In just 18 months the benefits of Reclaiming for families is very clear. The early findings from the LSE evaluation report conclude:

> 'Taken together, data indicate that Reclaiming Social Work is having an overall positive effect on the **management of risk**, the **quality of care** and the **response to families**, when compared to previous practice both at Hackney and elsewhere.

> Reclaiming Social Work **enables better learning systems**, more **opportunity for critical reflection**, a more appropriate **mix of skills** in dealing with families and a better balance between **meeting performance indicator targets and responding to family needs** professionally. When compared with previous practice, Reclaiming Social Work shows an improved approached to **decision-making** in child protection, and improved approach in **interaction with families** and other professionals, **fewer constraints** on practice and better **prioritisation and consistency of care**.'[4]

We currently have 34 of the 48 units live and continue to be reliant on agency staff based in our remaining teams (although these teams too have access to clinical input) and have to manage all the operational challenges this poses. There is an increased polarisation between units and the agency teams with regards to the quality of work. We know that the management arrangements around the SWU, is no longer the right one and we are in the process of a radical redesign of the social work management role and task. Our Fostering and Adoption Services, Statutory Reviewing Service and Child Protection Conferencing arrangements also need to be closely aligned with Reclaiming and will undergo extensive change over the next 18 months. Our recording systems present the most difficulty for practitioners and there is a pressing need to progress this work to alleviate this frustration. We also question whether we have the balance right yet – whilst practitioners spend much more time thinking about children and doing direct work with families we are posing the question as to whether we now talk too much! When does the conversation need to stop and the doing need to start?

---

[4]   Professor Eileen Munroe *Reclaiming Social Work – Early Findings* (London School of Economics, 2009).

CONCLUSION

The last 3 years have been hard work, frustrating, sometimes exhilarating and ultimately very rewarding. Reclaiming has created a critical mass of highly intelligent, thoughtful and committed practitioners enthused by this different way of working and constantly encouraged by each other's presence. Its initial impact on families is demonstrated through the early findings report, external casework audit and perhaps in particular the frequent letters we receive from professionals and families offering thanks for the work practitioners have done.

There is still much to do.

We are at a crossroads as a profession. The political context for child protection is such that we believe the time is ripe for some of our learning to be translated across the national social work landscape. So, in the meantime we continue to move forward, with determination and passion for our work, and hope.

CONFERENCE PRESENTATION

At the conference Steve Goodman described children's social care as a very difficult job that must be done in complex and risk-laden situations. The level of expertise needed to do the job is on a par with that of psychologists. National and local government has put in more and more checks and balances to try unsuccessfully to take out the risk from an inherently risky business. Good social workers have voted with their feet and left local authorities.

When Steve arrived in Hackney he was concerned at the low level of practice ability he encountered and realised this would not be changed through 'tinkering'; something radical needed to be done. The whole system was the challenge and needed to be reformed, through Reclaiming Social Work. Delegates were asked whether this approach represented a way forward for children and social care, and what difficulties could be foreseen.

A PARTNERSHIP APPROACH TO THE DELIVERY OF CAMHS AND CHILDREN'S SOCIAL CARE SERVICES

Karin Courtman

London Borough of Lewisham

and

Sandie Chatterton

Service Manager, Lewisham CAMHS

SUMMARY OF PAPER

'Therapeutic Networking' is the method adopted by Lewisham to facilitate joined up service delivery for children with emotional and behavioural problems. It also informs collaborative working, for example between Children's Social Care and Child and Adolescent Mental Health Services (CAMHS).

The difficulties of families with complex problems that are seriously affecting the well-being of children are dynamic and multi-layered. Therapeutic Networking involves a way of working for all in the multi-agency Team Around the Child/Family. Where possible interventions are targeted at an early stage to turn things around/rehabilitate families at crucial times, hoping to prevent Care episodes or other social/educational breakdowns/exclusions.

Therapeutic Networking is a model that uses compatible and overlapping conceptual frameworks to address the complexity of serious family problems. It is essentially systemic and draws heavily from group-work models, attachment theory and 'the coordinated management of meaning' to approach and address interventions at different levels. This networking process begins in a 'reflective group' which includes all significant involved professionals and parent(s), wherever possible. The shared objective of the group is to promote the welfare of the child, but each member brings their own agenda and responsibilities. During each meeting progress against agreed objectives is reviewed, priorities are revised and related action plans agreed. Using the 'coordinated management of meaning' interventions at different levels are addressed simultaneously and prioritised. The process is iterative: the group will repeat the process over and over again, building on previous understanding and achievement, with the aim that the family become self-sufficient and able to ask for help in the future if needed. Where this is not possible a good outcome for the child may be to move to a permanent, alternative carer.

Therapeutic Networking is one approach to collaborative working between Children's Social Care and CAMHS in Lewisham. In addition, Therapeutic Social Workers have been recruited and are based within frontline Social Work Teams to offer an assertive outreach therapeutic service to children and families who cannot, or will not, access traditional services. These Social Workers are supported by clinical consultation and support from a CAMHS Senior Family Therapist. Also, one full-time Social Worker with a therapeutic background is based half-time at CAMHS and half-time in the local Family Centre. This Social Worker helps identify families where the parent(s) would benefit from co-working with any of the mental health assessment and treatment services available within CAMHS. Two specialist Adoption Social Workers are deployed similarly between Social Care and CAMHS to support foster carers and post-adoption families where children's placements are at risk of disruption. Finally, an Independent Reviewing Officer and a CAMHS Worker co-facilitate 'Reflective Practice' groups for Social Work and CAMHS practitioners to consider the impact of these stressful families on themselves and their work.

THE PAPER

Lewisham have developed a partnership approach to delivering a joined up Team Around the Child (TAC) service that is not about large scale structural reorganisation and not about Child and Adolescent Mental Health Services (CAMHS), Children's Social Care (CSC) and others working in separate silos. This paper describes both 'Therapeutic Networking', a method of facilitating joined up service delivery for children with emotional and behavioural problems, as well as outlining examples of collaborative working informed by the Therapeutic Networking approach.

CONTEXT

Lewisham (child population of 58,500) has the largest child population in Inner London.[1] It is a diverse borough in terms of income and ethnicity. Parts of the borough are leafy and prosperous, such as Blackheath. 72% of the school age population are from black and minority ethnic groups.[2] Lewisham has 166 'super output areas', 8 of which are in the 10% most deprived in England, and 64 are in the 20% most deprived.[3]

CAMHS and CSC are relatively well resourced and we have enjoyed a period of relative staff stability having successfully recruited to specialist CAMHS and hard to fill child protection social work posts, so that now only 7% of posts are covered on a temporary/agency basis. This is important because we have found that a critical success factor in delivering joined up services is the way professionals communicate and interact with each other. Good working relationships between people in the network and the ability to trust and appropriately challenge each other are key to delivering good outcomes for children.

In terms of the National Service Framework for CAMHS, Lewisham has a robust comprehensive range of services (see Appendix 1 – Specialist areas of work within CAMHS).

THERAPEUTIC NETWORKING

One way of explaining the Therapeutic Networking approach is that what the multi-agency group must do together is to hold the sides of a trampoline on which the family in crisis is bouncing around. Sometimes the parent(s) can climb down from the trampoline and help us to steady the trampoline for the child(ren). Hopefully, the family and their network will manage their own trampoline without specialist help in the future.

The difficulties of families with complex problems that are seriously affecting the well-being of the children are dynamic (they change over time) and multi-layered in the way they are understood by, and affect, all in the family/community/professional network. Our approach involves a way of working for all; families, social workers, other professionals, and voluntary sector groups, in the multi-agency Team around the Child (TAC).[4] Where possible we are

---

[1] ONS Lewisham Population Mid-Year Estimate (2007).
[2] Lewisham Schools Survey (2009).
[3] IMD Briefing Note (2008).
[4] Department for Education and Skills *Every Child Matters: Change for Children* (London, 2004).

targeting interventions at an earlier stage to turn things around/rehabilitate families at critical times, hoping to prevent Care episodes or other social/educational breakdowns/exclusions.

The approach is one best suited to meeting the needs of children who are in the wider community. They are the children who cross backwards and forwards over the formal Child in Need (CIN) and Child Protection thresholds. The difficulties these families face are usually complex and often long-standing. Using the *Every Child Matters* hierarchy of needs the children have needs that warrant a *targeted* and, at times, a *specialist* response (see Appendix 2).

Our model of Therapeutic Networking addresses how to maximise the effectiveness of the TAC in a way that effectively addresses the complexity and 'stuckness' of serious family problems.

The conceptual frameworks used to help us all make sense of this complexity are:

- systemic;

- narrative and the coordinated management of meaning;

- resilience based;

- risk monitoring/management;

- attachment; and

- the holistic model which underpins all social work.

(See Appendix 3 for descriptions of these conceptual frameworks.)

Using these related, complimentary and overlapping conceptual frameworks facilitates effective inter-agency working.

Conceptual Framework	How we use it	How this adds value and meaning
Systemic and the Holistic social work model	To understand complexity across multiple levels of meaning, ie from the micro level (the child) to the macro level (the societal context).	Helps individuals not to blame themselves.
	To understand families and individuals within their social context and over time (the history of individuals, families and communities is important).	Helps us target our interventions and to recognise when an intervention is not helping.
Coordinated Management of Meaning	To organise our thinking about the above in order to decide where to focus our intervention, or when stuck, to widen our information/view.	Helps us focus in and out between hierarchical levels of intervention until we get to the one that works.
Narrative	To help us listen to and understand what others are saying.	Narrative helps people make sense of what has happened to them. It helps create 'coherent stories'. Coherence promotes safety and good mental health.
Resilience	To identify people's strengths and build on those. To balance the negatives and to help reframe attributes as positive, when appropriate.	Builds self esteem. Helps children and adults deal with adversity and become more self sufficient.
Risk monitoring/ management	To assess safety for the child but also to ensure *good enough parenting* while therapeutic work is undertaken.	Ensures that the safety and well-being of the child is at the centre of what we do. Helps us understand which risks to take and when.
Attachment	To understand the nature of the relationship between children and their caregivers and then to establish the best way of working with the family and significant others in order to improve family relationships.	Helps us to build trust and understanding within the family and within the professional network. Once trust has been established in one relationship, it becomes more possible to transfer trust building to other relationships.

THERAPEUTIC NETWORKING IN ACTION

To understand Therapeutic Networking in action see Figure 1 below. The process looks simple, but implementing it calls for some determination and the ability to hold in mind wide ranging information and multiple levels of meaning. Essentially it involves a systemic inter-agency way of working which facilitates the use of the conceptual frameworks above. Use of these frameworks begins in a *reflective group* led by someone who has the skill to help others to be *reflexive*, ie to understand their individual roles and relationships and how they complement each other in the action plan.

The reflective TAC group should include all significant involved professionals and parent(s) whenever possible. Membership of the group changes over time depending on the needs of the family, so at times it may include teachers, housing officers, members of faith communities, health visitors, community drugs workers, adult mental health workers and voluntary agencies as well as the social worker and the CAMHS worker.

The shared objective of the group is to promote the welfare of the child, but in addition each member adds their own agenda and responsibilities. These need to be made transparent. The Chair and the Social Worker (if different) will facilitate reflection on how these perspectives, roles and responsibilities differ, overlap, conflict or converge. This systemic way of thinking invites *curiosity* to think about new ideas. Members of the reflective group are allowed space to have their say, as well as space to listen. The group are encouraged to reflect on what the information means for them and might mean for the family.

Where strong feelings are apparent, sufficient opportunity needs to be given for their expression. As time goes on and the group experiences containment of strongly expressed emotion, then people begin to understand the impact and meaning of emotionality for relationships at all levels. Within the safety of the group, new ways of dealing with conflict can emerge.

The normal rules of group-work apply; confidentiality, commitment to attend, respect, and listening to others. These promote understanding and ownership and some sharing of responsibility. Inter-agency relationships are strengthened by this process, which also indirectly facilitates the promotion and safeguarding of other children in the community.

During each meeting progress against agreed objectives is reviewed and new ones set. This task-focused activity should contain people and reduce anxiety if the focus on agreed priorities is appropriately held. Using the *coordinated management of meaning*[5] interventions at different levels are addressed simultaneously and prioritised. Security is built in the group as members become more aware of their roles and responsibilities, those of others and as individuals they begin to experience not being alone. This reduces anxiety.

Often at this point the relationships between the professionals and the family become more relaxed and can model ways of better communication, problem solving and build trust for the family and network. This establishes containment all round.

A *virtuous circle* emerges, which allows issues to be dealt with in more depth. Issues which members previously avoided are raised. Members begin to understand things in a more complex way, but they can tolerate this increased complexity because of the growing trust and sense of shared responsibility. At this stage members will often explore solutions not previously tried. This maximises creative energy, a sense of achievement and the motivation to keep working together. At this point it is particularly important for the group to remain grounded and focused on the child(ren). Often one person in the group will hold this role (not always the same person).

The meeting ends when there is a clear set of priorities and related action plan, however, the conversations carry on outside the group, either through liaison commitments built into the action plan, or because people have become excited by a new sense of efficacy. An important part of the role of a good Chair person is giving praise and recognising each individual's strength and contribution (building resilience).

The Therapeutic Networking process (shown in Figure 1) is iterative in that the group will repeat the process over and over again, building on previous understanding and achievement. Different members will join or leave the group, depending on the focus of priorities and risk

---

[5]   Salmon, G and Faris, J 'Multi-agency collaboration, multiple levels of meaning: social constructionism and the CMM model as tools to further our understanding' (2006) 28(3) *Journal of Family Therapy* 272–292.

Figure 1

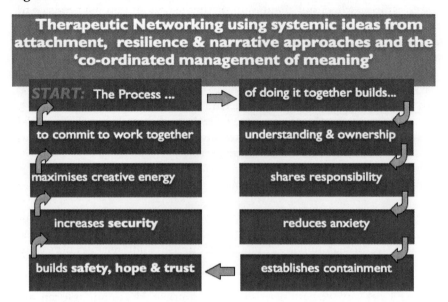

monitoring. As family difficulties reduce, with the agreement of the group, different members will end their involvement with the group and the family. The aim is that families will become self-sufficient and able to ask for help in the future if needed (ie they are more resilient). On occasion this is not possible, particularly where parental drug or alcohol use or mental ill health is an issue. In these circumstances a good outcome for the child is to move to a permanent alternative carer (if necessary, as an outcome of care proceedings). Whilst at one level this might be thought of as a disappointing outcome, in fact the TAC contributes constructively to avoiding drift and sometimes to helping parents accept that their parenting is not, and never will be, *good enough.*

Working with children and parents with mental ill health, particularly where there are safeguarding issues, is stressful. This coupled with the different professional backgrounds, roles and responsibilities of members of the group, means that conflict within the TAC is common. Such conflict is expected because the group reflects the tensions within the family and between them and their context. Therapeutic Networking is a model which allows expression of conflict and tries to channel it creatively. By holding difficulties and conflict within the safety of the group there is more opportunity to pull together in the same direction. The family get a clear, realistic and coherent message. This openness for them is constructive and more containing as they know where they stand. The group is more likely to devise a clear achievable action plan and the family is more likely to succeed.

COLLABORATIVE WORKING BETWEEN CSC AND CAMHS

Therapeutic Social Workers based in CSC Child Protection Service

One of the challenges for us has been that the children and families most in need of therapeutic services have been the most difficult to engage, many of them not attending clinic-based appointments. Some families have been referred to therapeutic services a number of times over a period of years and never attended. For these hard to reach families, this has sometimes meant that difficulties have escalated to the level where they have become quite entrenched and the family is no longer able to safely care for the children.

Parents told us that they found it embarrassing, and anxiety provoking and difficult attending clinic settings, even though Kaleidoscope, our main hub for these services, is a new, child and parent friendly, beautiful building. A number of initiatives have been launched to address this problem and to help stop children's needs escalating.

Two Therapeutic Social Workers have been recruited to work in Family Support and Intervention (FSI), the CSC child protection social work service. They are qualified social workers with training in systemic methods of working. One is a qualified Family Therapist. They are managed within FSI, but receive clinical supervision from a Senior Family Therapist based in CAMHS. Their role is to offer an assertive outreach therapeutic service for children and families who cannot or will not access traditional services.

Work is allocated to them on the basis of families' presenting needs and includes individual work with children and parents, couple therapy, advice around behaviour management and family therapy. Families also have an allocated Social Worker. Where a longer-term adult counselling service or psychotherapy is needed, the Therapeutic Social Workers work with the family and act as a bridge between the family and CAMHS or Adult Mental Health Services in order to ensure engagement with the required service.

In most of the families co-worked by the Therapeutic Social Workers with the children are subject to a Child Protection Plan or/and are on the brink of care proceedings. Another important aspect of the Therapeutic Social Workers' role has been their involvement in cases where children are in foster care and the plan is rehabilitation.

The Therapeutic Social Workers have been persistent and determined in gaining engagement with families. Sometimes they have had to visit families three or four times before they are even allowed to enter the home. Many of the families are understandably wary of professional involvement, particularly if there have been previous court proceedings or the children are subject to a Child Protection Plan. Trust between the Therapeutic Social Worker and the family is built up over time.

Our analysis of the work undertaken over the past year shows that the involvement of the Therapeutic Social Workers has been highly valued by families, and has led to children being subject to Child Protection Plans for shorter periods. Their role in providing a bridge for families to access mainstream CAMHS and Adult Mental Health Services has been an unexpected bonus. Families who previously have resisted treatment are now engaging having realised that therapeutic work has helped them to feel better. Another unforeseen positive consequence of the Therapeutic Social Workers role is that families' understanding of the Child Protection Plan and their ability to work with the FSI Social Worker has improved. This *virtuous* circle has been reinforced through the use of TAC Therapeutic Networking (see Appendix 4 – Case example Jermaine).

Partnership between CAMHS and a Local Family Centre

There is a full-time Social Worker with a therapeutic background based half time at CAMHS and half time in the Family Centre. The Family Centre accepts referrals from all professionals, and prioritises working with under-5s and their families where there is a Child Protection Plan, letter of intention to issue court proceedings in place, or children are already the subjects of care proceedings. The Social Worker receives clinical supervision again from the Senior Family Therapist in CAMHS and helps identify families where the parent(s) would benefit from co-working with any of the mental health assessments and treatment services available within CAMHS parenting groups run jointly with CAMHS.

The worker also supports foster carers where children's placements are at risk of disruption due to the children's emotional and behavioural issues. She offers behavioural management skills to foster carers and helps the children with the transition from home to foster placement, a move that some children find traumatic.

Reflective Practice Groups

Lewisham is committed to allowing busy front line workers the opportunity to reflect on their practice. Not only does this add a layer of challenge which can help improve the quality of work, hence improving outcomes for children, but it also allows workers to process some of the strong feelings that child protection work gives rise to. The 2 hour sessions, led by an Independent Reviewing Officer and a CAMHS worker, are open to all CSC and CAMHS staff to provide a safe supportive forum to reflect.

WHAT HAVE WE LEARNED?

(1) The benefits of flexibility

As members of the TAC become more confident and knowledgeable about each others' roles and responsibilities it becomes possible to relax boundaries and to step into each others positions temporarily if required. This must be within a clear understanding that doing this is to implement the TAC action plan. Skills include being 'multi-lingual', ie becoming conversant in medical, social care, therapeutic and mental health languages.

(2) Developing trust between workers

This is facilitated by being based at or spending time at each other's locations and by working on a shared task. Better inter-agency relationships facilitate more effective working with other children, and other Teams Around other Children.

(3) Importance of keeping the child's profile and needs in mind

This includes clarity around the child's views and feelings, a detailed understanding of the child's needs and history and the quality of care the child is receiving. This can be a challenge for networks where parents are care leavers or have mental health or learning disabilities. Change must be within the child's time span. TAC action plans must have longer-term as well as short-term targets and specificity about how and when to meet them.

(4) The importance of meeting practical needs

This model deliberately addresses or holds in mind the necessity to ensure basic needs, such as housing and healthcare are met alongside safety and therapeutic ones.

(5) Reflective Practice and Reflexivity are key to good outcomes

Inter-agency effectiveness is much more than sharing information.

(6) The benefits of placing Therapeutic Social Workers within the child protection teams and the local family centre

This has been enormously helpful in engaging hard to reach and avoidant families. Also unexpectedly, the involvement of these workers has meant that non-attendance rates for specialist services, such as CAMHS for these families have improved.

APPENDIX 1 – SPECIALIST AREAS OF WORK WITHIN CAMHS

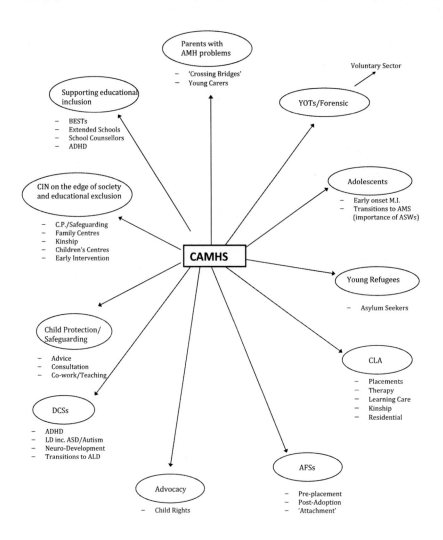

APPENDIX 2 – EVERY CHILD MATTERS HIERARCHY OF NEED

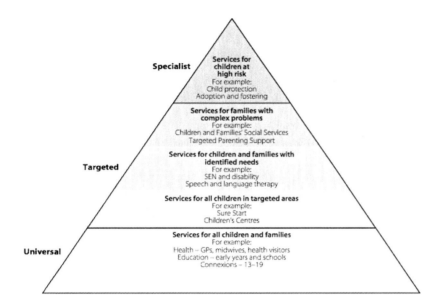

APPENDIX 3 – CONCEPTUAL FRAMEWORKS

These frameworks inform management, leadership and participation when using the Therapeutic Networking model. They are highly compatible and often overlapping in their ideas. They bring a richness of understanding to working with the complexity which the families bring to us.

Systemic and narrative approaches

Systemic practitioners are trained to appreciate that the *whole is more than the sum of the parts*. This means that we are always working with people in a social context and the many relationships which this means they are engaged in. As practitioners we try to stand back and understand the relationships between people at all levels in their lives. The overview amounts to more than the independent individuals or discrete parts of their lives which are transformed into quite different activities and meanings by their interactions. Systemic practice addresses the *relationships between* at all levels, ie between individuals, within individuals (internal dialogues), between family members and others in all contexts.[6]

This model addresses complexity, the chronic nature of some predicaments and crises in context. It considers *patterns* of relationships and events over time.

An important method which has been promoted by systemic practitioners in recent years is the *Coordinated Management of Meaning* proposed by Pearce and Cronen (1980)[7] and Cronen (1995)[8] – please see below.

A significant part of the systemic practitioner's role is to consider his/her own position in the network or group. So, *reflective practice* is vital to the ongoing understanding and the monitoring of change in situations. *Reflexivity* is about how the practitioner then decides to conduct herself/himself using insights from the reflections about others, thoughts about herself/himself in relation to others and her/his understanding of self in those relationships.[9]

Systemic practitioners in the last two decades have been particularly influenced by *Social Constructionism*,[10] ie that body of theoretical understanding which describes how we achieve a sense of our own *reality*. We *construct* beliefs about ourselves in relationships particularly through the use of language. Language allows opportunities to *deconstruct* and *reconstruct* our beliefs. Because words are not used like dictionary definitions but are *connotative*, ie they carry emotional and social meanings and symbolic associations, they are more open and accessible to change. We are able to create and recreate stories to explain our experience and why we behave as we do! These stories, or *narratives*, guide us and help us engage with others and allow us to move on when things seem stuck or unchangeable.

Narrative practitioners focus especially on the *stories* people have about their lives and the meaning that they place on their experience of relationships and events in their lives. Language, as described above, is important because it helps us make sense of things that have happened.

---

6   Salmon, G and Faris, J 'Multi-agency collaboration, multiple levels of meaning: social constructionism and the CMM model as tools to further our understanding' (2006) 28(3) *Journal of Family Therapy* 272–292.
7   Pearce, WB and Cronen, VE *Communication Action and Meaning: the Creation of Social Realities* (New York: Prager, 1980).
8   Cronen, VE 'Co-ordinated management of meaning; the consequentiality of communication and the recapturing of experience' in S Sigman (ed) *The Consequentiality of Communication* (New York: Hillsdale, 1995).
9   Flaskas, C and Perlesz, A *The Therapeutic Relationship in Systemic Therapy* (Karnac Books, 1996).
10 Salmon, G and Faris, J 'Multi-agency collaboration, multiple levels of meaning: social constructionism and the CMM model as tools to further our understanding' (2006) 28(3) *Journal of Family Therapy* 272–292.

People who can make *coherent stories* to explain what has happened to them are likely to be much more resilient and therefore able to cope.[11]

Attachment framework

Attachment theory is supported by over 50 years of research[12] and is a detailed developmental narrative to explain psychological, cognitive and mental well-being. It explains healthy psychological development and provides a series of concepts and reference points through which we may evaluate healthy relationships and how we might intervene to improve their development when they are unhealthy and unsafe. The theory articulates how health emerges from growth in a secure environment, from *a secure base,* through exploration and play, opportunities to protest and test out assertiveness, to experience loss in a supported way and develop through these experiences, *internal models* which help to build *resilience* to face future challenges. An important aspect of these experiences is developing *reflective capacity* and from that the ability to be *self-reflective* and use that ability in a *reflexive* way to improve constructive relationships with others.

The attachment framework helps us assess the security, or not, within close inter-personal relationships. The model is *dynamic,* ie it is open to change over time given safe, trusting relationships within which to test out different ways of doing things. The model is *maturational,*[13] ie different stages of development provide opportunities for change and so, even after poor beginnings or traumas, the potential exists for change given time and nurturing conditions.

The attachment model emphasises the importance of the *secure base* and this concept applies not only within the birth family but has potential for being provided by others, eg substitute families and, in our experience, by a strong TAC working well enough together.

Importantly, the attachment model is theoretically adaptable providing an easily accessible theoretical framework for all professionals. It therefore helps us to 'sing from the same hymn sheet' more readily. It promotes the construction of *coherent stories*[14] within the group with which the child and family can be supported.

RESILIENCE

Attachment and relationship-based theories help us to understand how people react when they are feeling things strongly and how they react and relate to others when under stress. People with good self-esteem, confidence in their own abilities and judgments and with a sense of their achievements in life, are better able to respond well under stressful conditions. *Resilience* comes from achieving *coherent stories*, ie the world makes cognitive sense and is strongly affected by the ability to be reflective (*self-reflective functioning*).[15] Supportive, strong resilience factors are high

---

[11] Fonagy, P, Steel, M, Higgitt, A and Taget, M 'Theory and Practice of Resilience' (1994) 35 *Journal of Child Psychology and Psychiatry* 231-257.

[12] Holmes, J *The Search for the Secure Base: Attachment Theory and Psychotherapy* (Bruner Routledge, 2001).

[13] See Dallos, R *Attachment Narrative Therapy* (Open University Press, 2006).

[14] See Fonagy, P, Steel, M, Higgitt, A and Taget, M 'Theory and Practice of Resilience' (1994) 35 *Journal of Child Psychology and Psychiatry* 231-257.
Geddes, H *Attachment in the Classroom* (Worth Publishing, 2006).
Howe, D, Brandon, M, Hinings, D and Schofield, G *Attachment Theory, Child Maltreatment and Family Support: A Practice and Assessment Model* (Palgrave Press, 1991).

[15] See Fonagy, P, Steel, M, Higgitt, A and Taget, M 'Theory and Practice of Resilience' (1994) 35 *Journal of Child Psychology and Psychiatry* 231-257.
Fonagy, P and Target, M 'Attachment and reflective function: their role in self-organisation' (1997) 9 *Development and Psychopathology* 679-700.

self-esteem, self-efficacy, the ability to reflect on relationships and be reflexive, having social empathy and autonomy. These attributes help us, in particular, to face and cope with adversity and come through it in turn a stronger person.

Secure attachments, developed from being nurtured in a *secure base,* facilitate the development of such psychological skills and resilience, ie social competence and mental health.

Different interventions are dictated by the type of attachment relationships people demonstrate and their levels of resilience. By strengthening a child's positive relationships within their family and with significant others and by providing a supportive and secure home-base, we can change their insecure internal experiences of the world into more secure and positive ones. Using these developmental, systemic and contextual models we can measure and monitor their progress towards good physical and mental health.

These models are valuable because they are accessible to being measured and evaluated over time.[16]

---

[16]   See Howe, D, Brandon, M, Hinings, D and Schofield, G *Attachment Theory, Child Maltreatment and Family Support: A Practice and Assessment Model* (Palgrave Press, 1991)..

APPENDIX 4 – CASE EXAMPLE: JERMAINE

This case demonstrates the Therapeutic Networking approach for a child who presented with challenging behaviour, which included absconding regularly from home. This placed him at risk whilst out in the community. The family were well known to Children's Social Care.

Background information

Jermaine was 13 years old and the eldest in the sibling group of five children. Jermaine is of Black Caribbean origin.

In July 1999, CSC received the first referral relating to Jermaine. It was from a Women's Refuge where his mother had fled domestic violence from Jermaine's father with whom she and Jermaine had been living. The next referral was received in 2004, from Jermaine's Primary School. Jermaine had told a staff member that his mother had kicked and beaten him that morning and that she had told him that she wanted him out of the family home. This was the first time that Jermaine had alleged physical abuse from his parents.

Jermaine began absconding in 2004. Jermaine's absconding became a serious issue and he was reported missing 30 times. Jermaine's stated reason for absconding so regularly was that he was not allowed out to play and that he was bored. During this time he also made an allegation of physical abuse against his father, which he later retracted. When he was picked up by the police he would give incorrect name and address details.

Jermaine was placed under Police Protection in September 2008. This followed a further allegation that he had been beaten by his father. He was placed in foster care with the agreement of his parents.

Throughout the involvement of the CSC, even when the case went into care proceedings, the parents were consistently resistant, verging on hostile, and extremely guarded. This only began to shift once the therapeutic SW was involved. The parents had refused to engage in any form of parenting assessment, including a Core Assessment, as they stated that there was nothing wrong with their parenting and the problem lay solely with Jermaine. They therefore agreed for therapeutic work with Jermaine, but wanted to be no part of it.

Jermaine returned home on an interim care order in December 2008. An assessment by a community based parenting assessment resource strongly recommended CAMHS involvement including work with the parents. CSC allocated a therapeutic SW and referred to CAMHS. This led to the provision of intensive, home-based family support.

Following the involvement of the therapeutic SW, the family continued to be mistrustful of professionals and remained hostile, however allowed agencies to work in their home, which was a significant step forward. The family began to engage with the therapeutic SW, with a view to this work continuing outside the home within the CAMHS environment.

The therapeutic SW helped the parents gain a better understanding of the triggers to Jermaine absconding. This involved a systemic approach, looking at their own parenting. It was identified that both parents had suffered physical abuse as children and they based their discipline/boundary setting on that approach. They were able to identify the problem and the need for the creation of a 'secure base'.

During this process the family began to have a better understanding about therapy and the role of CAMHS. They agreed for continued discussion with CAMHS, and eventually attended a TAC meeting supported by the therapeutic social worker. This emphasised to the family that the agencies were working together. The liaison between the agencies, which also included education, enabled the family to understand and change their previous behaviour that had led to confrontations, which in turn led to physical chastisement and concluded in Jermaine absconding.

During the sessions at home, Jermaine was able to see a change in his parents and how they addressed things. The family now have a good understanding of the partnership between CAMHS and CSC. They are engaged fully in the therapeutic work at home and are attending appointments with CAMHS. They are keen to establish a good understanding of Jermaine's emotional needs to ensure that he does not return to absconding. The family are able to identify the changes that they have made in order to ensure that Jermaine does not feel the need to abscond from the home.

The care proceedings have concluded and the collaborative work with CAMHS and CSC continues.

REFERENCES

Cabinet Office Social Exclusion Task Force *Think Family: Improving the Life Chances of Families at Risk* (London, 2008).

Department for Education and Skills *Care Matters: Time for Change* (London, 2007).

PLENARY 7

CONFERENCE ACTION POINTS

CONFERENCE RESOLUTIONS

The practice of agreeing resolutions began at the 5ᵗʰ Dartington Conference, 'Durable Solutions' and was put on a more formal footing at the 6ᵗʰ Dartington Conference 'Integrating Diversity'. It is hoped that these messages will be heeded by government departments and major players in the family justice system.

During the conference, the Resolutions Committee (which was chaired by Yvonne Brown and comprised Bruce Clark, Martyn Cook, Minna Daum, Liz Gillet and Deborah Ramsdale) met to distill the draft resolutions put forward by each small group. Where two or more groups proposed very similar resolutions these were amalgamated. Where two or more groups proposed opposing resolutions these were formulated in the alternative. Amidst lively debate a draft text, running to some 14 resolutions, was prepared.

Danya Glaser chaired the final plenary session in the course of which each proposed resolution was debated. Where necessary the wording was amended to achieve consensus. During the conference a number of matters had been discussed in breakout groups, which were not the primary focus of the conference. These nevertheless gave rise to proposed resolutions, and given the strength of feeling of delegates they were retained not as formal resolutions, but as 'invitations' to the Family Justice Council.

(1)   This Conference supports the concept, and anticipates the further evaluation, of 'problem solving' courts (such as the Family Drug and Alcohol Court) in their capacity as 'judge-led' (with judicial continuity) neutral, time-disciplined and non-adversarial environments where multidisciplinary teams can intervene early, with careful thought being given as to:

(a)   the expert assistance the family may need;

(b)   the assessment(s) that may already exist and proceedings that have previously have been concluded in respect of the relevant child/family member(s); and

(c)   the further focused assessment (including of the parents' capacity to change) the court may need;

in order to progress to a swift and lasting resolution.

There needs to be further consideration as to whether the same judge should hear care proceedings where families have failed or withdrawn from this process, and how this system can be extended to those cases where parties have mental health difficulties.

(2A)   This Conference believes that a framework should be developed between Adult Mental Health Services and Children's Services to assess the needs of 'young carers' and their parents, in order more effectively to determine the nature of the adult's needs, the relationship between the child and parent, and to identify what services are or should be made available to parent and/or child in order to ensure that the caring role of the child does not impair his or her development.

(2B)   This Conference also believes that there needs to be close collaboration between Adult Mental Health and Children's Services: there needs to be a more uniform implementation of the requirements of the Fair Access to Care Services (Guidance on Eligibility Criteria for Adult Social Care). Where an adult with mental health difficulties has parental responsibility there must be a mutual exchange of information between the services to keep each abreast of the development of/planning for the adult's mental health issues and the planning for the child(ren).

(3)   This Conference believes that litigants with mental health difficulties should, in addition to properly funded legal representation, have access to lay advocacy/support before and during the court process, and where appropriate the use of registered intermediaries. These services should be funded from the public purse, including through voluntary sector provision.

(4)   This Conference recommends that where intervention in a child's life including child protection and legal proceedings may be resolved by granting residence orders to kinship carers, these carers should be afforded the same rights of access to assessment and support services (both financial and practical, during and after the process) that is afforded under the auspices of special guardianship orders.

(5)   This Conference believes that there needs to be transparency as to the purpose of contact during care proceedings; it needs to be clear whether individual contact sessions are in order to maintain or to assess parent-child relationships. Parents should be made aware of when a contact session is specifically for the purpose of assessment. In the case of infants, careful thought must be given to the timetabling of contact in ways that will not harm the child's development.

(6)   This Conference believes that the MoJ and DCSF should commission research into the different models of assessment and intervention in entrenched private law cases, with a view to considering whether the Marlborough type of programme should be more widely available in the form of s 11 contact activity directions/conditions.

(7)   This Conference believes that the Family Justice Council (and if possible DCSF/Welsh Assembly) should explore how feedback could be given to judges as to the post final order outcomes for children and families in family law cases. The aim of this research would be to enhance judicial knowledge and awareness of medium and longer-term outcomes to assist their decision-making.

In addition to these resolutions, the Conference asked the Family Justice Council to take account of the following:

(a)   This Conference invites the Family Justice Council to consider the role, structure and effectiveness of Cafcass.

(b)   This Conference invites the Family Justice Council, when it reviews government proposals on openness, to consider the potential for harm to children and their parents.

(c)   This Conference invites the Safeguarding Committee of the Family Justice Council to consider whether children who are the subject of plans for permanence as looked after children should have their plans considered by the court.